CUSTOMER RELATIONSHIP MANAGEMENT

Sara Miller McCune founded SAGE Publishing in 1965 to support the dissemination of usable knowledge and educate a global community. SAGE publishes more than 1000 journals and over 800 new books each year, spanning a wide range of subject areas. Our growing selection of library products includes archives, data, case studies and video. SAGE remains majority owned by our founder and after her lifetime will become owned by a charitable trust that secures the company's continued independence.

Los Angeles | London | New Delhi | Singapore | Washington DC | Melbourne

CUSTOMER RELATIONSHIP MANAGEMENT

A Global Approach

Samit Chakravorti

Los Angeles | London | New Delhi
Singapore | Washington DC | Melbourne

Los Angeles | London | New Delhi
Singapore | Washington DC | Melbourne

SAGE Publications Ltd
1 Oliver's Yard
55 City Road
London EC1Y 1SP

SAGE Publications Inc.
2455 Teller Road
Thousand Oaks, California 91320

SAGE Publications India Pvt Ltd
B 1/I 1 Mohan Cooperative Industrial Area
Mathura Road
New Delhi 110 044

SAGE Publications Asia-Pacific Pte Ltd
3 Church Street
#10-04 Samsung Hub
Singapore 049483

Editor: Matthew Waters
Editorial assistant: Charlotte Hanson
Production editor: Nicola Marshall
Copyeditor: William Baginsky
Proofreader: Derek Markham
Indexer: Adam Pozner
Marketing manager: Sarah Jane Silvester
Cover design: Francis Kenney
Typeset by: C&M Digitals (P) Ltd, Chennai, India
Printed in the UK

Library of Congress Control Number: 2022941836

British Library Cataloguing in Publication data

A catalogue record for this book is available from the British Library

ISBN 978-1-5297-6742-1
ISBN 978-1-5297-6741-4 (pbk)

At SAGE we take sustainability seriously. Most of our products are printed in the UK using responsibly sourced papers and boards. When we print overseas we ensure sustainable papers are used as measured by the PREPS grading system. We undertake an annual audit to monitor our sustainability.

This book is dedicated to all positive cross-cultural endeavors

CONTENTS

ONLINE RESOURCES

This textbook is accompanied by online resources to aid teaching and support learning. To access these resources, visit: **www.study.sagepub.com/chakravorti** Please note that lecturers will require a SAGE account in order to access the lecturer resources. An account can be created via the above link.

For Lecturers

- **PowerPoints** that can be downloaded and adapted to suit individual teaching needs

ABOUT THE AUTHOR

 Dr. Samit Chakravorti is an Associate Professor of Marketing at Western Illinois University, Macomb, IL, USA. Dr. Chakravorti has a PhD in Business Administration-Marketing from Florida International University, Miami, FL and an MBA from Binghamton University, NY. Dr. Chakravorti's research and teaching are in the areas of CRM, Marketing Strategy, International Marketing and he has a growing interest in research on Wine Marketing. Dr. Chakravorti has published multiple articles in academic journals including a best paper in the *Journal of Personal Selling and Sales Management,* in proceedings of academic marketing conferences, and also a book on CRM.

Dr. Chakravorti grew up close to the city of Kolkata, India. In India after receiving a Bachelors in Science-Chemistry from Banaras Hindu University, Dr. Chakravorti worked for multiple years in B2B sales and marketing for multinational and national organizations. Dr. Chakravorti lives in Chicago, IL.

PREFACE

This book takes a fresh and a much needed global perspective on managing customer relationships.

In the last two decades, application and implementation of the concepts, models, and practices of customer relationship management (CRM) have significantly increased and evolved. To respond to this increasing interest and demand from industry, a number of books have been authored by academics and practitioners to help business students and businesses grasp and implement the complex and broad topic. Each of these has its own merits and contributions but most come with an overriding drawback. One would be hard pressed to find a book on CRM that has significantly addressed and discussed international and cross-cultural issues that pertain to managing customer experiences and relationships globally. On the other hand, international marketing books have not addressed strategic and technical aspects of CRM even though CRM should be a major concern for marketing in any organization. In today's consumer-driven world, CRM initiatives have become important to organizations engaged in international business, but implementing them has become increasingly complex. This complexity comes from globalization of the world along lines of economy, culture, and lifestyles that has created both integration across countries and fragmentation within, opening up new opportunities and raising new challenges. These realities warrant significant insertions of global perspectives in CRM discussions. Complex and organization-spanning CRM strategies like any other business strategy are impacted by cross-cultural and cross-country forces, and if an organization is to succeed in building profitable and loyal customers across the globe, it is its job to understand this impact and adapt to it.

This book prioritizes discussion of global or international issues in CRM approaches and practices and helps to fill the gap left unaddressed by both mainstream CRM and international marketing books. It comprehensively discusses strategic, tactical, and technical areas and concepts of CRM and at the same time significantly entwines discussion of international issues within each. It is based on knowledge I have gained from an extensive collection of offline and online published secondary sources of information from both academia and industry, supported by my international marketing experience, my research in marketing and over 15 years of teaching customer relationship management, international marketing and international business.

The book is primarily targeted towards advanced undergraduate or graduate business students but also towards practitioners in CRM and marketing. The discussion is grounded in marketing and business theory but led by global practice in CRM. The book is replete with long and short case studies of companies from different countries operating internationally and also provides practical and current information, tips, and guidelines from the global market, in an easy-to-read format.

The discussion is spread across 11 chapters. Chapter contents are categorized under four conceptual and logical parts that help readers comprehend the impacts of culture on global CRM and gain a sound knowledge of the process of developing and implementing country-specific and cross-country CRM initiatives.

Part I: Establishing Foundations (Chapters 1–3): Chapter 1 introduces several core and strategic concepts of CRM, and connects them with the impact of cross-country diversity on implementation of these concepts. It stresses the importance of understanding the connection between CRM concepts and country-specific environmental forces and making necessary adaptations to implementation of the former. It underscores the book's overarching approach towards CRM that the application of the underlying foundations of CRM are global but planning and implementation need to be adapted to the country-level environmental realities. To stress that, Chapter 2 highlights the three primary country-level business environments and the diversity that lies across countries, and Chapter 3 discusses the foundations of and diversity in consumer behavior, and business practices across countries, and ways to approach cross-country segmentation and target segments with CRM interventions.

Part II: Planning and Implementation (Chapters 4–8): These chapters discuss interconnected elements of global CRM initiative development that follow a logical thought process. Chapter 4 lays down detailed processes and guidelines for planning and implementing CRM and Chapters 5–7 narrow the discussion to different types of specific CRM projects such as analytical, strategic, operational, and social CRM that need to be developed as part of the overall CRM initiative. Given the importance of small and medium sized enterprises (SMEs) to the global economy and their special needs, Chapter 8 discusses CRM imperatives and implementation for SMEs across countries.

Part III: Managing Stakeholder Relationships (Chapters 9 and 10): Strong customer relationships cannot be built without help from value-chain partners and employees. Chapter 9 discusses ways to manage relationships within cross-country value chains which can show significant diversity in formats, infrastructure, quality, and cultural make-up of power–cooperation relationships. Chapter 10 provides guidelines for managing people change within organizations operating in multiple countries to get employees to embrace CRM initiatives and become customer oriented.

Part IV: Improving Global CRM Implementation (Chapter 11): As organizations expand operations across countries, cultural intelligence becomes a critical skill to successfully manage customer relationships. This chapter highlights its importance and ways to develop mindfulness, cross-cultural skills and cultural intelligence.

I hope this book helps you to be more keenly aware of cultural impacts on consumer behavior, the importance of developing cultural intelligence, and to become effective at developing and managing customer and stakeholder relationships across cultures and countries.

Samit Chakravorti

ACKNOWLEDGEMENTS

My sincere acknowledgments and thanks go to several persons at Sage Publications for timely publication of the book: Matthew Waters (Editor) for approaching me with the concept of the book, helping to determine the ultimate shape and direction of it, and facilitating the process of proposal and contract approval; Charlotte Hanson (Editorial Assistant) for timely feedback on the chapter contents; Nicola Marshall (Production Editor) for expediting the process of editing, and printing; and William Baginsky (Copyeditor) for providing valuable inputs. Finally, I would like to acknowledge the contribution of authors of the numerous publications without whose collective knowledge the book would not have been possible.

PART I
ESTABLISHING
FOUNDATIONS

1

CRM CONCEPTS AND GLOBAL MARKETS

Case Study

Managing Customer Experience at Royal Bank of Scotland

After a rapid bout of expansion during the early years of the new millennium through multiple acquisitions, Royal Bank of Scotland (RBS) had a major setback during the financial crises that followed 2008. After struggling for a few years the bank, one of the largest in the world, realized that the only route to financial viability lies in concentrating on customers. In 2010 the Customer Charter was created, and the company set about on the operation of enhancing customer experiences. Customer experiences run the range from pre-purchase awareness to post-purchase satisfaction. These are influenced by the company, environment, and customer characteristics. Understanding the difficulty of implementing such a broad and nebulous concept, RBS knew it would have to start with something concrete: evaluation of its existing systems, processes, and products.

RBS developed an evidence-based strategy of taking a customer's viewpoint in assessing product and service experience and quality, determining the cost of providing these services and making changes where necessary. This was implemented by RBS through a series of four steps. The first step was to define the customer journey in accessing its products and services. This included identifying all products and services that are experienced by customers. Once the products and service deliveries were mapped out, the second step included determining both the performance quality of these products and services, and the costs of providing these. The third step was to understand how customers evaluate the service qualities by utilizing a combination of three pragmatic measures: customer satisfaction, net promotor score (NPS) and customer effort score, which reflects a customer's physical, emotional and mental costs in utilizing the services. This helped the bank gauge customer satisfaction levels with different service components and which components were considered critical by customers. Steps 1, 2, and 3 together provided a strong diagnostic tool to help

(Continued)

compare the performance quality and costs of service delivery components with the satisfaction and importance customers ascribe to the same. This indicated areas that were performing well but not important to customers and areas that needed improving. Finally, step 4 compared the outcome from steps 1 through 3 with commitments made to customers in the Customer Charter and any gaps and needed improvements addressed.

During implementation of this 4-step process the bank overcame challenges in multiple areas that included developing insights on costs and customer satisfaction with service delivery components of the different kinds of products the bank has (current account, mortgages, and credit cards), allocating costs of delivering each service because accounting systems did not connect costs with customer-defined journeys, and making sure that the program was applied across all three products knowing that customer satisfaction would depend on a combined experience across all the products.

Instead of being a top down approach the effort was led and coordinated by middle tier management with support from senior leadership. The program resulted in increased customer satisfaction, NPS, and revenues, and decreased costs and customer churn.

Source: Maklan, S., Antonetti, P., and Whitty, S. (2017). "A better way to manage customer experience." *California Management Review*, 59, 2, 92–115.

CRM Concepts and Global Markets

Introduction

The concept of customer relationship management (CRM) has substantially grown and matured over the last couple of decades. Significant research has been done on CRM during this time (Liu et al., 2020; Oblander et al., 2020). Organizations too have increasingly implemented CRM. However, the level of success has only been moderate on average with about a third of all implementations failing to meet their goals (Edinger, 2018).

Success Story

Boise Office Solutions

Boise Office Solutions—based in Itasca, Illinois in the United States that sells office products to other businesses—has seen increased customer retention after successfully implementing customer relationship management. The company took several complementary steps to implement CRM. Their first step was to have a clear objective, which is to "provide the customer with a clear economic value." The next step was to clearly understand customer needs and how these vary from customer to customer so that approaches can be customized to customer desires. The step that the company took after that, the one that is perhaps the most important of all, is mapping the various customer–company interaction touch points and then revamping their internal processes to match these touch points. In essence they built their processes with an "outside-in" perspective. Both business and IT employees were involved in this effort. This allowed IT people to have a clear understanding of customer needs, facilitating selection of technology tools that would support the processes and help achieve the objective. The last crucial step was transforming the organizational culture to be customer focused where all functions take the customer's perspectives. The CEO of the company was directly involved in this cultural change.

Summarized from "A CRM Success Story" by Christophe Milliken, *Computerworld*, Nov. 7, 2002.

The benefits that implementation of the CRM brought to Boise and Royal Bank of Scotland make it clear that CRM is of critical value to organizations. The failure, however, of a significant number of other organizations to successfully implement CRM and see returns from it has raised questions about what they did wrong or missed doing. The combined impact of successes and failures of CRM implementation across organizations spawned a debate and research on the nature of customer relationship management, what it entails and how to successfully implement it. In many cases marketing plays a leading role in this effort. However, successful implementation and adoption of customer relationship takes a concerted effort from all functions within the organization, including senior leadership. Research has found that the critical factors that contribute to CRM success span the organization. The importance of these factors are stressed in the starting case on Royal Bank of Scotland. These factors are listed below (Band, 2013; Keramati et al., 2012):

- Cross-functional coordination
- Presence of CRM business strategies
- Organizational process change
- Senior management active support

Snippets

CRM Implementation Hurdles

UK hotel chain—inconsistent data: Sales and Customer Service were not following the same process of entering data, leading to duplicate and inaccurate records. Processes of

(Continued)

data entry and data structure needed to be standardized across the organization to provide a consistent view of customers and their behaviors.

International bank: Processes for CRM were designed to suit technology but not to keep customer needs in mind. Technology is a critical facilitator of a CRM effort but it is organizational processes that need to drive CRM efforts.

Summarized from "Three CRM implementation case studies you can learn from" by Jane Tareen, *Discover CRM*, August 25, 2017.

These successes and hurdles have shaped the definition and importance of CRM. Today CRM is understood as a multifaceted business model and tool set that positively impacts organizational health through enhancing customer experiences, satisfaction, profitability, and loyalty. It achieves this by:

1   In-depth understanding of needs and wants of customers and consumers
2   Targeting profitable customers and consumers with profit potential
3   Promoting value-added products and services to these customers/consumers
4   Creating positive customer experiences through engagement
5   Motivating customers to engage in repeat purchase and non-purchase behavior such as brand advocacy and referrals.

The collective contribution of these activities is evident as are the complexities in implementing the same. Hence, there is a high rate of failure in implementing CRM but where it is done well, organizations have reaped significant benefits.

Customer relationship management (CRM): Business model that puts customers at the center of organizational operations. It holds that long-term organizational growth can only be achieved through developing profitable and loyal relationships with customers by offering value-added products, services, and experiences.

Opportunities for CRM increased in international markets as globalization of trade and investment grew in the last few decades. This raised the complexity for CRM as organizations have to work within the business environments that exist in different markets. Cultural, economic, political, legal, technology, competition, and consumer environments vary from country to country with different degrees of differences and similarities. Economic, political, and legal environments interact to impact culture and technology. Culture and technology in turn shape consumers, consumption patterns, and competition. CRM success in international markets will only come through intimate comprehension of cross-country environmental similarities and differences and necessary adaptation to these. Globalization and economic development have created a dynamic and complex duo of 1) increasingly aware and sophisticated consumers with distinct value orientations and expectations of consumption experiences, and 2) intense competition from both global and local players. These create challenges in enhancing customer experiences and satisfaction. The wealthy younger generations in fast growing and traditionally more collectivist countries such as China and India have shown increasing individualistic bents but within a collectivist fold. For example, their primary motivation to purchase luxury products is to fulfill a need for status. This contrasts with individualism as the primary purchase motivation of corresponding cohorts in developed western countries (Schaffmeister, 2015).

International successes of diverse brands such as Danone, Volkswagen, and IKEA have underscored the increasing necessity of localizing strategies. Customer relationship management in today's globalized world thus needs a global approach but local strategies and tactics. CRM's tried and tested foundations, facets, and tools remain the same globally with strategies, tactics, and application of tools adapted to business environments, competition, and consumers. McDonald's standardizes its overall value offering of convenience and happiness in a McDonald's experience but adapts other processes crucial to customer engagement and satisfaction. To consistently provide this value offering, McDonald's standardizes its digital communication media (Twitter and Facebook) and employee training across markets, but customizes promotional contents (local festivals and language), product development, and customer service (e.g. McDonald's delivery) (IBS Center for Management Research, 2014; Mujtaba and Patel, 2007).

What Customer Relationship Management Really Is: Foundational Concepts

CRM evolved from the complementary fields of relationship marketing and market orientation. Relationship marketing stresses the importance of relationship building, collaboration, and coopetition (collaboration between business competitors for mutually beneficial results) with stakeholders as the foundation of long-term organizational growth (Buttle, 1996; Kotler and Amstrong, 2010). Market orientation stresses that a combined existence of an organizational culture oriented towards the market (consumers and competitors) and an active behavior of collecting, analyzing, and utilizing market information to develop intelligence and capabilities impact customer satisfaction and profitability (Day, 2000; Jaworski and Kohli, 1993; Narver and Slater, 1990). It consists of three components of customer orientation, competitor orientation, and inter-functional coordination. Customer and competitor orientations are exhibited in the culture and behavior of developing knowledge about customers and competitors. Inter-functional coordination facilitates organization-wide spread of this. Figure 1.1 illustrates the three prongs of market orientation.

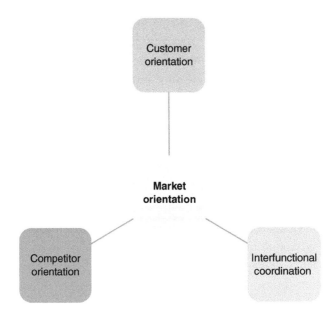

Figure 1.1 Market Orientation

So, what does customer relationship mean in the context of a market?

The Cambridge dictionary defines customer relationships as "the way in which a business and its customers feel and behave towards each other over a period of time, and the effect of this on the business" (dictionary.cambridge.org).

Relationships can be transactional or economic where a customer exhibits behavioral loyalty because of consistently low prices. Relationships can also be emotional, based on positive perceptions and attitudinal loyalty towards the brand. Both types are desirable. The first directly adds to organizational profits and the second to spread of word of mouth. Most customer relationships tend to lie somewhere in between the two extremes. Even though this would be true for all countries, country environments of culture, economy, consumers, and competition will determine the specifics of the kind of relationships desired by customers and the feasibility of providing and developing them. For example, in some developing countries such as India mom and pop stores dominate the retail sector. These are usually run by families and have long-term relationships with customers. These customer relationships are dependent on a particular desire of customers that retailers allow customers to pay in cash, in many cases on an interest-free monthly basis (Adhikari and Agashe, 2020). The retailer maintains accounts for different customers who pay at the end of the month, sometimes carrying forward the debt.

The next three subsections discuss the foundational concepts on which customer relationship management rests. In brief, when a customer consistently gets value and positive experiences from consumption of a brand, it generates trust and loyalty. This leads to increasing purchases and non-purchase behaviors that increases the monetary value of the customer to the brand. This can only be achieved and sustained if the brand is consistently oriented towards the customer.

Customer Value, Customer Experiences, Trust

All successful relationships of choice are founded in the concept of reciprocal values. In buyer–seller relationships the customer gets something of value from the organization in terms of offerings, services, and interactions and the organization in turn benefits from continued loyalty from the customer and increasing share of the customer's wallet.

The benefits can be tangible, such as effectiveness in removing dandruff of an anti-dandruff shampoo or intangible such as the trust that customer service will always resolve problems, and in the brand itself. The obvious cost is the price for acquisition and/or use but cost also includes cost of time for research, convenience, difficulty of usage, etc.

Customer value: The benefit that a customer receives from acquiring and using the product or service minus the costs borne to acquire and use.

Across countries, the value orientation of consumers, the expectation of value, and the perception of value received are impacted by economy, culture, and competition. Rice is sacred to the Japanese and so is the rice cooker. It is sacrilegious to suggest it be used for making anything else. Which is exactly what an international company introducing cake mixes to the Japanese suggested they do because Japanese homes tend to be small and many do not have western style ovens. Understandably, the suggestion backfired and the product did not take off. The perceptual quality and benefit of the product was negative because it went against cultural traditions and norms. Culture however is dynamic, does change slowly over the long-term, and may bring countries closer over time in terms of consumption trends. Despite this increasing closeness, countries will still exhibit sufficient differences to differently impact value perceptions and consumption. For example, American fast food became very popular in Japan some decades ago. However, eating habits, attitudes towards food, and food choices of Americans still differ substantially from the Japanese. Brands too have adapted their marketing strategies to cater to these market-based differences. In India for example, McDonald's has "Indianized" their menu by up to 70 percent and Frito-Lay came out with chips with "Magic Masala" flavor (Schaffmeister, 2015).

Consumers in a country are not homogeneous and thus value orientations and perceptions differ from segment to segment within a country and can be similar between two cross-country segments. "It is acknowledged that India is so heterogeneous that marketers have difficulty identifying common threads of Indian culture and core values" (Schaffmeister, 2015: 297), creating challenges in segmentation. Ford in China, depending on the segment, is perceived either as a foreign high end, an aspiring luxury or a quality mainstream American brand (Schaffmeister, 2015).

Neuroscience and psychology have shown that humans make decisions based on cognitive and emotional experiences (Sapolsky, 2018). Just as we are likely to appreciate the low price and energy efficiency of the air-conditioning system that we installed, we are also likely to be pleased (subconsciously most of the times) by the regular visits from the helpful and friendly technician for system checks, and helpful tips on maintaining other appliances in your household. Both experiences bring us closer to the brand. However, the impact on the cognition generated by the low price and energy efficiency fades over time faster than the positive experience of interacting with the technician. This leftover memory of a positive emotional experience helps create over time a positive perception towards the brand which impacts future purchases and other brand-oriented behaviors (such as spreading the good word). Customer experience thus consists of both cognitive and emotional reactions and creates and reinforces perceptions and expectations of value. The emotional component is particularly important in consumption of services worldwide and in consumer and luxury products in fast growing developing countries. Experiences through impacting value perceptions impact customer relationships. Customer experience management is now widely considered a core aspect of customer relationship management.

To truly generate both behavioral and attitudinal loyalty, superior value offering and a positive experience need to develop into trust in the brand. Positive customer experiences are crucial in CRM because over time they bolster trust. Trust is the foundation in any long-term buyer–seller relationship (Kotler and Armstrong, 2010). In the above example of the cake mix in Japan, the overall perception and mental experience of using the cake mix to bake a cake is marred by the recommendation of using a rice cooker to bake it, which is a cultural taboo for the Japanese and would be emotional to a large number of them. Such a recommendation does not enhance the feeling of trust. Either the cake mix never gets purchased, never used if purchased on an impulse, the rice cooker is used to bake the cake leaving the cook guilty of breaking a taboo or a different method of baking the cake is used that ends in sub-par results. At the end of the day, the perception of the value offering is negative and the experience of purchasing the cake mix and baking it is emotionally dissatisfying leading to an erosion of trust towards the brand.

Trust in a buyer–seller relationship has the added advantage of lowering costs of transactions and quicker decision making. For an organization to earn the trust it has to show that its actions are (Peppers and Rogers, 2017):

- Competent
- Responsible

- Ethical
- Proactive

Creating positive customer experiences and trust is a challenge in international markets. This is because cultural consumption patterns, economy, laws, competition, demographics (millennials vs. seniors), location (urban vs. rural), lifestyles, and interests create differences both across and within countries, in what consumers value, how they make decisions, and what they expect from brands. Even though across developed country markets Smart car is normally separated from any connection to Mercedes-Benz (its parent company) it would make sense to do the opposite in growth markets, where foreign (particularly German) autos have a strong quality image.

Customer Profitability and Customer Loyalty

Customer relationship management creates reciprocal values in a buyer–seller relationship. The value that the organization seeks from the customer are direct and indirect contributions from the customer to the organization's revenues and profits through repeated and increasing purchase of the organization's products and services as well as through advocating for the company and making referrals. Extent of profitability and loyalty of the customer together determine the value of the customer to the firm. It is important here to note that the relationship between customer loyalty and customer profitability is not always positive. Whereas loyalty only considers the nature and frequency of purchase and non-purchase behaviors, profitability considers the impact of the same on both revenues and costs. Increasing loyalty does not necessarily increase profitability. If the cost of catering to a loyal customer is higher than the revenue the company receives from that customer he/she will be considered loyal but not profitable (Reinartz and Kumar, 2002).

Customer Orientation and Customer Centricity

Appreciation of the complexities of global business, importance of customer profitability and loyalty to an organization's health, and increasing customer power and sophistication have pushed organizations to become more customer oriented. Companies have realized that to better serve, engage, and satisfy customers and to attract new ones their operations need to revolve around customers' needs and wants.

Customer orientation is one of the three components of market orientation. Customer-oriented organizational culture believes that making the interests of the customer the focal point that drives organizational operations and the interest of other stakeholders (partners, employees, etc.) helps develop a profitable enterprise (Deshpande et al., 1993). Customer centricity extends customer orientation by putting customers at the center of the organization.

Customer centricity is the organizational philosophy and culture which believes in the customer being the primary motivator for all operations, and that the sole reason for an organization's existence is to understand, engage, serve, and satisfy the customer profitably (Frankenberger et al., 2013).

A customer-centric organization allocates resources to acquire market information, analyzes it to gain knowledge, and creates innovative value-added offerings for customers. A customer-centric organization also creates strategies and policies to gain the customer's trust. A continuous process of knowledge development guides all organizational operations for the ultimate goal of profitable customer loyalty through enhanced customer value, experiences, and trust (Leavy, 2019). Customer centricity indicates a company's commitment to customer satisfaction and customer loyalty (Kumar and Shah, 2004). Figure 1.2 identifies the different actions that go into making an organization customer centric.

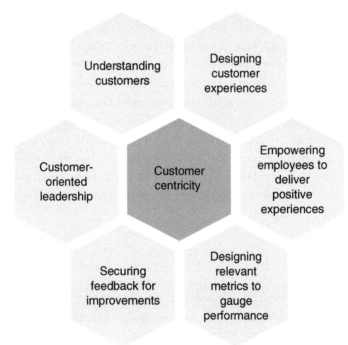

Figure 1.2 Customer Centricity

As organizations venture into international markets, developing relevant knowledge becomes critical to avoid missteps and incorrect assumptions. Mattel belatedly realized that Japanese girls did not like the look of the Barbie doll that was popular with girls in the

US (Keegan and Green, 2011). Finding relevant information in international markets can be challenging. Governments or private parties may not regularly collect information, the particular information needed is not collected, information is collected in a foreign language or consumers' contact information or addresses are not easily available for surveys. There are a few ways to overcome these challenges and get the right information.

- Private research companies such as MarketResearch.com publish and sell a wide variety of reports from different countries and industries
- Market research companies operating across countries collect and analyze primary data required for specific purposes
- A company's CRM technology and systems can feed data collected from sales, marketing, and customer service into built-in market research functions and capabilities

Table 1.1 below highlights the top global market research companies.

Table 1.1 Global Market Research Companies

Nielsen (UK)	IRI (US)
Kantar (UK)	Westat (US)
Quintiles IMS (US)	Wood MacKenzie (UK)
Ipsos (France)	INTAGE Holdings (Japan)
Gfk (Germany)	Dunnhumby (UK)

Source: Brereton, M. and Bowers, D. (2018). "The 2017 AMA Gold Global Top 25 Market Research Companies." American Marketing Association, Oct 1, www.ama.org/marketing-news/the-2017-ama-gold-global-top-25-market-research-companies

Facets of Customer Relationship Management

Research has uncovered multiple facets of customer relationship management. Over the decades, definitions of CRM have concentrated on one or more of these facets. Research on CRM implementation and experience of organizations have, however, shown that the different facets of CRM need to be aligned and work together to achieve long-term benefits (Becker et al., 2010; Bracknell, 2000; Courchesne et al., 2019; Galla, 1999; Meyliana et al., 2016; Nour, 2012; Sarmaniotis et al., 2013).

Strategic CRM

Strategic CRM lays down the overarching organizational reasons for implementing CRM, the goals that the CRM effort is trying to achieve, and the organizational and functional strategies and processes that will help achieve these goals. Strategic CRM takes a process-based view and provides both the big picture and the interconnected links through building the processes. For example, an organization may be planning to implement CRM to improve customer experiences. Maybe one of the goals the organization is trying to achieve is lowering the rate of product returns. High frequency of product returns has a negative impact on customer experiences. In order to achieve this goal, the organization may engage in strategies pertaining to creation and revision of processes of customer service, hiring and training of customer service employees, product return, product promotion, and new product development.

Operational CRM

Operational CRM equates to automated processes. It includes technology infrastructure and software applications that help automate organizational processes and operations pertaining to developing customer knowledge and catering to them. These range from database technologies, marketing, sales and customer service software automation, customer-facing technology applications that impact customer experiences through aiding interaction with organizations and acquisition and usage of products and services, and to technologies that impact customer experiences indirectly such as in the area of product development and inter-functional communication and collaboration. Essentially, operational CRM provides critical tech-based support to strategic CRM. In very simple ways CRM can be implemented without technology. However, in today's complex business world, tech support of CRM is critical. Just imagine trying to manually analyze consumers' social posts from a host of social media to unearth perceptions and behaviors! Facebook and other companies use artificial intelligence (AI) to recognize faces in photos and analyze conversations to identify patterns, and LinkedIn uses AI to analyze a mountain of data to recommend jobs (Kaput, 2019, 2020). Chapter 6 discusses operational CRM.

Analytical CRM

Metrics that objectively measure the success of CRM initiatives and software analytical tools that analyze data and information stored in databases form the core of analytical CRM. Together, these provide a granular view into the market, help the organization comprehend where they stand in terms of meeting CRM goals, and also provide a guide to future strategies. There are different types of metrics that help the organization objectively understand relevant issues such as customer selection, customer acquisition, customer activity, and customer management. Chapter 5 discusses analytical CRM.

Analytical software tools analyze information stored in databases and other operational CRM-process automation to provide meaningful patterns, trends, and predictions. There are specific tools that pertain to specific marketing activities that impact customer relationship management (Cao and Tian, 2020). For example, a cluster analysis tool aids the overall process of market segmentation by breaking down the market into clusters and recommending segments to target, and a conjoint analysis tool aids the process of product development by determining and recommending the most attractive set of attributes to be incorporated into a new product offering.

Collaborative CRM

Collaborative CRM helps with cooperation and coordination of people and activities in the value chain both within and outside the organization (partners such as market research organizations and advertising agencies, distributors, retailers, and logistics providers) to positively impact customer experiences and satisfaction. The value chain, which helps provide the value promised to consumers, commonly consists of entities that work with each other to achieve this goal. Organizations have realized that it is not possible for just one entity (organizational function or overall organization) in this value chain to truly provide long-term customer satisfaction. This is because each entity performs different complementary functions (human resources hires qualified employees and marketing brings in profitable customers; one organization makes the product and the other stores the product) that come together seamlessly to maximize awareness, access, purchase, consumption, experiences, and interactions. Employee and partner relationship management is thus intimately connected to customer relationship management. Recent research has shown that relationship quality in the value chain impacts both the management of the value chain and hence the performance of the focal firm (Işık et al., 2020). Table 1.2 highlights the different facets of CRM.

Table 1.2 CRM Facets

CRM Facet	Facet Characteristics
Strategic CRM	A process view of the firm determines the overarching CRM goals and the organizational and inter-functional processes required to achieve the same
Operational and CRM	Technology infrastructure that supports all organizational CRM processes
Analytical CRM	Metrics and analytical software that enable development of market knowledge and determination of the effectiveness of CRM actions
Collaborative CRM	Cooperation with value-chain partners to facilitate customer relationship management

Tools of Customer Relationship Management

What tools do organizations need to successfully manage customer experiences and relationships? Experience of organizations and research findings have shown that CRM implementation requires a three-pronged tool approach (Chen and Popovich, 2003; Ledingham and Rigby, 2004). These tools can be categorized as process tools, people tools, and technology tools. It is critical that the three types of tools align with each other. The process tools lay down what activities are involved in implementing CRM strategies. These process tools are automated by technology tools, and people tools assisted by technology tools put these process tools in action. Thus, by complementing each other, the three tools together help implement CRM strategies.

Process Tools

Like interconnected blood vessels in the human body, organizations can be viewed as a system of interconnected processes that impact each other and that need to be aligned for the proper functioning of the organization. This is the process-based view of organizations.

Process: A sequence of activities or actions that achieves a goal.

Depending on the breadth of CRM implementation (in a particular function or the whole organization), process tools will include all processes that directly and (in some cases indirectly) impact CRM goals and strategies.

If one of the goals of CRM is to reduce returns and cancellations, then some of the processes that would together impact returns and cancellations are customer prospecting processes, customer communication processes, both handled by the marketing and sales function, and customer service processes. Better prospective processes should make sure that the "right" customer is being targeted; better communication with the customer through various channels should help in alleviating difficulties in using the product or service and reinforcing the relevancy and benefit of the product and service. And finally, better customer service processes should complement the customer communication processes by answering any queries and solve any problem the customer may have, and facilitate consumption of the product. Improvements in these three processes together should help lower the chances of product returns.

Given the overarching goal of CRM, at the core CRM success directly depends upon effective and efficient marketing, sales, and customer service processes. Some organizational processes indirectly aid in CRM efforts. Hiring and training processes make sure customer-facing employees are qualified and customer oriented, knowledge management helps understand realities of the market, product management makes products competitive and user friendly, and sales management makes sales employees motivated, competitively compensated, and trained. Given the organization-wide nature of CRM initiatives, many of these processes that benefit CRM are cross-functional in nature (Gryna, 2001). Table 1.3 below provides a list of common organizational processes that facilitate CRM efforts.

Table 1.3 Processes that facilitate Global CRM

Process	Key Functions	Contribution to CRM
Market Research	Collection, storage, analysis, and interpretation of market data	Helps develop market knowledge
Market Segmentation	Breaks up the market into segments based on a combination of different variables (e.g. income and lifestyle)	Helps unearth characteristics of segments
Targeting	Selects segment(s) to target for CRM interventions	Helps more focused resource allocation
Customer Journey Mapping	Determines the sequence of steps customers would like to take to access, purchase, consume, and discard products and services	Helps in increasing customer value, experiences, and satisfaction
Product Development	Develops new products	Helps increase consumer interest, customer value, and revenues
Customer Communication	Interacts with customers across multiple channels and promotes products and services and other company activities	Helps increase customer engagement, experiences, value, and brand perception
Distribution	Transports and stores products through marketing channels	Helps increase customer value by streamlining product movement, safeguarding product quality and increasing service quality
Sales	Acquires and retains customers	Helps increase customer experiences, satisfaction, loyalty, and profitability through cross-selling, upselling, and relationship building
Customer Service	Interacts with customers to answer questions and solve problems	Helps increase customer experiences, satisfaction, loyalty, and retention

Technology Tools

Technology tools include different hardware, software, and applications that directly and indirectly aid in CRM implementation. There are dedicated CRM technology suites and platforms with different functionalities and varying degrees of sophistication to suit different CRM implementation needs of organizations. Technology tools commonly aid CRM in:

- Gathering, storing, and analyzing market information
- Collaborating within the organization and across the value chain
- Communicating and interacting with customers and other stakeholders
- Developing new products
- Marketing, sales, and customer service operations

Increase in competition, the significant role of social media and smartphones in consumers' lives, and the growth of omni-channel shopping behavior (consumer utilization of multiple offline and online channels to aid in purchase decision making) have made technology tools all the more critical for CRM. CRM technology tools enhance the efficiencies and effectiveness of decision making in processes. Technology-supported process automation seamlessly coordinates all process-related tasks, documentation, and reports and keeps all members of the process team updated. Technology-supported process customization facilitates customer access to, and enhances usability of, products and services, thereby increasing customer value and experience.

TECH BOX: AMAZON, WALMART TELL CONSUMERS TO SKIP RETURNS OF UNWANTED ITEMS

Retailers now have a new strategy to facilitate the process of returning an item by allowing customers to keep it! Amazon.com Inc., Walmart Inc. and other companies are taking help from artificial intelligence to determine whether it is economically feasible to process a return. For items that are inexpensive or large it is often cheaper to refund the purchase price because of high shipping charges to return the item. The customer gets to keep the product or donate it. This saves the customer the hassle of returning the product and saves the company shipping dollars. The relatively new approach presented itself as a solution and became more popular during the Covid-19 pandemic, as consumers turned to increased online shopping, forcing retailers to handle a surge in return issues.

"We are getting so many inquiries about this that you will see it take off in coming months," said Amit Sharma, chief executive of Narvar Inc., which processes returns for retailers.

Source: Suzanne Kapner and Paul Ziobro Jan. 10, 2021, www.wsj.com/articles/amazon-walmart-tell-consumers-to-skip-returns-of-unwanted-items-11610274600

People Tools

Just as an organization can be considered as a grouping of interconnected processes, it can also be viewed as a grouping of interconnected roles that operate these processes.

These roles are almost always filled by people. Except for some repetitive processes that are automated and run by robots, all the processes are still designed and run by humans with some help from machines. This may, however, change as AI grows up.

The people tool of CRM is critical to CRM efforts because it is the people who make or mar the effectiveness of a process. Product development, marketing, sales, logistics, and customer service are all crucial for CRM and all have significant people components. There is evidence of the importance of human capital in high-performing, resilient organizations (Periera et al., 2020). The people tool is also by far the most tricky to effectively develop and manage. People are cognitively, emotionally, and socially complex beings. For employees to effectively contribute to organizational growth in general and CRM in particular, they need to be capable and motivated. Change management efforts by senior management supported by human resources initiatives in hiring, training, compensating, and motivating are necessary to get buy-in from employees.

Despite the importance of all three tools to CRM, process tools are at the forefront and foundation of CRM implementation, given the criticality of processes to organizational health and growth (Chakravorti, 2009; Lambert, 2010; Mitussis et al., 2006; Pisharodi et al., 2003). Process management takes a holistic approach in managing organizational operations that help achieve core values and frequently these operations cut across organizational functions (Badreddine et al., 2009). Technology and people tools provide support to facilitate effective functioning of CRM processes. Process tools lead the way forward, but success will only come with adequate support from tech and people tools. Figure 1.3. illustrates the three-pronged nature of CRM.

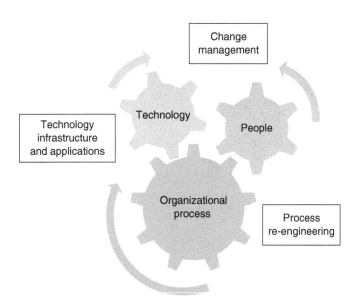

Figure 1.3 CRM Process, People, and Technology Tools

As CRM goes international, the tools themselves remain critical to CRM efforts. For example, both the process and the technology tools are important for CRM in both conventional banks and Islamic banks that exist in many Islamic countries (Lebdaoui and Chetioui, 2020). However, different business environments existing in different countries force some level of adaptation to the tools, most notably the process and people tools.

Home Depot's business model relies on do-it-yourself (DIY) consumers hauling away home improvement items and their CRM processes are geared around the needs of DIY consumers and the way they shop. They have been very successful in the United States market because of the significant percentage of consumers who prefer DIY home improvements (Corcoran, 2013). Around the world, DIY culture as well as access to vehicles to haul away large home improvement items are far less predominant. As Home Depot ventures into diverse international markets, they will need to overhaul a good percentage of their processes if they want to effectively cater to a significant portion of the world population of a country.

Expected behaviors across countries are governed by cultural norms. These norms set the standards of interpersonal communication between employees (sales people, customer service) and customers and help determine what will be effective. For example, the extent of use of the word "no" varies among countries and is also perceived differently (Cateora et al., 2013). Differences in economic development and culture also mean that employees across countries are motivated by different things (money vs. recognition), may need different kinds of training (technical vs. cultural) and have different expectations from and exhibit different types of interactions with their colleagues and supervisors. Harmony is more important than honesty in many East Asian cultures, leading teams to take collective blame for non-performance vs. identifying the actual person within the team primarily responsible for the lower performance (Cateora et al., 2013).

Case Study

Kaya Clinic's Efforts at Differentiation through Customer Relationship Initiatives

Kaya Skin Clinic, an Indian beauty clinic company established in 2002 had successfully established itself in a majority of countries in the Middle East by 2015. In just over 12 years Kaya had 23 beauty clinics in this region. Facing stiff competition and difficulty in differentiating its offering, Kaya was wondering what strategies would help differentiate its offering and further expand in the region.

Business Model

Kaya's business model is to differentiate itself with customized innovative solutions and personalized service from dermatologists all offered in an aesthetic, luxurious, and comfortable clinic setting.

Offering

Kaya Clinic's value proposition is about facilitating the achievement of flawless skin with the help of skincare and haircare. Kaya's research department has developed 15 different skin care product lines to address a variety of client needs and customize solutions. Customers could select from different skin care categories and regimen. Apart from such customized solutions Kaya also provide an appearance-enhancing beautification service with 50 standard products. Dermatologists at the clinics provide this service. The clinics are comfortable and pleasing to the eye and are equipped with the latest beauty technology which has been approved by the US government's Food and Drug Administration (FDA). All employees are regularly trained on product, technology, and customer service aspects of the business.

Kaya delivers the beauty service with personalized attention. A dermatologist assesses the individual needs of each customer and in consultation with the client develops a customized plan with available options and a desired and assured outcome. Its excellent customer service has been awarded the "Super Brand" citation for multiple years.

Customers

Many of Kaya's customers in India are working women who have less time for elaborate skin care. Hence in its efforts to differentiate its offerings Kaya Clinic in India has complemented its clinic offerings through other retail offerings. The Kaya Skin Bar is a downsized version of the Kaya Skin Clinic and more conveniently located. The Kaya "shop-in-shop" concept provides the entire range of Kaya's standard skin products within other lifestyle stores and hypermarkets.

In the Middle East, however, most of Kaya's clients are wealthy, and have enough time to engage in an elaborate beauty ritual. Beauty treatment and skin quality are very important to Arab women. Price and location convenience is thus not an issue here, unlike in the Indian market.

Customer Relationship Management (CRM) Efforts

Expansion through a combination of customer acquisition and retention via increased customer satisfaction are dual CRM goals of Kaya.

Customer acquisition efforts include conventional TV (in Arabic channels), magazine, and digital advertisements to increase brand awareness as well as social media communications to enhance brand equity.

Customer satisfaction and retention efforts include a combination of product and service quality, localization, and rewards. The clinics have an Arabic look and feel, multilingual employees and regular emphasis is made on the qualities of "customer care, concern, customer centricity and transparency." The company also makes sure an Internet search will lead consumers to the Middle East Kaya website, not Kaya's Indian website.

The company also has a loyalty program "Kaya Smiles" that includes a tiered point-based reward system with five categories of customers. These customer categories

(Continued)

were created based on frequency of visits and types of transactions and signified the value of the customer. Rewards include converting points into cash discounts and also customized offers at regular intervals.

Challenges Ahead

As competition in the skin care industry has heated up in the Middle East, Kaya has seen its differentiation based on customization being easily copied by competitors. At the same time research has shown that customers care more about the ingredients than about the product, making Kaya's model of utilizing dermatologists to develop and provide the solutions through a clinic-based experience vital to success. To feed its aggressive expansion strategy amid strong competition and dwindling differentiation, Kaya is having to rethink its strategy for the Middle East. Kaya has learned that in the Middle East the retail and clinic experience are most likely the differentiator. However, it has to decide if continuing with its current strategy of providing expert and customized services in a pleasant location is enough or if the brand value proposition direction needs to be revamped for the Middle East.

Source: Waheed, K.A. and Jham, V. (2017). *Kaya Skin Clinic: Creating a Sustainable Competitive Advantage with Customers*. ID: 9B17A022. Richard Ivey School of Business Foundation. Distributed by www.thecasecentre.org

Summary

Customer relationship management is an organization-wide business model to develop and manage relationships with customers. CRM's objective is to create loyal and profitable customers. The foundation of what helps achieve this objective is adoption of a customer-oriented organizational culture and taking customer-centric actions that consistently provide differentiated customer value and high-quality customer experiences. CRM implementation is a complex undertaking given its multiple facets and organization-wide reach that frequently involves value-chain partner organizations. Multiple faces of CRM include Strategic, Operational, Analytical, and Collaborative. All these facets are essential and thus a holistic approach to CRM implementation that incorporates all these is needed. These facets are holistically implemented through a three-pronged CRM tool set. These are process, technology, and people tools. Process tools direct the CRM implementation supported by technology and people tools. As organizations expand their CRM operations into international markets, business environments such as culture, economy, laws, competitive actions, and consumers existing in different countries raise additional challenges. The foundations on which CRM rests, its facets and its tools remain the same. However, what goes into making these effective changes from country to country, making it necessary to adapt aspects of the CRM initiative.

References

Adhikari, A. and Agashe, R. (2020). "The digital payments push: What 50 micro-merchants in India are saying." *Center for Financial Action, Blog post*, June 29, www.centerforfinancialinclusion.org/the-digital-payments-push-what-50-micro-merchants-in-india-are-saying

Badreddine, A., Romdhane, T.B., and Amor, N.B. (2009). *"A new process-based approach for implementing an integrated management system: Quality, security, environment."* Proceedings of the International MultiConference of Engineers and Computer Scientists 2, 2–6.

Band, W. (2013). "How To succeed with CRM: The critical success factors." *Forrester Research* (July 31), https://www.forrester.com/blogs/13-07-31-how_to_succeed_with_crm_the_critical_success_factors/

Becker, U., Greve, G., and Albers, S. (2010). "Left behind expectations: How to prevent CRM implementation from failing." *New Strategies*, 2, 34.

Bracknell (2000). "Ten steps to successful CRM implementation." *Powergrid International*, www.power-grid.com/smart-grid/ten-steps-to-successful-crm-implementation

Buttle, F. (1996). *Relationship Marketing: Theory and Practice*, Paul Chapman Publishing, London, 1–16.

Cao, G. and Tian, N. (2020). "Enhancing customer-linking marketing capabilities using marketing analytics." *The Journal of Business & Industrial Marketing*, 35, 7, 1289–99.

Cateora, P.R., Gilly, M.C., and Graham, J.L. (2013). *International Marketing*, 16th edn. New York: McGraw-Hill Irwin.

Chakravorti, S. (2009). "Extending customer relationship management to value chain partners for competitive advantage." *Journal of Relationship Marketing*, 8, 4, 299.

Chen, I.J. and Popovich, K. (2003). "Understanding customer relationship management (CRM): People, process and technology." *Business Process Management Journal*, 9, 5, 672–88.

Corcoran, E. (2013). "70% of Americans prefer do-it-yourself home improvements." *The Street Inc.*, May 28, www.prnewswire.com/news-releases/70-of-americans-prefer-do-it-yourself-home-improvements-209184081.html

Courchesne, A., Ravanas, P., and Pulido, C. (2019). "Using technology to optimize customer relationship management: The case of Cirque du Soleil." *International Journal of Arts Management*, 21, 2, 83–93.

Day, G.S. (2000). "Managing market relationships." *Journal of the Academy of Marketing Science*, 28, 1, 24–30.

Deshpande, R., Farley, J.U. and Webster, Frederick E., Jr. (1993). "Corporate culture, customer orientation, and innovativeness." *Journal of Marketing*, 57, 1, 23–38.

Dictionary.cambridge.org. "Customer relationship," https://dictionary.cambridge.org/dictionary/english/customer-relationship

Edinger, S. (2018). "Why CRM projects fail and how to make them more successful." *Harvard Business Review*, Dec. 20, https://hbr.org/2018/12/why-crm-projects-fail-and-how-to-make-them-more-successful

Frankenberger, K., Weiblen, T., and Gassmann, O. (2013). "Network configuration, customer centricity, and performance of open business models: A solution provider perspective." *Industrial Marketing Management*, 45, 5, 671–82.

Galla, J. (1999). "Team-building key to CRM implementation." *Strategy*, https://strategyonline.ca/1999/03/01/24671-19990301

Gryna, F.M. (2001). *Quality Planning and Analysis*, 4th edn. McGraw-Hill, New York.

IBS Center for Management Research (2014). "McDonald's: Using social media to connect with customers." *ICMR*, www.icmrindia.org/casestudies/catalogue/Marketing/MKTG319.htm

Işık, Ö., Yumurtacı, H., Kotzab, H., and Teller, C. (2020). "Supply chain relationship quality and its impact on firm performance." *Production Planning & Control,* 31, 6, 470–82.

Jaworski, B. and Kohli, A. (1993). "Market orientation: Antecedents and consequences." *Journal of Marketing*, 57, 3, 53–70.

Kaput, M. (2019). "9 AI tools to streamline your social media strategy." *Hubspot.com*, Nov. 25, https://blog.hubspot.com/marketing/ai-social-media-tools

Kaput, M. (2020). "What is artificial intelligence for social media?" *Marketing Artificial Intelligence Institute*, Dec. 22, www.marketingaiinstitute.com/blog/what-is-artificial-intelligence-for-social-media

Keegan, W.J. and Green, M.C. (2011). *Global Marketing*, 6th edn. Harlow: Pearson.

Keramati, A., Samadi, H., & Nazari-Shirkouhi, S., and Askari, N. (2012). "Identifying and prioritising critical success factors for CRM implementation: A case study." *International Journal of Electronic Customer Relationship Management*, 6, 235–52.

Kotler, P. and Armstrong, G. (2010). *Principles of Marketing*. Saddle River, NJ: Pearson Education.

Kumar, V. and Shah, D. (2004). "Building and sustaining profitable customer loyalty for the 21st century." *Journal of Retailing*, 80, 4, 317–29.

Lambert, D.M. (2010). "Customer relationship management as a business process." *The Journal of Business & Industrial Marketing*, 25, 1, 4–17.

Leavy, B. (2019). "Decoupling: Customer-centric perspectives on disruption and competitive advantage." *Strategy & Leadership*, 48, 1, 3–11.

Ledingham, D. and Rigby, D.K. (2004). "CRM done right." *Harvard Business Review*, November.

Lebdaoui, H. and Chetioui, Y. (2020). "CRM, service quality and organizational performance in the banking industry: A comparative study of conventional and Islamic banks." *The International Journal of Bank Marketing*, 38, 5, 1081–106.

Liu, W., Wang, Z., and Zhao, H. (2020). "Comparative study of customer relationship management research from East Asia, North America and Europe: A bibliometric overview." *Electronic Markets*, 30, 4, 735–57.

Meyliana, Hidayanto, A.N. and Budiardjo, E.K. (2016). "The critical success factors for customer relationship management implementation: A systematic literature review", *International Journal of Business Information Systems*, 23, 2, 131–74.

Mitussis, D., O'Malley, L., and Patterson, M. (2006). "Mapping the re-engagement of CRM with relationship marketing." *European Journal of Marketing*, 40, 5/6, 572–89.

Mujtaba, B.G. and Patel, B. (2007). "McDonald's success strategy and global expansion through customer and brand loyalty." *Journal of Business Case Studies*, 3, 3, 55–66.

Narver, J.C. and Slater, S.F. (1990). "The effect of a market orientation on business profitability." *Journal of Marketing*, 54, 4, 20–35.

Nour, M.A. (2012). "An integrative framework for customer relationship management: Towards a systems view." *International Journal of Business Information Systems*, 9, 1, 26–50.

Oblander, E.S., Gupta, S., Mela, C.F., Winer, R.S., and Lehmann, D.R. (2020). "The past, present, and future of customer management." *Marketing Letters*, 31, 2–3, 125–36.

Peppers, D. and Rogers, M. (2017). *Managing Customer Experiences and Relationships*, 3rd edn. Hoboken, NJ: John Wiley and Sons.

Pereira, V., Temouri, Y., and Patel, C. (2020). "Exploring the role and importance of human capital in resilient high performing organisations: Evidence from business clusters." *Applied Psychology*, 69, 3, 769–804.

Pisharodi, R.M., Angur, M.G., and Shainesh, G. (2003). "Relationship strategy, effectiveness, and responsiveness in services marketing." *Journal of Relationship Marketing*, 2, 1–2, 3–22.

Reinartz, W. and Kumar, V. (2002, 07). "The mismanagement of customer loyalty." *Harvard Business Review*, 80, 86.

Sapolsky, R.M. (2018). *Behave*. New York: Penguin Books.

Sarmaniotis, C., Assimakopoulos, C. and Papaioannou, E. (2013). "Successful implementation of CRM in luxury hotels: Determinants and measurements." *EuroMed Journal of Business*, 8, 2, 134–53.

Schaffmeister, N. (2015). *Brand Building and Marketing in Key Emerging Markets*. Cham, Switzerland: Springer.

2
COUNTRY BUSINESS ENVIRONMENTS

ZipDial—Reaching Customers across Emerging Countries

Having successfully established their business in South Asia, ZipDial was hoping to expand into other developing countries in that region and in the future to other emerging markets across the world.

ZipDial is a mobile marketing and analytics company founded in 2010 in Bangalore India. The brainchild of Sanjay Swamy and Valerie Rozycki Wagoner, the company was formed to help marketers run targeted marketing campaigns and increase engagement with customers. Its offering consists of a mobile marketing solution piled on top of a user database, making it possible for marketers to get a granular level of analysis and insight into consumer behavior.

Consumer Behavior Traits

Marketers in developing countries such as India needed a tool that would facilitate such targeted engagement. Consumer behavior traits in India make it very difficult for marketers to gather information. Unlike in developed countries where consumers regularly engage in online activities and use credit cards for multiple purchases, a large percentage of consumers in emerging countries only do business in cash.

Mobile phone usage in India has grown rapidly, providing retailers and brands a means to connect with customers through mobile. The market is fragmented with many companies competing nationally and regionally. Unlike developed country consumers, most Indian consumers are prepaid customers with a small percentage using smart phones with Internet capabilities. Being very cost conscious, South Asians rarely use text messaging for communication. More common are "missed calls," which consumers use to save money. It has been estimated that more than 50 percent of mobile subscribers use missed calls. "It's exceptionally prevalent peer-to-peer user behavior, where users dial a friend's number and then hang up on purpose in order to signal something such as 'Call me back' or 'I'm thinking of you,' or 'I've arrived home safely'" (Techcrunch, 2013).

(Continued)

The Missed-Call Mobile Solution

Popularity of the "missed call" behavior and the difficulty faced by marketers in tracking consumer behavior and in engaging them meaningfully helped Swamy and Wagoner decide on offering a "missed call" mobile solution to marketers. The solution is simple, language agnostic, and doesn't cost anything, making it compelling. One example of a missed call solution application is getting feedback on customer service by having customers make "missed calls" to specific numbers, which results in the system sending a survey based on the call. The company thought up multiple applications for "missed calls" that would generate customer information and also engage them.

Before implementation the "missed call" solution was tested by 1) polling fans of cricket to vote for the team they think will win by calling a number assigned to that team and 2) offering a free dial-for-score update service for cricket games where consumers would dial a number to get an automated text update on the score. Within four months, millions of consumers were dialing millions of times a day to respond to the surveys and to get the score.

The functionality of the product was further expanded by adding the following features to allow for more engagement between marketers and customers.

- Friends referral—customers refer friends to the brand and share experiences on Facebook
- Solutions for marketers to address different campaign goals such as acquisition, retention, retargeting, referrals and trials
- Customized targeting of consumers based on the particular user's profile, behavior, and mobile device capabilities. Voice, WAP, SMS and mobile apps were available consumer interaction interface options

A Boon for Marketers

The product was a big success. In a country where reliable and detailed customer profile data is not available, this unique capability of the ZipDial product allowed brands to learn more about their customers, engage them through customized communication, and facilitate customer relationship management and customer loyalty. ZipDial functionalities also allowed brands to measure the effectiveness of their mobile marketing campaigns relative to campaigns on traditional media.

Several brands creatively used ZipDial's "missed call" solution successfully to boost customer engagement. Gillette India took advantage of the dial-for-cricket-score functionality by sending a Gillette ad along with score updates. Kingfisher, one of India's largest beer brands introduced a mobile cricket game that utilized "missed calls" as a point-scoring mechanism. UTV Bindass, a national TV broadcast channel primarily targeting youth, also ran a similar "missed-call" advertising campaign to gauge opinions on dating and relationships which went viral on Facebook. Disney successfully created a fan base by using ZipDial's "missed call" solution for a contest that involved gathering points by calling the different ZipDial numbers that flashed across the screens on cartoon planes. Results were particularly impressive considering that a significant percentage of participants did not have access to Facebook or the Internet.

In less than five years ZipDial built a successful end-to-end mobile marketing and analytical platform, ran over several hundred campaigns for brands, and secured clients that included multiple global brands such as Coca-Cola, Pepsico, Proctor and Gamble and Unilever, and significantly grew revenues.

To replicate its success in other distant emerging markets, however, the company will have to overcome several challenges. These lie in the areas of 1) substantial investment in infrastructure and sales, 2) accurate forecasting of revenues because of changes in pricing structure from campaign based to subscription based, and 3) increased consolidation and new competition in the mobile technology and advertising industries.

Source: Clara, Laurent, D. and Sorensen, J. (2014). *ZipDial: Reaching the Next 3 Billion Consumers*. ID: IDE-07. Stanford Graduate School of Business. Distributed by www.thecasecentre.org

Introduction

The story of ZipDial's success in South Asia and its potential expansion into other emerging economies highlight two important takeaways that are relevant to global CRM: 1) Consumer behavior varies from country to country and in order to be successful it is important to understand these differences and develop creative customer-focused strategies for each country that align with consumer behavior, and 2) the importance of actively looking for similarities in business environments and consumer behavior across countries so that competencies, strategies, and tactics can be leveraged in another geographical market where substantial similarities exist.

Why does consumer behavior vary from country to country? The reason lies in the nature of the country environments that exist in every country. Consumption is influenced and shaped by the nature of the country-level macro environments. These environments vary from country to country in different degrees bringing about differences in consumers and their behaviors (Lowe et al., 2019). For example, macro environments have helped shape a stronger environmental consciousness in a certain set of customers in certain countries more than in other countries. These consumers prefer to consume products and services that are environmentally friendly (BEMG Global Scan Sustainability, 2012). Country environments also shape business practices which in turn impact consumer behavior. For example the acceptance and legality of coupons vary from country to country because of culture and laws. In order to operate effectively in a country, organizations thus need to work within the limitations imposed by macro environments and the realities of consumer characteristics.

Chapter 1 highlights customer value and customer experiences as critical to customer relationship management. To provide meaningful and differentiated value and enhance experiences in a country with specific macro environments it is critical to 1) understand consumers, particularly their perceptions, motivation, expectations, and traits related to consumption, and 2) develop effective and efficient business processes and operations.

As companies venture into multiple countries, effective global CRM will require first understanding and then managing differences and similarities in both macro environments and consumer behavior. It will be necessary to make adaptations to the process, people, and technology CRM tools and to leverage existing competencies from one country market to another.

Country Macro Environments

The primary macro environments in a country are the economic environment, the cultural environment, the political environment, and the legal environment. These together interact to impact what consumers desire, how they engage in the consumption process, nature, and extent of competition and business practices. Over time the impact of these environments helps create specific country-level consumer and business traits. Environments, however, are dynamic and change by different degrees across countries, setting the pace at which consumers, competition, and business practices change. For example, the economic environments of developed countries such as the US or Australia change at a much slower pace than those in developing countries such as India or South Africa. Given the important role that these environments play in consumer behavior and customer relationship management initiatives, it is imperative for brands to keep abreast of any changes. Figure 2.1 illustrates the macro country environments.

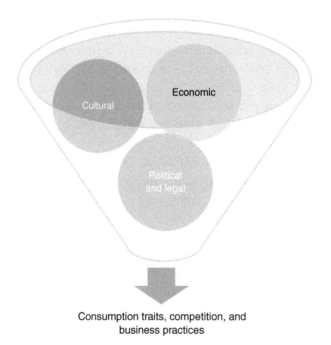

Figure 2.1 Country Environmental Forces

Economic Environment

There are two types of economic systems: a market economic and a mixed economic system.

Economic environment: The foundational economic system of a country and associated indicators.

1   *Market economy*: This is characterized by completely privatized production based on the forces of demand and supply. For most consumer and industrial products, consumption behavior and competition determine demand, supply, and the prices of products and services. A good percentage of the developed world has a market economy.

2   *Mixed economy*: Most countries in the world can be categorized as mixed market economies. In a mixed market economy, some industries are completely privatized, some partially privatized, and some owned and operated by the government. Mixed market economies are seen in both developed and developing countries with significant differences in the extent and type of privatization versus government ownership or control of production. The United Kingdom, for example, has far less government ownership and far more privatization than Brazil. China and Russia are atypical examples where despite extensive privatization, the governments maintain strong sway on the operation of private companies.

Economic Indicators

To achieve a granular understanding of the nature of the economy and the extent of impact of economic environments on consumer behavior and business operations it is important to monitor indicators that impact the economic system (BDC, n.d.).

Table 2.1 includes some major economic indicators.

Table 2.1   Economic Indicators

Economic Growth Rate (%)	Average Income
Inflation (loss of currency value/increase in prices)	Educational attainment (literacy rate, and percentage of population with primary and secondary education levels)
Interest rates (%)	Demand for products and services
Tax rates (%)	Competition (type and extent)
Unemployment rates (%)	Availability and quality of suppliers (manufacturers, distributors, retailers)
Currency exchange rate (exchange relationship between two currencies)	Quality of infrastructure and quality of distribution

Cultural Environment

A set of universal human values form the foundation of culture across countries (Rokeach, 1973). Geert Hofstede, the eminent organizational anthropologist, defines culture as the "collective programming of mind which distinguishes the members of one human group from another" (Hofstede, 1984: 21). This mental programming consists of a set of values and value-based norms that act as a framework for living among a group and distinguishes one group from another (Hill and Hult, 2020).

Values are the foundation of a country's culture. Values are abstract concepts that govern a culture's perceptions and attitudes towards life and lifestyle issues such as the role of women, marriage, justice, corruption, health, environment, travel, business, and consumption (Schwartz, 2004). Values are thus imbued with emotions. Cultural values give rise to norms. Norms are rules that govern a culture's behavior and consumption (Schwartz, 2004). For example, cultures approach time differently. Behavior and consumption of time is more discrete on average in northern Europe with meetings and trains running on exacting schedules compared to southern Europe, Latin America, and the Middle East where time is approached more fluidly (World Science Festival, 2020).

Elements of Culture: What to Look out for

To understand cultures well we need to know what elements to look for to identify values and norms so that effective CRM strategies and tactics can be developed. Figure 2.2 illustrates the elements of culture.

Hofstede's cultural value types: Geert Hofstede identified six value dimensions along which cultures vary. These dimensions have been researched extensively and have held their relevancy for organizations engaged in international marketing (Hofstede. com, n.d.). The six dimensions on which countries vary are Individualism, Power Distance, Masculinity, Uncertainty Avoidance, Long Term Orientation and Indulgence. Each dimension is a continuum with scores from 0 to varying maximum scores. The higher the score the more the culture exhibits that dimension. Table 2.2 highlights and describes these cultural dimensions.

Rituals: Every culture has rituals that showcase the values and norms of that culture. Rituals are activities of life and lifestyles that are either of common or uncommon occurrence. These rituals can be mundane, such as daily dining patterns (sitting around the table with extended family members vs. eating out alone or with friends); special, such as a wedding (a bride decked in a red shimmering sari in an Indian wedding vs. a bride decked in pristine white in a typical Christian wedding); and festivals and customs such as the activities surrounding Chinese New Year (Cateora et al., 2019).

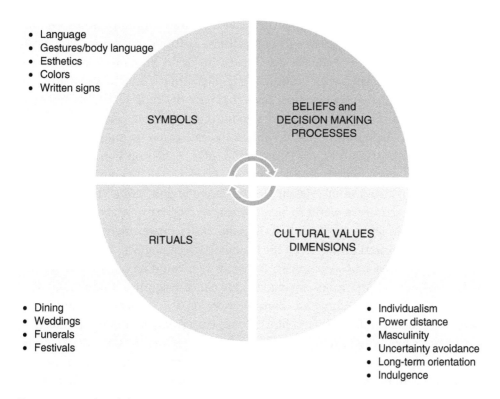

- Language
- Gestures/body language
- Esthetics
- Colors
- Written signs

SYMBOLS

BELIEFS and
DECISION MAKING
PROCESSES

RITUALS

CULTURAL VALUES
DIMENSIONS

- Dining
- Weddings
- Funerals
- Festivals

- Individualism
- Power distance
- Masculinity
- Uncertainty avoidance
- Long-term orientation
- Indulgence

Figure 2.2 Cultural Elements

Table 2.2 Hofstede's Cultural Dimensions

Dimensions	Descriptor
Individualism–Collectivism	Individual vs. group societal structure. The higher the score the more individualistic is the country. More individualistic countries believe in individual achievement but more collectivist countries believe in group achievement
Power Distance	Extent to which power differential exists and is accepted between different individuals and groups, such as between social classes. The higher the score the larger the power differential
Uncertainty Avoidance	Extent of society's acceptance of ambiguity and uncertainty as a normal aspect of life. The higher the score the less the acceptance of uncertainty. High uncertainty avoidance countries showcase a strong desire for security, rules, and regulations
Masculinity–Femininity	Emotional make-up of gender roles. The higher the score the more masculine the country. In a masculine society gender roles between men and women are clearly demarcated. Men are expected to be tough, materialistic, and competitive. In a more feminine society competition is lower, genders are emotionally closer, and consumers do what they like to do
Orientation (long term–short term)	Attitude towards and acceptance of change vs. sticking to tradition. This is exhibited through instant vs. delayed gratification, and attitudes to time. The higher the score the more positive the attitude towards change and the looser the attitude to time
Indulgence–Restraint	Extent to which a society controls its materialistic desires and impulses. The higher the score the more indulgent the culture

Symbols: Cultural symbols are signs that have meanings within a culture. Cultural symbols include spoken languages (colloquialisms), gestures (head nods to indicate yes, no, or maybe), colors (white is associated with death in many Asian countries whereas black is associated with death in western countries), esthetic standards such as type of clothing, and actual written signs that have meaning such as the swastika (signifying good luck) in India or a STOP sign (directing traffic to come to a complete stop) in the US. The meanings these symbols indicate could be unique or could be shared among other countries. For example the color of the stop sign in most countries is red but that's where the similarities end. Even though a handshake, which is said to have originated from Ancient Greece (Deep English, 2021), has been commonly adopted across the world to signify trust, respect, balance and equality, it is done differently in different countries (Wikipedia, 2021). Interestingly, the handshake is being slowly replaced in the US by the fist bump (Deep English, 2021).

Beliefs and decision-making processes: Beliefs, which could be religious or secular, impact ways in which decisions are made in life. Since a significant number of decisions made within a culture are consumption related, beliefs are particularly relevant to global CRM whether companies are engaged in promoting products or services, or negotiations with a channel member. Beliefs and the ways decisions are made show differences across countries. For example western countries in general believe in the unlucky nature of the number 13 and hotels try to avoid identifying a 13th floor in western markets. The Chinese belief of feng shui (harmony between energy and individuals) has an impact on home purchase in China. A particular point of difference that exists in consumer thought processes and decision making between Easterners and Westerners has implications for CRM efforts. Easterners on average consider a topic holistically and purchases are decided upon a holistic appreciation of individual details of the purchase. This involves a lot of back and forth across purchase elements such as packaging and warranties. Westerners on the other hand tend to think through each topic or elements of purchase sequentially with all details worked out sequentially before the decision is finalized (Cateora et al., 2019). It should be noted here that as much as it is important to be aware of belief systems and their impact on decision making it should not be generalized across all populations of a culture because there will be some differences between segments.

What Determines Cultural Elements?

The national cultural elements of a country that we see today have developed over a long period of time through the combined impact of several forces (Hill and Hult, 2020). These forces include:

- *The political and economic systems* of the country
- *Structure and divisions in society*: a) Is society primarily structured as groups or individuals? b) Are there divisions in society along racial, ethnic, tribal, class and/or caste lines?
- *Major religions followed*: In Islamic countries the concept of social justice in Islam creates a negative consumer attitude to interest charged by banks. This in turn impacts operations of financial institutions in these countries (Ziegler and Associates, 2021)
- *Primary languages spoken*: Where the English language has only a few terms to indicate snow or ice, the Sami language of Scandinavia has more than 180 words for the same (Magga, 2006)
- *Level of education*: As public education rises, values tend to become more secular and scientific and less traditional or dictated by pure religion (Baker, 2020). Education tends to promote values of equality, materialism, and concern for the environment

Figure 2.3 illustrates the forces that determine culture.

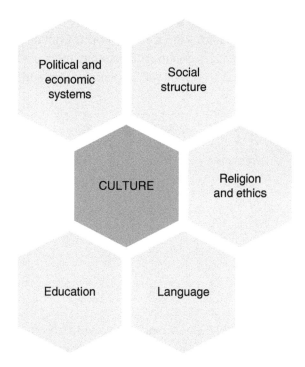

Figure. 2.3 Cultural Determinants

Cultural determinants have a mutually reinforcing relationship with cultural values, norms, and elements. As these determinants change over time they bring about a change in cultural values and norms which, as they evolve, in turn change the nature of the determinants. As countries grow economically "secular–rational" and "self-expression" values tend to replace "traditional" and "survival" values (Inglehart and Baker, 2000). Culture thus is always dynamic, although changes happen over medium to long periods of time.

Political and Legal Environments

The political and economic beliefs and philosophies (e.g. promoting education, investment, etc.) of a country's government are reflected in the laws of the country. The legal environment includes the "… the rules or laws that regulate behavior along with the processes by which the laws are enforced and through which redress for grievances are obtained" (Hill and Hult, 2020: 46). It consists of the legal foundation of the country and specific laws that regulate society and commerce.

Legal foundations: There are four main legal foundations in use across countries (World Factbook, n.d.). Figure 2.4 illustrates the legal foundations that exist across countries.

The most common type of religious law is Islamic law used in Islamic countries. Many countries utilize a mixed law system where aspects from different legal foundations are mixed to create the legal system. For example, India uses a combination of primarily common law mixed with civil and customary laws, and Algeria uses a mix of civil and Islamic laws.

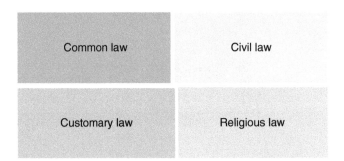

Figure 2.4 Legal Foundations

Legal indicators for global CRM: Countries have specific laws that reflect their legal foundation and indicate the ease or difficulty in operating. Table 2.3 highlights some specific areas where laws would impact customer relationship management and marketing operations.

Table 2.3 Types of Laws

Contracts	Intellectual property protection	Product safety
Anti-corruption	Property rights	Product liability
Privacy	Pricing	Promotion
E-commerce	Packaging and labelling	

The legal system and specific laws in a country impact international marketing and global CRM. For example, both the presence or absence and nature of laws that regulate promotion of products and services, product returns, pricing, and forming value-chain alliances impact marketing operations. It is thus important to know the relevant laws in a country and if they are implemented effectively. Laws and regulations vary across countries. This can pose a challenge in standardizing CRM practices across multiple countries.

Implications for Consumer Behavior and Business Practices

The economic, cultural, and legal environments in a country individually and collectively impact consumers (interests, lifestyle, perception, attitude, motivation), consumption behavior, and business practices. Since these country environments vary across countries, consumer behavior and business practices across countries also do. It is thus important to have a deep knowledge of the environments and critically understand their impacts before developing cross-country customer relationship management initiatives.

Consumer Behavior: Economy and culture have a combined impact on:

- Consumers' purchasing power
- Perceptions of value in and desirability for a) the types of products and services (e.g. a microwave oven, a skateboard, health insurance), b) the role these products play or can play in people's lives (e.g. good value, reliable, premium, exciting), and c) product and service attributes (e.g. easy to operate, free installation, multiple colors)
- Consumption behavior and trends (lifestyle—frequency of eating out, driving for weekend getaways—shopping frequencies, types of retail outlets frequented, leisure activities, etc)

These impacts create similarities and differences in consumption culture across countries.

Rural vs. urban: Within countries too economic development creates differences in consumption culture among segments, for example between rural and urban consumers. Unlike developed countries and smaller emerging countries, this difference is particularly stark in relatively fast growing, larger emerging countries such as India, China, Brazil,

Nigeria, South Africa, and Indonesia where rural consumers contribute significantly to consumption dollars. Whereas urban consumers across countries and their patterns of consumption have grown more similar, the perceptions, expectations and consumption of the rural segment have tended to remain more country specific. Because of differences in income, education, occupations, lifestyle, and access to technology between urban and rural segments, culture change in rural areas of these countries has been slower than their urban counterparts.

Providing superior value and experience to this challenging but lucrative rural segment, however, requires a deep understanding of them and creativity. Makers of household appliances such as Whirlpool not only lower prices but also reduce the complexity of the product for rural consumers. This serves to achieve both customer satisfaction and company profits. Reducing bells and whistles such as automatic dispensers in washing machines helps reduce manufacturing costs. Hindustan Lever, the Indian branch of Unilever, one of the oldest consumer goods companies and one that has had a long and successful presence in poorer countries, maximizes reach of these consumers in India by advertising in places where people congregate such as village centers, open markets, and village wells where people gather to wash clothing. The company also created audio entertainment-focused cell phone ads by using the "missed-call" strategy as discussed in the opening case on ZipDial. These advertisements are complemented by visits from salespeople during communal gatherings to display and explain products and give out free samples (Hill and Hult, 2020; Mahajan, 2016). Companies that can consistently create perception of higher quality of the product and service and provide value-added experiences through marketing activities are likely to see gains in satisfaction, profitability, and loyalty in this segment.

Luxury purchase: Increasing wealth in developing countries has created increasing potential for luxury brands. Even though consumption behavior of the luxury segment is quite similar from country to country, culture has subtle and complex impacts. Younger affluent consumers in today's China exhibit a unique combination of achievement orientation and a deference to hierarchy, the latter being an almost unchanging feature in Chinese culture and Chinese communist rule. This is unlike younger affluent consumers in the West. Young Chinese want to reach higher like their western counterparts but they also feel the need to conform and not stand out, which is very unlike their western counterparts (Doctoroff, 2012). The underlying motive for purchasing luxury for the young Chinese is to simply proclaim their status in society without any desire to express a unique individuality through this acquisition, as is more common in the West. It is therefore not surprising that this segment in China is only interested in purchasing luxury goods that are for public consumption such as automobiles but not goods for private consumption such as TVs. Similarities in luxury consumption among emerging and developing countries is expected to be stronger compared to consumption in corresponding cohorts in developed western-style markets.

As we consider the impact of both culture and economy we start seeing impacts which are more pervasive and complex. Cultural values, symbols, rituals, and ways of thinking impact what products and services are bought and how they are used. Success of food products, apparel, cosmetics, and other consumer goods are impacted by culture. Hence culture demands adaptation not only to the actual product but also service components in order to provide superior value and experiences. Successful companies such as Unilever, McDonald's and Coca-Cola have adapted and even invented products and services for different countries. McDonald's has adapted menu items to suit local tastes and Coca-Cola has introduced unique drinks for different local markets (Racoma, 2019; Stofsky, 2016). Beyond product adaptation and invention some companies may also have to adapt packaging. Many consumers across the world prefer to buy products such as shampoos, toothpastes, detergents in smaller packages for reasons of affordability and lack of storage space at homes. Consumer goods companies such as Proctor & Gamble, Colgate, and Nestlé have introduced small single-use sachets. For more expensive items such as electronics, automotive, and home improvement products such as water filtration systems, delivery, installation, and repairs are expected as part of service offerings in many developing countries.

Business practices: Economic development impacts distribution systems (e.g. availability of refrigerated trucks and warehouses for transportation and storage of perishables, and types of retail outlets) and quality of infrastructure such as bridges, roads, electricity, and Internet connectivity. This in turn shapes business practices, perceptions of brands, and the quality of service they provide. Marketers have become creative in working within these restrictions to find opportunities to differentiate themselves. For example, the concept of active selling by retailers, particularly for relatively expensive and complex consumer products such as electronics, is nonexistent or weak in many country markets. Many developing country consumers need this guidance, however, because of low awareness and experience with these products. International marketers thus have had to employ their own sales people on the retail floor. This increases cost but has helped create differentiation and increased awareness of the brand. Both Starbucks and IKEA have gone out of their way across country markets to create a differentiated value offering and exciting and learning experiences through their interactive stores (Cateora et al., 2013).

A country's laws and regulations also indirectly impact consumer behavior through their direct impact on business practices. Company operations are bound by the laws of the country. As Starbucks opens stores from country to country it considers economic, legal, and cultural factors to determine how to enter a country. This has led to utilizing different kinds of value-chain alliance strategies such as licensing, joint ventures, and wholly owned subsidiaries in different markets to best provide value and experience (Hill and Hult, 2020: 377). McDonald's in some developing countries had to vertically integrate back to supply some of the raw materials in order to maintain the same quality of food as elsewhere. This, although raising the cost of operations, has increased positively impacted customer satisfaction.

In many countries laws require companies to have a maximum price labelled on the product. In other countries comparative advertising is not allowed and neither is advertising to children. In countries with multiple languages packaging needs to have information in more than one language. In some European countries sales happen at specific times during a year (only a couple of times in some countries) and many types of sales promotion tactics that help to create value such as premiums or free gifts are not allowed. Laws such as these challenge companies to develop creative customer relationship management strategies and tactics that positively impact awareness, perceptions, superior values, and experiences.

In many countries in Africa, Latin America, and Asia, the combined impacts of economy, culture, and laws pushes organizations to innovate in ways that create a win–win situation for both brand and country. Brands can dip into an existing ecosystem and/or extend the brand to other products and services. This increases the potential for increasing revenues and awareness and improving customer values and experiences. Here are two examples:

- In Africa, Equity Bank innovated in the healthcare industry. It launched a network of medical centers called Equity Afia tied to its health insurance product. These medical centers are owned by medical graduates of the bank's scholarship foundation. The bank also helped these entrepreneurs to start the centers.
- 2U, a US-based educational technology company, acquired a South African startup GetSmarter to offer online certification courses through a partnership with top global universities.

In innovating provision of customer value and experiences these two companies not only addressed their commercial interests of growth, but also societal needs for health and education (Leke et al., 2018).

Superior and differentiated value of the product offering and, positive experiences from its consumption, are ultimately defined by the customer. Hence, creation of the desired perception of the brand is of prime importance. Desired perceptions may need to be adapted across countries to suit the culture or be standardized for creating a global position. This can be a challenging and expensive proposition. Often, however, it can be achieved relatively easily by creating incremental improvements that target the senses. Singapore Airlines developed a specific fragrance for their cabins designed to improve the air quality and also calm passengers. They also train their flight attendants to speak in a particular tone, courteously and with empathy (Dew and Allen, 2018).

This discussion makes clear the impacts of country level environments on consumer behavior and business practices and the importance of adaptation and innovation in marketing and CRM strategies and tactics to provide superior customer value and positive customer experiences. The next section discusses how to utilize the three prongs of the CRM tool set to help implement some of these strategies.

Success Story

Tesco's ClubCard in the UK

To improve its position in their domestic market of the UK Tesco PLC decided it wanted to differentiate itself by becoming a large and modern version of the UK's traditional corner grocery store. This led the company to engage in a strategy of concentrating on individual customers. The focus was to understand individual customers well and then cater to their desires and lifestyles with relevant products and services as the local grocery stores used to do. This would help achieve customer satisfaction and loyalty. To achieve both, the Tesco ClubCard loyalty program was born.

To make the loyalty program effective Tesco took a dive into multidimensional and complex segmentation strategies and analyzed a huge amount of data to understand customers at the individual level. Customers were first categorized into groups such as cost conscious, mid-market, and up-market and then further segmented by orientations towards health, gourmet, family, convenience, etc. These sub-segments were segmented again into smaller groups such as family into mothers with young children. This granular level of knowledge on individual customers was followed up by customized communications.

Working with RightNow's on demand CRM solution facilitated this overall CRM strategy. The CRM system allowed Tesco to get a 360 degrees view of the customer by logging customer communications across channels and then responding to them consistently with relevant offerings.

Since the inception of the Clubcard in 2010 coupon redemption has increased to 40 percent and costs of couponing have gone down. The company realized that increasingly higher-value coupons are not needed when an attractive and customized value proposition is offered at the right time. Sales have grown by more than 50 percent since the inception of the loyalty program and the rate of growth has increased over time.

Source:

Retail report. (2004). "The success of the Tesco Clubcard in winning customer loyalty" *International Journal of Retail & Distribution Management, 32*(6), 358–60. Retrieved from https://www.proquest.com/scholarly-journals/retail-report/docview/210901762/se-2

Creating Global Customer Values and Experiences with CRM Tools

It must be dawning on you now that it is a challenge to create customer value and experiences that are meaningful and differentiated across country markets. Some companies have, however, done it successfully. So how does a company operating in international markets actually create values and experiences that will aid in managing customer relationships?

The three-pronged process–technology–people tool set of CRM discussed in Chapter 1 facilitates this.

Process tool application: The first step is to establish processes for 1) knowledge management and segmentation processes to facilitate determination of value and experience propositions that will align with the market, 2) product and service development to bring to life the value propositions, 3) marketing and sales to communicate and facilitate purchase and consumption, 4) customer service to provide value added experiences, and 5) employee relationship management to make sure the people prong of CRM can support the processes.

It is important to always consider the realities of the country environments while developing one or more of the above processes. A process may look excellent on paper but be useless because something in the environment makes it cost prohibitive or technically impossible to implement. Here is an example that highlights the development of customer service and employee relationship processes. If consumers in a country want a repair service to be included in the offer for a washing machine, what will the overall process of identifying repair needs, customer access to repairs, delivery of such a service and feedback look like and how will it be implemented? Can part of this process be facilitated with technology? The company may have customers speed up requests by making them on the company's website. This will depend on the extent to which they have access to the Internet. People are at the helm of organizational processes. One requirement would be properly trained repair personnel. If a telephone option is provided then that will require developing processes of hiring and training customer service employees or outsourcing this to another company.

A good learning exercise would be to revisit some of the examples of value creation from the previous section and identify the steps that went into creating and implementing them. Tolaram, the Indonesian company that made Indomie noodles popular in Nigeria, supports its CRM efforts by a unique distribution method. It spreads its distribution strength through more than a thousand vehicles on the street, including motocycles, trucks and tuk-tuks (three-wheeled mini autos common throughout Africa and Asia) and even people on foot, to get their product to thousands of informal small outlets (Leke et al., 2018).

Technology tool application: Technology tools support CRM efforts by streamlining, automating, and customizing processes. In today's world of big data and omnichannel purchasing and consumption, CRM tech tools are a necessity. At the same time viability of tech tools in different markets will vary depending on the infrastructure and usage of technology and communication, and the popularity of different tools. Usage of the Internet, telephony, and social media tech tools varies across countries. WhatsApp, a social media communication app, is widely used in many countries by both companies and consumers in communicating with each other but is not so popular in the US market. Using technology for capturing market data for market research also varies across countries. Thus automation of processes through tech tools across markets will likely need some customization to suit the market. Table 2.4 highlights examples of usage of innovative technology tools in multiple markets.

Table 2.4 Global CRM Technology Tool Usage

Company	Technology Tool Application
Tecno (Chinese mobile phone maker)	• Phone includes specialized tech tools tailored to the African market** • Photo software to capture darker skin tones more effectively • Keyboard in Amharic, Ethiopia's official language
Shoprite (South African supermarket chain)	Utilizes sophisticated route planning technology to determine and maximize distribution efficiencies*
Equity Bank (Kenya)	To make banking accessible and less intimidating mini bank branches that could fit in the backs of vans were driven from village to village*
LafargeHolcim (Global cement company)	Developed a new process for Africa which allows homebuilders to create high-quality bricks, mostly from earth. The company provides training to customers, equipment to make the bricks, and also reduces their cost by 20 to 40 percent*
Volkswagen	To provide a unique and emotional brand experience Volkswagen in collaboration with BlackSpace developed a 3D brand logo and space identity. It comes as a modular architecture system which provides a 360 degree brand experience at any space: fairs, events, stores, etc.***

Sources:

*Leke, A., Chironga, M., and Desvaux, G. (2018). *Africa's Business Revolution*. Boston, MA: Harvard Business Review Press.

**Doctoroff, T. (2012). *What Chinese Want: Culture, Communism and China's Modern Consumer*. New York: Palgrave Macmillan.

***Blackspace (2019). "Vibrant Space,' 3D branding and space identity for Volkswagen, 2019." Blackspace, www.black.space/vibrant-space-3d-branding-and-space-identity-for-volkswagen

People tool application: Organizations are still operated by people and not by robots. Hence the effectiveness of CRM processes and technologies utilized to support them will depend upon the collective will and skills of people in the organization. Additionally, CRM efforts needs to bring into the fold value-chain partners. Effective application of people tools globally can be a challenge. Cultural mindsets and behaviors vary from country to country and can be quite entrenched. Change management, human resource management, and partner collaboration strategies will likely need to be adapted from one country to another to create an effective CRM people tool set. Particular responsibilities lie with senior leadership to make this happen.

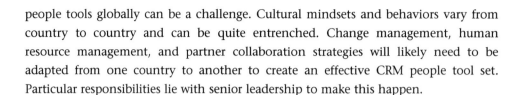

TECH BOX: VALUE CREATION

Marketers have been experimenting with two emerging technologies in enhancing customer value.

One such technology is mobile augmented reality technology. Research was conducted in France on the effects of augmented reality on tourist experiences in Chambord Castle in France. The tourists used the histopad, a digital mediation tool that interactively engages and is capable of creating 3D reconstructions. Observation of and interviews with such visitors revealed that there are both positive and negative impacts of the technology on value perception and experience. Augmented reality changed the spatial and time aspects of tourists' experiences as well as their perception of the value dimension (e.g. hedonic vs. aesthetic).

The second technology being utilized is Web personalization systems. These systems track consumer activities on websites and then create personalized websites. In-depth interviews conducted with Belgian consumers revealed that personalized websites complement personalized ads in terms of experience value. However, the interviews also revealed that personalization can both create and destroy value with value creation counterbalancing value destruction. Loss of control during navigation as the website automatically personalizes content is seen as frustrating, whereas the navigation guidance provided by the system is seen as helpful.

Sources:

Coutelle, P., Garets, V.des., Maubission, L., and Riviere, A. (2018). "The effects of mobile technology on overall tourist experience: The case of augmented reality used during a visit of Chambord Castle: An abstract," in P. Rossi and N. Krey (eds), *Finding New Ways to Engage and Satisfy Global Customers: Proceedings of the 2018 Academy of Marketing Science (AMS) World Marketing Congress (WMC)*. Cham, Switzerland: Springer, pp: 33.

Lambillote, L. and Poncin, I. (2018). "Web personalization experience: Value creation or value destruction," in P. Rossi and N. Krey (eds), *Finding New Ways to Engage and Satisfy Global Customers: Proceedings of the 2018 Academy of Marketing Science (AMS) World Marketing Congress (WMC)*. Cham, Switzerland: Springer, p. 49.

Case Study

Digital Gifting Trends in India

In the last decade the digital gifting industry has boomed in the Indian market. India has a long cultural heritage of giving gifts as part of social and business customs, meaning Indian consumers are quite passionate about giving gifts.

Traditionally gifts, whether personal or corporate, were given face to face and used to be either physical items or cash. Personal gifting used to be reserved for special occasions such as birthdays, weddings, anniversaries, and festivals. This pattern has shifted with digital gifting fast becoming the norm in both personal and corporate worlds.

Current Dynamics in the Indian Gifting Industry

India is poised to be one of the fastest growing gift giving markets in the world. It is estimated that the market will grow to 84 billion by 2024. The gifting industry in India, in line with global gifting markets, has increasingly moved online.

Gift giving in India has three categories: personal, festival, and corporate. Corporate gifting takes up a significant majority of this market.

Online gifting in general and online gift cards in particular have increased in popularity. Close to half of employees in corporate India prefer to receive online or digital gifts. This is particularly true for younger professionals. These gifts bring additional benefits too. Online gifts help lower the operation costs of managing corporate rewards, and online gift cards act as brand promoters.

The variety of items available for gifting has also significantly expanded to suit the changing tastes of consumers. Beyond flowers, chocolates, and cakes, consumers can send gift cards, travel packages, movie passes, dining vouchers, digital shopping options, and online coupons. Corporations too offer multiple gift options to employees and customers, including coupons for vacations, beauty services, health examinations, food, and entertainment.

This increase in variety reflects the changing tastes of consumers. "People looked for innovative ideas with a personal touch". Consumers are preferring to buy gifts that are "stylish, unique, personalized, matched their aspirations and reflected their status."

Multiple online gift retailers have stepped in to fill these changing market needs. They have matured over the years becoming a "one stop shop" for all kinds of gifts. To attract visitors these retailers utilize different kinds of discounts, cashback opportunities in collaboration with companies that offer digital payment and discounts, and flexible delivery options. This has substantially increased online traffic, particularly during the traditional gifting season between October and December. The table includes a list of some of the most successful companies and highlights their offers.

(Continued)

Giftoxo	Primarily caters to corporate clients with unique and experience-based offers. These are packaged in elegant boxes as keepsakes. The offers are also available on its app (Frogo)
Qwikcilver Solutions	App (Woohoo) has gift options from more than a hundred leading brands and allows consumers to store gift cards received from anywhere
Giftease	Gift offers for different budgets for a broad range of products. Particularly popular with youth because of the large number of affordable, quirky, cool, and fun items
Askmygift	Provides a channel for social-media-based gift makers to reach customers. Specializes in "handmade, customised, and DIY gifts"

Impacts of Country Environment on the Rise of the Online Gifting Industry

Several environmental changes happening in the Indian market facilitated the popularity of the digital gifting industry. Strong economic growth of India not only increased disposable incomes of a large segment of consumers but also attracted investors from across the world. A diverse range of media companies have increased consumer awareness of and desire for western and more globalized products and lifestyles. This impacted consumer aspirations and outlook, broadening gift type and variety. Technological innovations happening in parallel increased access to computers and smartphones for consumers and allowed e-commerce companies to satisfy these newly evolving desires, particularly of the younger generation.

Challenges Ahead

While the digital/online gifting market is forecast to grow in India, some challenges do remain for organizations to overcome if they want to succeed. There is always the challenge for gift companies to create awareness of the company's offering in a crowded market where products are not that differentiated. Much more difficult is to offer a combination of the "right" gift and maximum value at low prices. This demands serious innovations on the part of these companies. Additionally there is the danger of losing a customer forever through a mistake. Given the personal and emotional nature of the product, a dissatisfied customer is not likely to return.

Source: Das, S. (2019). *Online Gifting in India: The Next Big Thing of Ecommerce*. ID: 319-0060-1. Amity Research Center Headquarters. Distributed by thecasecentre.org

Summary

Chapter 2 introduced the primary country environments, their characteristics, and the environmental indicators to look for within each country. Country-level environments are economic, cultural, political, and legal. Environments across countries are both similar and different. The differences and similarities should be considered before developing cross-country customer relationship management goals and strategies. This is because consumption in countries is shaped by the influence of macro-level country environments. The chapter discussed how environments impact consumption behavior and business practices and how to use the three CRM tools of processes, technology, and tools to adapt to these environments.

References

Baker, D. (2020). "Why the spread of public education is unlikely to yield a secular world." *Brookings Education Plus Development*, March 20, www.brookings.edu/blog/education-plus-development/2019/03/20/why-the-spread-of-public-education-is-unlikely-to-yield-a-secular-world

BDC (n.d.). "Economic environment." www.bdc.ca/en/articles-tools/entrepreneur-toolkit/templates-business-guides/glossary/economic-environment

BEMG Global Scan Sustainability (2012). "Regeneration roadmap: Rethinking consumption." www.slideshare.net/sustainablebrands/regeneration-roadmap-rethinking-consumption

Cateora, P., Gilly, M., and Graham, G., (2013). *International Marketing*, 16th edn. New York: McGraw-Hill Education.

Cateora, P., Graham, G., Gilly, M., and Money, B. (2019). *International Marketing*, 18th edn. New York: McGraw-Hill Education.

Deep English (2021). "Handshake history." *Deep English*, https://deepenglish.com/lessons/handshake-history-listening-fluency-116

Dew, R. and Allen, C. (2018). *Customer Experience Innovation*. Bingley, UK: Emerald Publishing.

Doctoroff, T. (2012). *What Chinese Want: Culture, Communism and China's Modern Consumer*. New York: Palgrave Macmillan.

Heslop, A.D. (2020). "Political System." *Britannica*, June 30, www.britannica.com/topic/political-system

Hill, C.W.L. and Hult, G.T.M. (2020). *Global Business Today*. New York: McGraw-Hill Education, p. 11e.

Hofstede.com (n.d.). "6D model of national culture." https://geerthofstede.com/culture-geert-hofstede-gert-jan-hofstede/6d-model-of-national-culture

Hofstede, G. (1984). *Culture's Consequences: International Differences in Work-Related Values*. Beverly Hills, CA: Sage, p. 21.

Inglehart, R. and Baker, W. (2000). "Modernization, cultural change, and the persistence of traditional values." *American Sociological Review*, 65, 1, 19–51.

Leke, A., Chironga, M., and Desvaux, G. (2018). *Africa's Business Revolution*. Boston, MA: Harvard Business Review Press.

Lowe, B., Mort, G.S., and Hasan, M.R. (2019). "Connecting with consumers in subsistence marketplaces: An abstract," in P. Rossi and N. Krey (eds), *Finding New Ways to Engage and Satisfy Global Customers: Proceedings of the 2018 Academy of Marketing Science (AMS) World Marketing Congress (WMC)*. Cham, Switzerland: Springer.

Magga, O.H. (2006). "Diversity in Saami terminology for reindeer, snow, and ice", *International Social Science Journal*, 58, 187, 25–34.

Mahajan, V. (2016). "How Unilever reaches rural consumers in emerging markets." *Harvard Business Review*, Dec. 14, https://hbr.org/2016/12/how-unilever-reaches-rural-consumers-in-emerging-markets

Racoma, B. (2019). "How McDonald's adapts around the world." *Day Translations blog*, Jan. 4, www.daytranslations.com/blog/how-mcdonalds-adapts-around-the-world

Retail report. (2004). "The success of the Tesco Clubcard in winning customer loyalty" *Inter- national Journal of Retail & Distribution Management, 32*(6), 358–60. Retrieved from: http://www.proquest.com/scholarly-journals/retail-report/docview/210901762/se-2" www.proquest.com/scholarly-journals/retail-report/docview/210901762/se-2

Rokeach, M. (1973). *The Nature of Human Values*. New York: Free Press.

Schwartz, S.H. (2004). *Mapping and Interpreting Cultural Differences around the World*. Leiden, Netherlands: Brill.

Stofsky, M. (2016). "11 international Coca-Cola products you can't buy in the U.S." *Mental Floss*, May 16, www.mentalfloss.com/article/79458/11-international-coca-cola-products-you-cant-buy-us

Wikipedia (2021). "Handshake." https://en.wikipedia.org/wiki/Handshake

World Factbook, The (n.d.). "Field listing—Legal system." CIA.gov, www.cia.gov/the-world-factbook/field/legal-system

World Science Festival (2020). "How do different cultures think about time?" *YouTube*, www.youtube.com/watch?v=4klDmEViusA

Ziegler, H. and Associates (2021). "Islamic banking." *Helen Ziegler and Associates*, www.hziegler.com/articles/islamic-banking.html

3

GLOBAL MARKET SEGMENTATION AND CONSUMER BEHAVIOR

Case Study

Pro-Hijab—Nike and Muslim Women Athletes

In spring of 2018 Nike launched a new sportswear product targeted at Muslim women athletes (MWAs) in general, and particularly in the Middle East. The piece of clothing is a performance headscarf named "Pro Hijab." It allows MWAs to cover their heads according to the dictates of Islam while taking part in a performance sport.

This innovation was inspired by a cultural change—the increasing participation of Muslim women in performance sports and particularly by the Saudi Arabian runner Sarah Attar who competed in the London Olympics in 2012 and Amna Al Haddad, a weightlifter from the United Arab Emirates. Both women competed wearing a hijab.

Reasons for Nike's Decision to Target the MWA segment

Several factors contributed to Nike's decision to target this segment. Some of these factors were macro environmental and others were Nike's expansion goals and its strategic approach to competitiveness.

In 2016 Muslim women athletes were increasingly making a statement by competing with a hijab in the Olympics but also acknowledging the difficulty of participating with a traditional hijab unless it was pinned down. Simultaneously several professional sports organizations such as the International Basketball Federation, the Federation of International Football Association, the

(Continued)

International Judo Federation and the American Boxing Federation started allowing women athletes to play and compete wearing a hijab. This brought the culture of wearing a hijab to the attention of and acceptance by mainstream sports, giving rise to an industry of "sports/ competition friendly hijabs." On the other hand, increasing Islamophobia in particular parts of the world due to perceptions related to extremism and sensitivities surrounding immigration created a niche culture of Muslim women going out of their way as a protest to wear the hijab to showcase it as part of their faith. Mainstream apparel companies jumped at this opportunity created by a booming market for modest clothing. Thomson Reuters' "The Global Islamic Economy Report 2015/2016" estimated that there would be a sharp increase in the amount of money Muslim consumers would spend on apparel and clothing reaching US$ 327 billion by 2019. What made this market even more attractive was the relative youth of Islamic consumers. The Muslim world had one of the largest number of millennials and the Muslim population was growing twice as fast as non-Muslim populations.

Inability of relatively weaker regional and local competition to fully satisfy the wants of Muslim women athletes also played a part in Nike's decision to target the segment. Athletes complained that existing products were not comfortable, were heavy, and did not allow for proper breathing. This opened up the opportunity for Nike to engage in innovation and market it worldwide.

Lastly, Nike also wanted to safeguard its own performance and financial success. It wanted to invest in this segment not only for expansion through a more diverse market portfolio but also as a cushion against a potential decline in performance in fast growing but highly competitive emerging markets such as China.

Launch of "Pro Hijab"

Nike launched "Pro Hijab" to mixed responses. Even though most MWAs were enthusiastic and Nike was praised for raising and supporting sensitive issues such as religion and gender inclusiveness, it was criticized by some women in the Middle East on its controversial ad which, according to these women, misrepresented the lives of Muslim women in the Middle East. Criticism also came from other quarters; some people said that Nike was exploiting and commercializing religious sentiments and others who were against the hijab criticized Nike for supporting it. However, many analysts believed that this launch would "normalize Muslim and Islamic culture" where well known Muslim women athletes supported the product launch by associating feelings of empowerment with wearing the hijab.

Overall Nike was successful in identifying and targeting a unique segment and introducing "modest, Muslim-friendly clothing into the mainstream." With its global reach Nike may encourage more Muslim women to follow their passion for sports. Amna Al Haddad stated, "[It will] encourage a whole new generation to pursue sports without feeling there is a limitation because of modesty or dress code."

Source: Sadia, S.T. and Perepu, I. (2017). "Nike 'Pro Hijab': Targeting Muslim women Athletes." ID: 517-0132-1. IBS Center for Management Research. Distributed by thecasecentre.org

Introduction

Segmentation is the backbone of marketing. Effective segmentation of markets makes CRM strategies and tactics more impactful by helping to target segments that will see value in the organizations offering and facilitating creation of superior customer value (Harrison and Ansell, 2002; Weinstein, 2002). For global CRM, segmentation is particularly beneficial because it opens up opportunities across markets, as shown in the Nike case above, and also helps to overcome the challenge in balancing differences and similarities across countries by allocating and leveraging resources efficiently and creating strong value offerings in each (Papadopoulos and Martín Martín, 2011).

Segmentation for global CRM is challenging because of its increased complexity compared to single-country segmentation. Optimal segmentation needs to be a dual-stage process that includes both cross-country and within-country segmentation. Complexity in spotting lucrative segments and efficiently allocating resources arise because of the difficulties in identifying and analyzing similarities and differences among countries. The segmentation process highlights that the same or very similar market segments may exist across multiple countries and that countries may have segments unique to them. Given this complexity it is critical but challenging to select appropriate segmentation variables that will help unearth the most lucrative segments both across and within countries.

Global Market Segmentation: Identifying Unmet Needs and Creating Value

The "lost generation" in China is a unique segment with few parallels in other big countries. An equivalent segment (based just on birth years) would be the "baby boomer" generation in the US. Both generations were born between 1946 and 1960. Where, in large democracies such as the United States and India, this generation grew up with a certain cynicism towards governmental authority based on their views on the corruption they witnessed, in China the same generation grew up during the Cultural Revolution venerating the "cult of Mao" (Erickson, 2009). The Cultural Revolution led to the collapse of most social institutions including educational institutions. Large numbers of young people without access to schools joined Mao's cadres and learned whatever little they could from Chairman Mao's "Little Red Book." This generation grew up believing loyalty to the state would be rewarded, education was unimportant, and anything foreign was not good. When the Cultural Revolution dissolved, this generation were left angry and frustrated. Today, without the benefits of a formal education, they have a difficult time operating in a modern society.

At the other extreme is the youth culture, which became globalized after spreading from the West. It has retained modern individualism at its core but has in some cases been imbued with local elements as it crossed cultures. Youth across the world tend to share aspects of lifestyle and consumption such as music, movies, and clothing as well as underlying preferences for having fun and seeking thrills, and values such as caring about the environment. At the same time global "youthness" is influenced and expressed locally—for example, in local rock music under the umbrella of global rock music (Kjeldgaard and Askegaard, 2006; Moses, 2000). This means that the youth segment is universal but with stylized variations across countries.

It is only through creative and disciplined market segmentation that such segments can be identified and new ones created. Global marketplaces are filled with a variety of consumption behaviors shaped by country environments. This variety hides unmet needs and wants, promise of new segments, and opportunities for innovations in value creation for global CRM (Bowonder et al., 2010).

Global Market Segmentation Strategies

Traditionally, international marketers viewed each country as a single segment and clustered countries together based on similarities in economics, culture, and other broad macro traits to create a mega segment to be targeted with standardized marketing offerings and interventions (Budeva and Mullen, 2014). The benefit of such an approach is economies of scale from standardization. Many scholars, however, raised concerns about this approach on two grounds: 1) the assumption of a country being a homogeneous market is simplistic and 2) segmentation that does not include behavioral traits of consumers is not actionable (Hassan and Katsanis, 1993; Helsen et al., 1993; Nachum, 1994).

A second more contemporary and critical approach is to consider consumers across countries (sometimes even across major cities in different countries) and group them based on their demographics, lifestyles, psychographics, values, and attitudes. This has the advantage of having a customer orientation to the process, leading to higher likelihood of satisfying segments being targeted (Burgess, 1992; Cleveland et al., 2011; Hassan et al., 2003). Research has shown the importance of having information on individual consumers for CRM efforts to be successful. Samli (2013) states that "International markets must be segmented by consumer needs or behavior." Behavioral data has been shown to be more effective as a segmentation variable compared to demographic data (Lindenbeck and Olbrich, 2019). At the same time there is a drawback to this approach. Countries can be vastly different in economics, laws, politics, culture, and competition. Simply grouping consumers across vastly different countries just on the basis of similarities on individual characteristics would end up ignoring the environmental differences that can hinder the effectiveness of customer relationship management effort. For example let's assume that consumers of two countries A and B share the same values and attitudes towards consumption of frozen foods but the technology and transportation infrastructure of these two countries are quite different. A's infrastructure is excellent whereas B's is poor. Additionally, country B is three times larger in size than A. If it is determined that one-day delivery is something that consumers between the two countries will value, it will be much more difficult to successfully implement this strategy in country B than country A.

Current research now recommends a two-step process that retains the advantages and reduces the disadvantages of both the previously mentioned approaches (Hassan et al., 2003). The first step includes clustering countries based on macro environmental bases, eliminating countries that are unattractive and difficult to operate in. In the second step, for each of the country clusters that are deemed viable, the consumers are divided into segments based on individual-level characteristics (Cavusgil et al., 2004; Hassan and Craft, 2012; Hassan et al., 2003). This provides the best chance of 1) identification and creation of both cross-country segments across countries in the cluster and unique segments within individual countries in the cluster and 2) delivering on the value proposition given the environmental similarities across different countries in the chosen cluster. This two-step segmentation allows for a clearer picture of the extent of interconnectedness across countries and opportunities for new standardized, and/or differentiated offerings, a more accurate prediction of outcomes in future countries and for easier transfer of expertise and competencies to new countries (Budeva and Mullen, 2014).

Step 1: Macro Segmentation

This first step includes researching macro environmental characteristics of countries of interest and utilizing these as segmentation variables to create country clusters where clusters are homogenous within and heterogeneous between. Both broad and more focused economic, cultural, and legal realities in the markets need to be utilized as segmentation variables to create meaningfully homogenous country clusters (Budeva and Mullen, 2014; Hassan and Craft, 2005). This process ends with creation of one or more country clusters with multiple countries within a cluster. Step 1 ends with selection of one or more country clusters based on relative attractiveness of the clusters. Attractiveness is determined by a cost, benefit, and risk analysis of entering different country clusters. Table 3.1 shows a list of commonly utilized macro environmental segmentation variables.

Table 3.1 Macro Environmental Global Segmentation Variables

Broad Environmental Variables	Focused Environmental Variables
Level of economic development	Market orientation of economy
Per capita income	Communication infrastructure
Level of industrialization	Energy consumption
Form of government	Media availability and usage
Political stability	Level of engagement in the retail sector
Level of technological innovation	Convenience orientation
Type of dominant religion	Quality of life
Languages spoken	Brand image perceptions
Cultural distance based on Hofstede's cultural dimensions	Percentage employed in services
Life expectancy	Customer receptiveness
Literacy rate	Cosmopolitanism
Legal environment	Average length of work week

Step 2: Micro Segmentation

In step 2 a deeper look is taken into consumer-level characteristics across countries within a selected cluster. This includes information on demographics, psychographics, lifestyle, attitudes, behaviors, and benefits sought from the focal product category.

A relevant combination of variables across different types of consumer characteristics (such as income bracket and a certain lifestyle) is then selected as an additional layer of a segmentation variable set for determining and developing cross-country segments within the selected cluster and unique segments within specific countries. For example, travel companies would likely include, at the minimum, lifestyle information such as interest in travel, reasons for desiring to travel, attitude towards different aspects of travel such as mode of transportation, accommodation, etc., travel experience, age group, and income bracket. The more relevant variables included the richer the picture of the consumer will be and the deeper the insight into consumer values and wants. Including multiple consumer characteristics as segmentation variables thus facilitates creation of targeted customer experience and relationship-enhancing offerings and provides a greater chance of profitably satisfying customer needs (Cleveland et al., 2011). Table 3.2 highlights some common and not so common consumer characteristics that have been used as variables in step 2 of the segmentation process.

Table 3.2 Global Consumer Based Segmentation Variables

Consumer Characteristics: Category	Specific Consumer Variables
Demographics	• Age group • Income group • Ethnicity • Geographic location (urban vs. rural)
Psychographics	• Brand perception (global vs. local; premium vs. mainstream) • Level of involvement with the product category/brand • Motivation for consumption
Lifestyle	• Interests • Activities such as grilling/barbecuing
Attitude	• Beliefs, and positive, negative, or neutral orientation towards relevant consumption-related aspects such as cooking products and services targeted on cooking • Benefits sought
Behavior	• Adoption of innovation • Adoption of technology • Social media activities • Channel used for research and purchasing • Frequency and recency of purchase • Monetary value of purchase • Brands purchased

It is important to critically examine the two-step global marketing segmentation strategy and process for effectiveness. The diversity across countries in both the environmental and consumer levels makes it crucial to determine and select the most relevant variables for segmentation so that the company can identify unmet needs, lucrative segments, and take advantage of the most promising opportunities to create differentiated value creation and customer relationships.

The two-step segmentation strategy is particularly beneficial for Global CRM in the light of the convergence in economic, cultural, and legal environments across countries, as it makes it increasingly feasible to identify similar segments across countries and to implement CRM interventions effectively across these countries. This aids efficiency of expansion and increases the chances of success as tried and true strategies are extended to other countries. Effective regional segmentation allowed Honda, the Japanese automaker, to identify a universal segment across Europe with large similarities in lifestyle and to successfully position their Honda HR-V as the "Joy Machine" to this cross-country segment. The two-step segmentation process also helps to identify unique segments that do not cross borders but which can be profitable to serve.

Porsche, the German luxury auto brand, with the aid of segmentation was also able to identify two unique and distinct segments within the United States: the Top Guns and the Proud Patrons.

It is crucial to realize here that all consumers within a cross-country segment that this two-step segmentation process creates, are usually not exactly the same in all aspects of consumer characteristics and behavior. In a cross-country segment, consumers within that segment (they come from multiple countries—that is why the segment is cross-country) are significantly similar in a large number of relevant consumer characteristics (e.g. lifestyle) but usually different in few other aspects (e.g. perception of global vs. local brands). Such differences may necessitate some adaptation to CRM strategies and tactics to be implemented in these different countries that are part of the cross-country segment. This will depend on the variables on which the segment consumers differ and how important those variables are to the consumers themselves and for creating value. For example, the body-care company The Body Shop positions its brand in exactly the same way across all markets despite some differences between the markets. This is because the cross-country segment that The Body Shop targets has the same attitude towards environmental consciousness and related usage behavior across countries, the most important segmentation variable for The Body Shop. On the other hand, Miele, the German appliance manufacturer positions its products differently across the cross-country premium segment in the US and EU. These two segments, though similar across a vast range of characteristics, is different in one aspect: benefit sought. Where EU customers are seeking durability, US customers seek maintenance-free appliances in a variety of designs (Hassan and Craft, 2005). So the cross-country segment that The Body Shop targets would be considered universal or global but the segment that Miele caters to is not. Table 3.3 highlights some universal or global segments or traits that have been identified during the segmentation process and examples of brands which have successfully targeted these segments and traits through a globalized and standardized image.

Table 3.3 Global Segments and Global Brands

Universal/Global Segments and Traits	Global Brands Targeting Universal Global Segments and Traits
Children	McDonald's
Youth	MTV
Women	Redd's by SAB Miller
Elite	Rolex
Seniors	Ford (autos), Danone (food), L'Oréal (beauty)
Coffee lovers	Nestlé
Beer lovers	Budweiser

Universal/Global Segments and Traits	Global Brands Targeting Universal Global Segments and Traits
Cosmetics	Dove, Avon
Cosmopolitanism	Heineken
Americanness	Levi's jeans

Over time, some country environments change and so does consumer behavior. This is particularly true for fast growing developing and emerging countries. These changes may bring about new similarities and differences across countries. It is thus important to regularly evaluate the relevancy of selected segmentation variables and perform segmentation iteratively to identify new cross-country and country-specific unique segments. Across countries, increasing environmental consciousness, usage of e-commerce, and desire for do-it-yourself based on rising labor costs, may necessitate changes in CRM strategies.

Now that we have covered the mechanics of the two-step segmentation it is important to consider the outcome of the segmentation process: the segments created. A segmentation strategy is successful only when it results in segments that are accessible, substantial in size, can be communicated to, and is expected to respond to, brand communication (Hassan and Craft, 2012). The disciplined and creative method of considering similarities and differences both at the country and consumer levels that the two-step segmentation process follows, helps to create segments that will fulfill the above-mentioned characteristics of a good segment. Figure 3.1 illustrates the two-step global segmentation process.

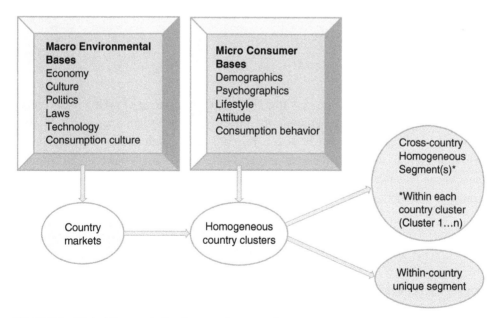

Figure 3.1 Global Segmentation Process Framework

TECH BOX: SITEZEUS

Segmentation, like many other marketing operations, has also hit the technology high road. SiteZeus, a location-based intelligence platform, has introduced an artificial intelligence (AI) segmentation feature in its platform in partnership with Spatial.ai and Uber Media, leading data providers.

The segmentation feature utilizes billions of social media conversations on lifestyle and interests provided by Spatial, and then integrates that with mobile data provided by Ubermedia on locations of consumers. This helps the AI system to know where consumers are going within a few hours before and after a store visit or purchase, find patterns in consumer behavior and create multiple unique segments. The AI has created 70!

The feature should help stores understand customer behavior at a more granular level that would normally not be available to them and allow them to effectively customize communication and offers that positively impact customer relationship building and store performance. The feature also allows stores to predict how sales and performance will likely be affected by changing certain variables.

Source: PRNewswire (2019). "New customer segmentation technology allows multi-unit brands to build stores with greater accuracy." MartechSeries, Aug 21, https://martechseries. com/analytics/behavioral-marketing/location-data/new-customer-segmentation-technology-allows-multi-unit-brands-build-stores-greater-accuracy

Global Consumer Behavior

The two-step segmentation process highlights the importance of taking into consideration relevant consumer behavior for effective global segmentation. It is thus important to understand some basic tenets of global consumer behavior. This should help marketers to understand consumers and behaviors across countries, to segment them more effectively and to develop effective customer relationship management strategies and tactics.

Beliefs, Perceptions, Attitudes, and Preferences

Consumer behavior has been widely studied in marketing. Commonly researched areas are 1) belief that gives rise to perceptions, 2) attitude and motivation that impact preferences, and 3) how perceptions, attitude, motivation, and preferences impact purchase decision making. Beliefs, especially cultural belief systems, over time give rise to perceptions about the world of consumption. Through repeated experience with different stimuli these perceptions develop into attitudes (positive or negative thought processes and feelings) towards different consumption phenomena and objects. Perceptions and attitudes over time create preferences.

Several theories have been developed in marketing to explain these relationships. These have been tested in the marketplace many times. The theory of planned behavior states that whether a consumer will engage in a certain behavior or not starts with beliefs. Consumers hold salient beliefs about possible positive or negative consequences of a behavior. These impact attitude towards that behavior. Ultimately the actual possibility of the behavior happening is impacted by how the consumer perceives and feels about the social pressure of engaging or not engaging in the specific behavior (Azjen, 1991).

The means–end theory (MEC) utilizes this belief–attitude–behavior relationship in a product or service consumption context to explain consumer behavior. It states that consumer choice and purchase happen through a series of hierarchical and increasingly abstract evaluation processes from attributes to benefits to value end states. Consumer choice starts with an evaluation of attributes of the product offering. This evaluation helps the consumer realize if consumption of the product will lead to desired benefits and how such benefits would help the consumer achieve an ultimate value state that is important for the consumer (Olson and Reynolds, 2001). For example, the ultimate value state from purchase of an insurance product could very well be peace of mind. This theory explains the process of consumer preference and choice by connecting perceptions and knowledge of product attributes held by consumers to desired benefits and value states the consumer thinks can be achieved through acquisition and consumption of the product (Mulvey and Olson, 1994). Product attributes can be both physical such as the shape of the packaging, or abstract such as taste. Benefits can be functional such as comfort while driving an automobile, psychological such as perceiving the automobile as a source of identity, and social such as perceiving the automobile as being an ideal conveyance for travel with friends. Values are desired end states and underlying reasons for consumption such as convenience, status, and socialization (Barrena et al., 2017; Huang et al., 2019). Product attributes impacting desired benefits and value-based end states have been studied in a broad range of consumer products such as perfumes (Valette-Florence, 1998), coffee (Silva de Oliveira et al., 2021, beverages (Gutman, 1984) and wine (Overby et al., 2004). We can view the cross-cultural consumption of wine through the lens of these theories. Some cultures frown upon alcohol consumption as a part of a lifestyle or social ritual and hence consumption is uncommon. This belief system negatively impacts consumer perceptions about and knowledge of the product, which in turn impacts benefits, values, and desired end states from consuming wine. In order for a wine brand to change this belief and perceptions about wine consumption from negative to neutral positive it will have to provide rich information about the product, its benefits, and how the consumer can reach a valued end state with consumption. This may be feasible if product benefits (e.g. health related) and value end state (a happier life) that would be attractive to consumers of that country can be effectively highlighted and communicated.

Cultural Values and Consumer Behavior

Some researchers have argued that all investigation of consumer behavior should have national culture and lifestyle values as the starting point (Johnson, 1998; Roth, 1995). This is specifically meaningful as products and services cross country borders. This would be in line with the two-step segmentation process discussed above. National cultural values have been shown to impact purchase and consumption of a broad range of products such as mineral water, Internet access, luxury products, wine, and financial services by impacting beliefs about identity and image, emotions, motives, and attitude (Chui and Kwok, 2008; DeMooij, 2004, 2010; Overby et al., 2004). Under the national culture value umbrella lie other lifestyle and segment-specific values that can also cross cultural borders and have been found to be both similar and different across and within countries. For example, some consumers may have a utilitarian orientation and some a purely hedonic orientation when it comes to consumption of products such as clothing, automobiles, and cosmetics. Considering both national and lifestyle-based values should thus help identify similarities and differences in consumer behavior across countries.

Global Consumer Behavior and Purchase Decision Making

Beliefs, attitudes, and the attribute–benefit-value cycle are therefore crucial impact factors in a consumer's purchase decision-making process (Engel et al., 1968). Beliefs and perceptions about consumption help guide need recognition and search. Effective marketing communications help increase awareness and knowledge of the product and give rise to a certain attitude towards consumption of the product and a desire for specific benefits and value states. These preferences regarding attributes, benefits, and value states play a crucial role in evaluation of alternative offerings and ultimate purchase.

Motivation

The underlying and essential force that propels the consumer to move from need recognition to purchase in the decision-making process, is motivation (Reynolds and Gutman, 2001). Motivation involves both cognition and emotion and is impacted by values and benefits consumers are looking for in a product category. Research shows that motivation to achieve specific desired values and benefits are impacted by underlying consumer factors such as income (De Mooij and Hofstede, 2011) and age, identity (Webster, 1994; Zeugner-Roth et al., 2015), utilitarian vs. hedonic lifestyle orientation (Baumgartner and Steenkamp, 1996), and involvement, knowledge of the product, and past experience with it (Hernández-Ortega et al., 2008). All of the above are impacted by country environments and show both differences and similarities across countries. A highly motivated pet owner may appreciate an opportunity from a brand for co-creation of specific benefits and values (customization of pet food or pet services such as obedience training). A less motivated consumer on the other hand may see more value in hassle-free standardized offerings. If national culture of a country values pet ownership then there will likely be a high number of motivated consumers for pet products. This reality will determine the kind of CRM initiatives that will be effective. Porsche, the German luxury auto brand, caters to two unique segments in the United States that exhibit very different motivations for purchasing a luxury auto brand. The Proud Patrons are elitists and fantasists who desire to have the best just for the internal satisfaction it brings. On the other hand, the Top Guns purchase a luxury auto brand to be noticed. Marketers thus should actively utilize motivation as a segmentation variable. Motivation information can also be used as an indicator for stepping up customer relationship management efforts to actively enhance motivation of consumers where it is low and involve them more in the purchase decision process. This can be achieved through communication of product and brand benefits and values that facilitate consumer knowledge development and increase the possibility of involving consumers cognitively and emotionally. This product knowledge–motivation connection is particularly crucial for complex products and services such as insurance, travel, and high-end tech products where there tends to be a significant asymmetry in knowledge level between the seller and the buyer. This is particularly true in less developed countries where level of education and access to technology and information are lower. It is important for marketers to bridge this asymmetry for the sake of generating preferences. Signaling theory explains how information asymmetry between two parties can be minimized (Spence, 2002). When applied to consumer behavior, signaling theory states that information asymmetry between buyers and sellers can be lowered through communication of various signals in the form of organizational, product, and brand-related information that indicate to buyers the quality of the product, the credibility of the seller and the overall value of the offering. This has the added benefit of reducing the buyer's information costs and risks (Pan, 2011; Wells et al., 2011). Signaling theory has also been applied to explain consumer behavior in multiple consumer product categories and signals have been shown to shape the perception and preferences of consumers (Asahan et al., 2018). Figure 3.2 summarizes the consumer behavior phenomena and Table 3.4 highlights the different consumer behavior theories discussed.

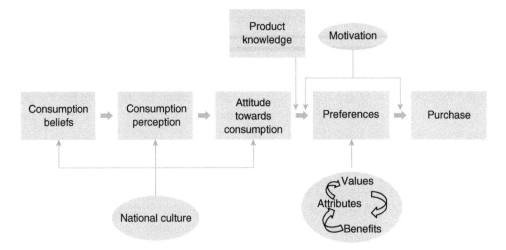

Figure 3.2 Global Consumer Behavior Phenomena

Table 3.4 Consumer Behavior Theoretical Concepts

Theory	Highlights
Theory of planned behavior	Determines behavior. Behavior is impacted by: • Beliefs about consequences of a behavior • Attitudes which are impacted by beliefs • Thought processes and emotions about social pressure to engage or not engage in the behavior
Means–end theory	Explains consumer choice and purchase. Choice is determined by the sequential evaluation of the following: • Evaluation of product attributes • Evaluation of how product attributes will provide desired benefits • Evaluation of how benefits from consumption will help achieve desired end value state
Signaling theory	Explains minimization of information asymmetry between buyers and sellers. Sellers can increase buyers' knowledge and reduce this asymmetry by communicating product- and brand-related information that signals quality, credibility, and value

Success Stories

Segmenting and Creating Value for Bottom of the Pyramid (BOP) Customers in Emerging Markets

The bottom of the pyramid (BOP) (also known as the base of the pyramid) refers to the approximately two to three billion people in the developing world who survive on between $1 and $5 per day. Most live in rural areas or shanty towns in urban areas, do not own their dwellings or place of business, have little to no formal education, work mostly in the informal economy as drivers, farm hands or construction workers, and cannot be reached through traditional channels of communication, distribution, and credit. They tend to consume inexpensive consumer products for day-to-day usage. Despite this, they strive for better education and employment, and a better life.

Typically, most organizations lack the resources such as skills and cost structures to profitably reach these poor consumers. Yet increasingly researchers, corporations, and non-profit organizations have identified this segment as a vibrant but largely hidden consumer market. They say satisfying this market profitably is possible by being innovative in segmenting the market and creating both private value for the segment members and public value for their community.

First, instead of viewing them as a homogeneous bloc, brands need to use demographics to segment this population into two subgroups because these groups exhibit varying characteristics and have different needs (the $1–$3 segment and the $3–$5 segment). Second, brands need to go beyond demographics to consider co-creation of values. They need to realize that these subgroups can play a role both as consumers and producers in value-creation relationships. Including both roles and differentiating between them in a segmentation scheme sets up a clear dual goal of organizational profit and value creation for these atypical segments.

To create value for the consumer role these groups can play, companies need to introduce innovations in offerings for education, credit, and items for regular consumption that are easy, cheaper to use, and of good quality. Vast improvements in technology sophistication and global reach should facilitate this process.

- Manila Water, a private consortium in Philippines brought higher connectivity and lower costs of water access and usage for this segment resulting in a win–win situation of increased volumes of sale for the organization and improved quality of water for the consumers.
- In the 1990s, Nirma Ltd of India, an Indian company, and Hindustan Lever, the Indian arm of Unilever, a global leader in consumer product industry, realizing the opportunities that lay in the BOP market, came up with laundry detergent product offerings specially for rural areas that included innovations such as a new product formulation (lower ratio of oil to water to suit the common laundry practices of this segment of washing clothes at wells or at the river), low-cost manufacturing, and special packaging for daily usage.

(Continued)

To cater to the segment's role as a producer, companies have provided work, income, and some technical assistance. The following are examples of how companies have successfully created both private and public value in the bottom of the pyramid segment. Actions taken by these companies have helped create commercial value for themselves through increased sales and profits, private value for segment members through increased income, and public value when this additional income is spent on purchasing.

- Nestlé sources milk from small dairy farmers in Asia, McDonald's sources lettuces from farmers in Asia, and Mars sources coffee from farmers in West Africa. Technical assistance allows these people to play a better role as producers, distributors, and retailers.
- Hindustan Lever, a leader in the bottom of the pyramid segment has trained thousands of women to become door-to-door sales entrepreneurs for their consumer products.
- M-pesa, a mobile phone based money transfer company established in Kenya and operating across multiple African countries, depends on thousands of mom and pop stores to distribute its mobile money transfer service.
- African telecommunications company Safaricom utilizes small retailers to sell and distribute additional airtime. These millions of micro payments add up and the company's operation remains economically hassle free because these retailers manage and consolidate these small payments.
- Roshan, a mobile network operator in Afghanistan, has grown its network as well as increased BOP access to cellphones by encouraging Afghans to act as network members to distribute SIM cards and phones to other consumers. From its eight stores it has grown to 3500 stores and 3.5 million users.

Experts caution, however, that BOP markets are hard to crack. Profits are not guaranteed and many companies have made missteps to treat this segment as a traditional one. Since individual purchasing is small, scaling up through increased sales volumes is the only way to profitability. Sufficient volumes will materialize in this segment only when both private and public values are co-created.

According to experts creating and sustaining a thriving BOP market needs fulfilling four key elements:

1   *Increase purchasing power*: Create opportunities to increase purchasing power, for example by providing easier access to credit
2   *Help achieve aspirations*: The BOP segment wants to strive for a better life so helping them to aspire educationally and economically is key—for example, provision of micro credit to remote villages to help them bring electricity and creation of jobs for operating these electrical systems through a revolving loan fund

3 *Improve access through lower price and improved distribution:* Ruf and Tuf jeans in India are sold as $6 kits (parts to be assembled) and sold through local tailors, many in rural areas. Ruf and Tuf jeans are the largest selling jeans in India, surpassing the sales of many multinational companies operating in India

4 *Adapt to local conditions:* Create local solutions to nurture local markets. The operations of Amul Milk Cooperative in India originate with local dairy farms which take small quantities of milk to a local collection place and get paid daily. The milk is transported to processing centers and final products are transported to urban centers. The cooperative helps improve the quality of milk, its profits and the economic wealth of the farmers by providing vet services and cattle feed to them

Sources:

Prahalad, C.K. and Hart, S.L. (2002). "The fortune at the bottom of the pyramid." Worldview, Jan. 10, issue 26, updated by Deepa Prahalad in 2019 for Strategy+Business, www. strategy-business.com/article/11518

Rangan, V.K., Chu, M., and Petkoski, D. (2011). "The globe: Segmenting the base of the pyramid." *Harvard Business Review*, https://hbr.org/2011/06/the-globe-segmenting-the-base-of-the-pyramid

---

Case Study

Blair Athol Coal Mine's Customer Value Identification and Evaluation

Rio Tinto's Blair Athol Coal Mine (BAC) in Australia was facing problems with satisfaction and loyalty from one of their long-term customers Japan Electric Power Company (JEC).

During a meeting with their client, BAC's team was informed that the client was planning to shift part of their orders to Adaro, a competitor based in Indonesia. The coal from the two companies would be blended. JEC explained that this was becoming necessary to lower expenses in meeting environmental regulations that forced companies to dispose of ash and sulphur dioxide (SO_2). Adaro's coal, though lower quality than BAC's, had less ash and SO_2 content.

BAC had successfully held on to JEC's business by providing what it saw as value-added components. The company had offered the client a 10 percent lower price than the strongest competitor in Australia, Hunter Valley (HV), strong technical support, and reliability. BAC, however, had ongoing problems with their coal being lower in energy and higher in moisture (high energy and lower moisture are desired qualities for Asian clients) compared to HV's and delays in shipments because of maintenance problems at the facilities.

(Continued)

The Thermal Coal Market had become increasingly competitive and clients more cost sensitive. Companies fought tooth and nail to gain and retain clients in a largely undifferentiated product category. HV heavily promoted the lower moisture content and higher energy of their coals but BAC had not done the same regarding the lower ash and SO_2 content of their coal.

BAC's analysis of its problem with JEC showed them that BAC 1) did not know enough about the client's need and 2) had failed to offer a solution that impacted their client's bottom line. Such an offering would "show them the money." BAC decided it was time to change the strategy of engaging in the usual price-based competition and deeply understand the client's needs and problems and provide solutions for them. This they thought would be a sustainable source of competitive advantage and customer loyalty.

BAC's Customer Value Identification and Evaluation

As part of implementing this changed strategy of higher customer orientation, BAC hired a technical marketing manager whose responsibility was first to conduct a "value-in-use assessment" working together with the BAC commercial team. This would help the team to understand the customer's business from multiple angles.

To guide the value-in-use assessment a value-in-use model would be developed. Data on industry, competition, coal technology, operations, and supply-chain costs would be collected and fed into this model.

The value-in-assessment would help BAC find answers to the following critical issues, which would guide marketing decisions:

- *Differentiation*: Ways to meaningfully differentiate (differentiation that will positively impact the customer's bottom line) BAC's offering from HV's and Adaro's. Identification of similarities and differences in offerings across the three companies
- *Target segment*: Identify BAC's ideal customer segment considering BAC's differentiation. Describe this segment and what makes them perfect customers
- *Value proposition*: Write a value proposition statement that includes BAC's offering
- *Pricing*: Determine pricing strategies and tactics vis-à-vis the two competitors

Sources:

Ulaga, W. (2015). "Japan Electric Power Company (A): Can this customer be saved?" ID: IMD-7-1575. IMD Lausanne, Switzerland. Distributed by thecasecentre.org

Ulaga, W. (2015). "Japan Electric Power Company (B): The Customer Value Assessment Project." ID: IMD-7-1576. IMD Lausanne, Switzerland. Distributed by thecasecentre.org

Summary

Segmentation is the backbone of marketing and customer relationship management. Effective segmentation identifies viable, substantial, and accessible segments helping an organization develop and implement focused CRM strategies and tactics that profitably increase customer satisfaction and loyalty. The unfamiliarity with highly diverse and dynamic foreign country environments, and the oversized impact of these on consumer behavior and business practices make effective segmentation both critical and challenging in global ventures. This chapter introduced the reader to the importance of segmentation to global CRM initiatives, discussed how segmentation helps create value for global customers, and described the two-step segmentation process that leads to creation of both cross-country segments and within-country unique segments. Since effective segmentation and value creation is only possible with an adequate and deep knowledge of consumer behavior, the last part of the chapter also described global consumer behavior phenomena and trends.

References

Asahan, H., Prybutok, G., and Prybutok, V.R. (2018). "Insights into the antecedents of fast-food purchase intention and the relative positioning of quality." *Quality Management Journal*, 25, 2, 83–100.

Azjen, I. (1991). "The theory of planned behavior." *Organizational Behavior and Human Decision Processes*, 50, 2, 179–212.

Barrena, R., Garcıa, T., and Sanchez, M. (2017). "The effect of emotions on purchase behaviour towards novel foods: An application of means–end chain methodology." *Agrekon*, 56, 2, 173–90.

Baumgartner, H. and Steenkamp, J.-B.E.M. (1996). "Exploratory consumer buying behavior: Conceptualization and measurement." *International Journal of Research in Marketing*, 13, 2, 121–37.

Bowonder, B., Dambal, A., Kumar, S., and Shirodkar, A. (2010). "Innovation strategies for creating competitive advantage." *Research Technology Management*, 53, 3, 19–32.

Budeva, D.G. and Mullen, M.R. (2014). "International market segmentation: Economics, national culture and time." *European Journal of Marketing*, 48, 7–8, 1209–38.

Burgess, S.M. (1992). "Personal values and consumer research: An historical perspective." *Research in Marketing*, 11, 1, 35–79.

Cavusgil, S.T., Kiyak, T., and Yeniyurt, S. (2004). "Complementary approaches to preliminary foreign market opportunity assessment: Country clustering and country ranking." *Industrial Marketing Management*, 33, 7, 607–17.

Chui, A.C.W. and Kwok, C.C.Y. (2008). "National culture and life insurance consumption." *Journal of International Business Studies*, 39, 1, 88.

Cleveland, M., Papadopoulos, N., and Laroche, M. (2011). "Identity, demographics, and consumer behaviors: International market segmentation across product categories." *International Marketing Review*, 28, 3, 244–66.

De Mooij, M. (2004). *Consumer Behavior and Culture: Consequences for Global Marketing and Advertising*. Thousand Oaks, CA: Sage.

De Mooij, M. (2010). *Global Marketing and Advertising: Understanding Cultural Paradoxes*, 3rd edn. Thousand Oaks, CA: Sage.

De Mooij, M. and Hofstede, G. (2011). "Cross-cultural consumer behavior: A review of research findings." *Journal of International Consumer Marketing*, 23, 3–4, 181.

Engel, J.F., Kollat, D.T., and Blackwell, R.D. (1968). *Consumer Behaviour*, 1st edn. New York: Holt, Rinehart and Winston.

Erickson, T. (2009). "Generations in China", *Harvard Business Review*, https://hbr.org/2009/03/generations-in-china

Gutman, J. (1984). "Analyzing consumer orientations toward beverages through means-end chain analysis." *Psychology & Marketing*, 1, 3, 23.

Harrison, T. and Ansell, J. (2002). "Customer retention in the insurance industry: Using survival analysis to predict cross-selling opportunities." *Journal of Financial Services Marketing*, 6, 3, 229–39.

Hassan, S.S. and Craft, S. (2005). "Linking global market segmentation decisions with strategic positioning options." *Journal of Consumer Marketing*, 22, 2, 81–9.

Hassan, S.S. and Craft, S. (2012). "Examining world market segmentation and brand positioning strategies." *Journal of Consumer Marketing*, 29, 5, 344–56.

Hassan, S.S. and Katsanis, L.P. (1991). "Identification of global consumer segments: A behavioral framework." *Journal of International Consumer Marketing*, 3, 2, 11–28.

Hassan, S.S., Craft, S. and Kortam, W. (2003). "Understanding the new bases for global market segmentation." *Journal of Consumer Marketing*, 20, 5, 446–62.

Helsen, K., Jedidi, K., and DeSarbo, W.S. (1993). "A new approach to country segmentation utilizing multinational diffusion patterns." *Journal of Marketing*, 57, 4, 60–71.

Hernández-Ortega, B., Jiménez-Martínez, J., and Martín-DeHoyos, M.J. (2008). "Differences between potential, new and experienced e-customers: Analysis of e-purchasing behavior." *Internet Research*, 18, 3, 248–65.

Huang, L., Mou, J., See-To, E.W.K., and Kim, J. (2019). "See-to consumer perceived value preferences for mobile marketing in China: A mixed method approach." *Journal of Retailing and Consumer Services*, 48, 70–86.

Johnson, M.D. (1998). *Consumer Orientation and Market Action*. Upper Saddle River, NJ: Prentice Hall.

Kjeldgaard, D. and Askegaard, S. (2006). "The glocalization of youth culture: The global youth segment as structures of common difference." *Journal of Consumer Research*, 33, 231–47.

Lindenbeck, B. and Olbrich, R. (2019). "Improving Targeting by Taking Long-Term Relationships into Account", in P. Rossi and N. Krey (eds), *Finding New Ways to Engage and Satisfy Global Customers: Proceedings of the 2018 Academy of Marketing Science (AMS) World Marketing Congress (WMC)*. Cham, Switzerland: Springer, p.29.

Moses, E. (2000). *The $100 Billion Allowance: Accessing the Global Teen Market*. Hoboken, NJ: John Wiley and Sons.

Mulvey, M.S. and Olson, J.C. (1994). "Exploring the relationships between means–end knowledge and involvement." *Advances in Consumer Research*, 21, 1, 51–7.

Nachum, L. (1994). "The choice of variables for segmentation of the international market." *International Marketing Review*, 11, 3, 54–67.

Olson, J.C. and Reynolds, T.J. (2001). "The means–end approach to understanding consumer decision making", in T.J. Reynolds and J.C. Olson, (eds), *Understanding Consumer Decision Making: The Means–End Approach to Marketing and Advertising Strategy*. Mahwah, NJ: Lawrence Erlbaum, pp. 3–20.

Overby, J.W., Gardial, S.F., and Woodruff, R.B. (2004). "French versus American consumers' attachment of value to a product in a common consumption context: A cross-national comparison." *Journal of the Academy of Marketing Science*, 32, 4, 437–60.

Pan, Y. (2011). "Eliminating the cyber 'lemons' problem with the e-reputation in e-commerce market: Theoretical model and practice." *International Journal of Networking and Virtual Organisations*, 8, 3/4, 182–91.

Papadopoulos, N. and Martín Martín, O. (2011). "International market selection and segmentation: Perspectives and challenges." *International Marketing Review*, 28, 2, 132–49.

Reynolds, T.J. and Gutman, J. (2001). "Laddering theory, method, analysis, and interpretation", in T.J. Reynolds and J.C. Olson (eds), *Understanding Consumer Decision Making: The Means–End Approach to Marketing and Advertising Strategy*. Mahwah, NJ: Lawrence Erlbaum Associates, pp. 25–62.

Roth, M.S. (1995). "The effects of culture and socioeconomics on the performance of global brand image strategies." *Journal of Marketing Research*, 32, 163–75.

Samli, A.C. (2013). *International Consumer Behavior in the 21st Century: Impact on Marketing Strategy Development*. New York: Springer.

Silva de Oliveira, A., Souki, G.Q., Gandia, R.M., and Henrique de Barros Vilas Boas, L. (2021). "Coffee in capsules consumers' behaviour: a quantitative study on attributes, consequences and values." *British Food Journal*, 123, 1, 191–208.

Spence, M. (2002). "Signaling in retrospect and the informational structure of markets." *The American Economic Review*, 92, 3, 434–59.

Valette-Florence, P. (1998). "A causal analysis of means–end hierarchies in a cross-cultural context: Methodological refinements." *Journal of Business Research*, 42, 2, 161–6.

Webster, F.E. (Jr.) (1994). *Market-Driven Management: Using the new marketing concept to create a customer-oriented company*. New York: John Wiley & Sons, Inc.

Weinstein, A. (2002). "Customer retention: A usage segmentation and customer value approach." *Journal of Targeting, Measurement and Analysis for Marketing*, 10, 3, 259–68.

Wells, J.D., Valacich, J.S., and Hess, T.J. (2011). "What signals are you sending? How website quality influences perceptions of product quality and purchase intentions." *MIS Quarterly*, 35, 2, 373–96.

Zeugner-Roth, K., Zabkar, V., and Diamantopoulos, A. (2015). "Consumer ethnocentrism, national identity, and consumer cosmopolitanism as drivers of consumer behavior: A social identity theory perspective." *Journal of International Marketing*, 23, 2, 25.

PART II
PLANNING AND IMPLEMENTATION

4

GLOBAL CRM PLANNING AND IMPLEMENTATION

TD Bank's Data Transformation Initiatives for Customer Relationship Management

Between 2002 and 2016, the Toronto-Dominion (TD) Bank Group, one of the largest banks based in Canada saw considerable and continuous growth after entering the US market. This growth created challenges in data management. The amount of available data increased sharply with the growth in the number of customers utilizing mobile and Internet services and associated personalized customer data.

Data Management Challenges

TD realized that the only way to compete better is to more effectively utilize this wealth of information for enhancing customer value and customer experience. However, an evaluation of its data system showed that despite having good data policies, processes, and controls regarding data privacy and security, data was being managed separately within each line of business without overarching, centralized, enterprise-level policies and processes for data management. This lack of a centralized umbrella impeded the organization's ability to trace sources of data and introduced inefficiencies in sharing data analytics reports across multiple business lines. Further, it impacted negatively the organizations's ability to fully utilize human resource capabilities and enhance customer value and experiences.

Data Transformation Program Initiative

In 2013 TD decided to initiate a program of data transformation to more effectively manage data for customer experience management. As part of this transformation journey the bank needed to do the following:

(Continued)

- Develop an enterprise data strategy
- Build a team to manage the data
- Design and implement data policies
- Develop processes and tools to monitor and enforce compliance with data management policies

People, Process and Technology Changes

To achieve the above, TD took several initiatives to better align people, processes and technology.

People changes: In 2013 it created a new position of Chief Data Officer (CDO) to lead the data transformation. This senior management position was in charge of utilizing information as a strategic asset, to align TD's data strategy with its strategic business priorities and to highlight the implications for data of any strategic business initiatives to be undertaken. As part of building a team for enterprise data management the Office of the CDO established a data stewardship role within each business line to make sure data management was consistent throughout the organization. Data stewards were responsible for maintaining overall data quality standards by identifying and managing data elements, data issues, and data changes across their line of business. In 2015 TD had more than 300 data stewards. Given the importance of resources for bringing about a transformation in data management, executive buy-in was critical. TD appointed senior executives from each line of business to be executive data sponsors who would be responsible for making sure business line data strategies were aligned with enterprise-wide data strategy. As part of their role executive sponsors would provide funding, champion data quality issues and appoint data stewards.

The office of CDO was vacant for 9 months and was thus left without a rudder. The lack of leadership in that office created fragmentation and lack of a sense of direction. The new CDO Glenda Crisp, appointed in 2015 needed to bring her team back on the same boat along with other stakeholders in the different lines of business.

To create more consistency in organization-wide processes the CDO decided to implement several changes to data management policies across all business lines. These changes resulted in significantly increasing the workload for data stewards. Under the previous CDO data stewards were only allocating 25 percent of their time to data management. Crisp realized she had to do something to address this issue. However, since data stewards reported to their business line supervisors and not the CDO, addressing the overload issue would entail not only changes to responsibilities for data stewards but also reporting structure.

The massive restructuring that TD engaged in also created several difficulties for the new CDO in performing her role adequately. With restructuring, departments changed, taking on new responsibilities and roles. The restructuring also negatively impacted the CDO's ability to access all relevant data. To complicate things further, the newness of the CDO office created inconsistencies in how employees perceived the role of CDO. The CDO would need to regularly work with executives in the different lines of business to build new relationships and clarify roles, responsibilities and reporting hierarchies.

Process changes: TD decided to implement three main processes to achieve a common understanding of and approach towards data management. These were:

- *Data issues and governance*: To ensure a common approach to data governance across all business lines
- *Data quality management*: To ensure quality of data
- *Data impact assessment*: To ensure all projects aligned with the enterprise's data strategy.

The CDO realized, after interviews with multiple senior executives, that the 141-page document highlighting all processes and policies was needlessly long and complicated and needed to be shortened and simplified.

Technology changes: In order to make sure the changes in people and processes were supported by effective technology TD decided to implement a combined approach of "build your own" and licensed solutions. TD built its own tool for the data issue and changed the governance processes to allow the CDO to see and solve issues across the organization that impacted multiple stakeholder units. To ensure data quality and large data management, TD licensed IBM's Infosphere® Information Governance Catalog and its Infosphere® Information Analyzer. The former standardizes approaches to understanding data sets and the latter helped derive more meaning from data, ensured incorrect data was minimized, facilitated delivery of valid content and lowered data integration costs.

Source: Kristal, M., Crisp, G., Bonnello, C., and Heighington, K. (2018). "TD Bank Group: Building an effective enterprise data management policy." ID: 9B18E007. Ivey Business School Foundation. Distributed by www.thecasecentre.org

Introduction

In the past 20 years organizations have increasingly considered CRM as one of the core tools for organization growth, but a significant number of implementations have failed to deliver desired outcomes of customer satisfaction, loyalty, and profitability (Rigby and Bilodeau, 2013, 2009; Santouridis and Tsachtani, 2015; Steel et al., 2013). The lack of a strategic approach to CRM is the number one reason for failure. A strategic approach takes into consideration the competitive position of the organization, the operational environment, the availability of resources and expense of securing new ones, and organizational structure and culture (Frow and Payne, 2009; Frow et al., 2011; Kim and Kim, 2009). A strategic approach guides the organization in developing feasible and needed CRM objectives, strategies, and tactics that will have a higher chance of success.

The second reason for failure is a solely inward-looking, firm-centric approach to CRM not balanced by an outward-looking customer-centric approach (Frow and Payne, 2009; Frow et al., 2011; Nguyen and Mutum, 2012). A solely firm-centric CRM approach hinders fully understanding and engaging customers and hence does not deliver (or care to deliver in some cases) differentiating and superior customer value and experiences. An "only me" CRM approach also does not develop trust in the consumer's mind that the company is acting competently, ethically, and proactively towards her. As discussed in Chapter 1, trust is an essential component that impacts both the customer's perception of value of the company's offerings and her experiences of interacting with the company and consuming its products and services.

A strategic organization-wide approach to CRM tied to an unrelenting focus on customers is effective. However, it increases the complexity of implementation. This complexity lies in the management of data and changes to and alignment of processes, people, and technology aspects of the organization to meet the demands of effective CRM implementation.

Over the years some organizations have become better at successfully managing this complexity. The case above provides a view into aspects of complexity and its management. Effectively managing data and information is core to CRM success (Frow and Payne, 2009). Efforts made in consciously gathering consumer, competitor, and environmental information helps organizations to understand these deeply. This understanding then helps develop effective CRM strategies and processes supported by people and technology to create sustainable, win–win relationships with customers.

The role of information becomes particularly crucial with the advent of technology-enabled omnichannel modes of communication, interaction, and purchase, and the increasing internationalization of organizations (Aliyev, 2021). Both increase the diversity and amount of information that needs to be managed well for effective CRM.

CRM Planning and Implementation Process

A strategic approach to planning and implementing a CRM strategy needs to be an organization-wide initiative. It includes a change in and alignment of processes, people, and technology for effective flow of adequate and relevant information needed to develop the capability to create and deliver a win–win value proposition for both the firm and the customer. Planning and developing an effective CRM strategy usually starts by evaluating the competitive situation of the organization and environmental realities. This information provides a guide to creating the CRM vision and developing a plan for the core value proposition for the customer. This proposed value umbrella helps determine changes required in organizational processes, culture, and technology and develop a business case for the CRM initiative (Frow and Payne, 2009). Figure 4.1 illustrates the process of development of the CRM strategy.

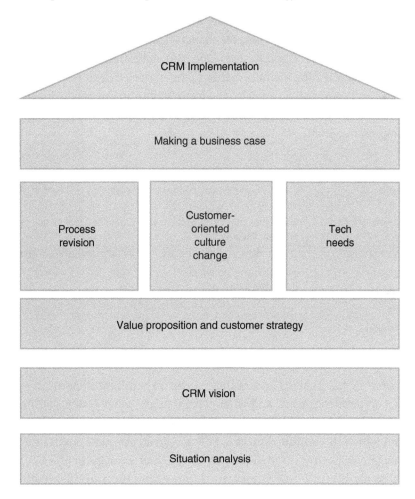

Figure 4.1　Strategic Plan for CRM

Implementation of this CRM strategy then happens as a series of separate but connected functional and cross-functional projects under this umbrella, aided by an organization-wide customer-oriented culture, and a capability to manage information, channels of communication and distribution, and to engage willing and able partners such as distributors, retailers, and logistics providers (Becker et al., 2009; Finnegan and Currie, 2010; Frow et al., 2011).

Development of CRM Strategy
Situation Analysis

In this step the organization takes stock and evaluates 1) its environmental and operational realities within and across countries, and 2) its current competitive position in view of current environments and possible changes. Essentially, the organization analyzes its Strengths, Weaknesses, Opportunities, and Threats from the market (SWOT).

Environmental scanning includes assessing the macro environments (cultural, economic, legal, and competitive) and also the micro environment of consumer behavior. Table 4.1 identifies some environmental areas particularly relevant to global customer relationship management.

Table 4.1 Macro and Micro Environmental Factors

Income levels	Consumer perception of product category	Availability and type of middlemen
Technology infrastructure	Consumer level of acceptance of product category	Extent and type of competition
Physical infrastructure	Consumer usage of technology	Value propositions of competitors
Marketing laws:	Availability of and types of consumer segment(s)	
Product safety		
Advertising		
Sales promotion		
Pricing		

An environmental analysis and evaluation helps highlight opportunities, market demands, competitive threats, and what is feasible and what is not. During its early forays into the European market Campbell's soup company of the United States, being confident of its continued success, failed to do an adequate environmental scan of the market. Following its tried and tested product strategy in the US market it offered its soups in cans to the European customers and was surprised that they were not well received. What Campbell failed to discover was that Europeans were used to buying soup in powder or bouillon form and Campbell's value proposition was at odds with their cultural habit.

Once opportunities and threats in the market are identified, a further analysis of strengths and weaknesses vis-à-vis competitors provides a clear picture of what strengths can be exploited and what weaknesses need strengthening. Table 4.2 identifies areas where strengths or weakness can impact customer relationship management efforts.

Table 4.2 Areas that Impact CRM

Segments being targeted	Relevancy of customer value proposition	Channels utilized: Sales, distribution and communication
Consumer awareness of the brand	Differentiation in customer value proposition	Sales Trends
Organizational management of information		

This first step is crucial because it sets in place a foundation of knowledge on which the CRM strategy will be built. For the knowledge foundation to be sound and useful it is important that information flows well within the organization and is not siloed. For global CRM, a major deterrent in analyzing the current situation is the lack of high-quality, adequate, current, and correct market information in many countries.

CRM Vision and Objectives

A situation analysis should provide enough knowledge to help the organization clearly envision the desired impact of their CRM effort and develop 1) an overarching vision for CRM and 2) goals and objectives for the whole organization as well as for functional areas involved in the CRM initiative.

A CRM vision is a statement that identifies and states what the CRM initiative will mean for customers, do for customers, and in what way it will change the organization. At its core a CRM vision underscores the value proposition of the organization, the value customers will receive from the CRM effort. Irrespective of country the CRM vision of an organization should remain the same. It provides strategic guidance to all things CRM across all markets. Table 4.3 showcases some examples of CRM vision statements.

Table 4.3 Examples of CRM Vision Statements

Organization	CRM Vision Statement
Westin Hotels	"Year after year Westin and its people will be regarded as the best and most sought after hotel and resort management group in North America"*
Tata Steel	"TATA Steel enters the new millennium with the confidence of learning, knowledge based and happy organisation. We will establish ourselves as a supplier of choice by delighting our customers with our service and products. In the coming decade we will be the most competitive steel plant and so serve the community and the nation"*
Farm Fresh Produce	"We help the families of Main town live happier and healthier lives by providing the freshest, tastiest, and most nutritious local produce: From local farms to your table in under 24 hours"*

(Continued)

Table 4.3 (Continued)

Organization	CRM Vision Statement
IKEA	"To create a better everyday life for many people" (https://crm.org/articles/vision-statement-a-guide-to-writing-a-great-vision-with-examples)
Amazon	"To be the earth's most customer-centric company; to build a place where people can come to find and discover anything they might want to buy online" (https://crm.org/articles/vision-statement-a-guide-to-writing-a-great-vision-with-examples)

*Sources

1 www.pe.com/2014/08/03/moving-from-vision-to-ambition/

2 Saiyadain, M.S. (2001). "Modernization of Mind at Tata Steel", *Indian Journal of Industrial Relations*, 36 (3), 363.

3 www.mindtools.com/pages/article/newLDR_90.htm

To be implementable a CRM vision needs to be translated into concrete and quantifiable objectives. Overarching organizational objectives can vary from country market to country market based on a SWOT analysis in each market. For example, an objective in one market where the brand is the market leader could be improving customer experience by 20 percent in three years through innovation, whereas in another market where the brand is less well known and new it could be improving customer perception of the brand by 10 percent in one year through promotional efforts. Based on the country-level objective, different functional objectives need to be agreed upon such as for sales, marketing, customer service, logistics, HR, R&D, and manufacturing. It is important to actively involve employees working in these functions to collectively develop these objectives based upon an open discussion and analysis of requirements.

Value Proposition and Customer Strategy

After the organization-wide CRM vision and objectives are established it is time to drill down to the core of CRM: the customer. CRM exists to attract, acquire, and retain profitable and high-value customers through provision of a higher than expected customer experience. To provide this experience an organization has to provide an offering (product + service) that has value in the eyes of the customer.

Value proposition: "A multifaceted package of product, service, process, price, communication and interaction that customers experience during their relationships with a company" (Kumar and Reinartz, 2018).

In formulating the value proposition for a customer or a customer segment across country markets, an organization must clearly address the following issues:

- What facets of the value proposition do segment members (customers and non-customers) value more than others—for example, do they value the high quality of the product more than the intimacy of the service?
- What is the extent of similarities and differences across countries in value perception of cross-country segment members?
- How do segment members perceive the current offering of the company vis-à-vis competitors' offerings. How do these perceptions differ across countries?
- How aligned or mismatched is the organization's own perception vs. customers' perceptions of the value proposition? Are both on the same page?

An overall value proposition is only the start. Because organizations usually have a portfolio of different types of customers at different stages of acquisition and retention across different countries, a CRM effort should strive to sustain this diverse portfolio. This means diverse and granular customer strategies (ideally one for each consumer or customer segment at different stages of acquisition or retention, with tweaks built in to adapt to country environments) need to be developed under the overall umbrella of the value proposition.

A customer strategy should be both for customer acquisition and retention. In order to have an effective customer strategy the organization needs to:

- Analyze and understand existing customers and their expectations at a granular level. This will help in developing more relevant and meaningful retention strategies
- Engage in a customer segmentation process that crosses country borders to develop relevant acquisition strategies. Variables such as past purchase patterns and expectations of value should yield valuable cross-country segments that would be potentially profitable and whose expectations can be met
- Consider value propositions of competitors to develop competitive acquisition and retention strategies. These could very well be different in different countries leading to tweaking of the value proposition for specific countries
- Consider customers' societal networks to develop customer experience enhancement strategies for retention. These should include customized offers for cross-selling and upselling

Organizational Process Redesign and Alignment

Customer relationship management is a process-driven strategy. Processes are the foundation of an organization and any organizational goal is achieved through processes.

Process: A flow of inputs and information into and through a specific sequence of activity steps that results in an outcome.

Processes are vital because the flow that happens through the different steps in a process connects and integrates the effects of complementary inputs and activities that together achieve a goal. Process flows relevant to CRM include inputs and activities that include the value proposition, customer needs, and CRM goals. The process flows connect and integrate these inputs and activities to deliver the offering. This offering, as discussed before, is multifaceted and can include product delivery, service fulfillment, complaint resolution, and social media communication and interaction to name a few (Lambert, 2010).

For example the personal selling process connects and integrates multiple inputs and activities such as development of knowledge of customers' needs, knowledge of competitors' products, approaching the customer, making a presentation to the customer, handling objections, asking for an order, and finally following up with the customer to achieve the goal of revenue generation and customer satisfaction.

There are multiple types of business processes that are crucial for achieving CRM. These are customer-facing processes such as customer complaint handling, purely back office processes such as R&D, processes straddling both customer-facing and back-office processes such as order fulfillment, horizontal cross-functional processes such as new product development, and vertical function-specific processes such as customer acquisition housed within the marketing function (Rababa et al., 2011). In order to make sure that all business processes collectively help achieve CRM objectives they need to be audited and then revised to the extent necessary.

Table 4.4 highlights different types of organizational processes that would be relevant to an organization-wide CRM initiative.

Making processes cross-functional: The overarching goal of CRM is acquisition and retention of high-value customers. Hence marketing and sales should rightfully take the lead in such an initiative. However, for CRM to bear fruit, other functions such as IT, customer service, human resources, supply chain, engineering, R&D, manufacturing, and finance need to be actively involved and connected. Some individual processes across these functions need to be redesigned and aligned to create cross-functional processes. It is important to build feedback into these cross-functional processes to facilitate continuous improvements (Lambert, 2010).

One example of such a cross-functional process would be that of product development where the team represents multiple organizational expertise areas and steps in the process involve inputs from multiple functions such as marketing, sales, R&D, manufacturing, and finance. Many organizations now bring the market closer by having customer and value-chain partner representation at the product development team.

Table 4.4 Processes that Impact CRM

Operational Processes	Administrative Processes	Decision Making Processes	Communication Processes	Information Management and Learning Processes
Create, produce and deliver offerings to customers • New product development • Manufacturing • Marketing • Selling • Order fulfillment • Supply chain • Customer service	Support operational processes • Strategic planning • Budgeting • Performance evaluation • Human resource management • Research & development	Determine the underlying cognitive parts of operational and administrative processes	Determine the underlying interpersonal parts of operational and administrative processes	Acquisition, analysis and interpretation of information leading to new applicable knowledge

Source: Garvin, D.A. (1998). "The processes of organization and management." *MIT Sloan Management Review*, July 15, https://sloanreview.mit.edu/article/the-processes-of-organization-and-management

Aligning processes: It is also important to align processes more closely so that they work in tandem to fulfill CRM goals (Lambert, 2010). For example, the process of handling customer complaints should be aligned with product development processes so that customer complaints on product usage and product quality can be incorporated into new product development. Table 4.5 highlights important measures for evaluating processes for a CRM initiative.

Table 4.5 Process Evaluation Metrics

Efficiency: Considerations of • Cost • Resource productivity	Degree of alignment with other related processes
Number of bottlenecks	Reliability
If feedback is built into the process for continuous improvements	Time to completion
Effectiveness: • Type and degree of value added by process • Critical to objective achievement	Compliance with third-party regulatory, safety, and environmental standards

Source: BEM (2020). "9 ways to measure a business process." Business Enterprise Mapping, Jan. 2, www.businessmapping.com/blog/9-ways-to-measure-a-business-process

A useful tool for process evaluation and revision is mapping (Pombriant, 2016). A process map helps to clearly visualize all flows throughout the process from start to finish and points of connections between processes. To improve an individual process and create better alignment between processes, it is important to view process flows through the eyes of customers and keep in mind the customer value proposition. Customer experience enhancement comes when business processes deliver customer value in a way the customer expects it to be delivered. Figure 4.2 shows a process map of multiple services in the credit card business developed by the Royal Bank of Scotland during their CRM initiative. The maps shows different service aspects and their alignment. Service aspects are color coded to indicate customer satisfaction levels. Green indicates high satisfaction, red low and orange medium. Some service aspects (cells marked by "x"s) were not evaluated.

Mapping and revising processes to be effective in providing a high-quality customer experience across countries will need consideration of a country's consumption culture and behavior, and business culture and requirements. Given the differences and similarities in environments and consumer value perceptions, expectations, and behaviors across countries, there will be some overlap in CRM processes across country operations with some tweaking needed to suit country-specific needs. It is important to coordinate across countries to create synergies in processes and leverage process-based competencies.

Market demand for new products and the kinds of new products may not be exactly the same or happen at the same time. Brazilians, for example, don't like to touch food with their hands. For a fast food provider, a new product development process needs to keep this mind. What form should chicken wings take in Brazil so that they can be conveniently consumed using utensils rather than fingers. Customer service processes, product returns, and repair and maintenance issues may need to be incorporated differently across countries because of different consumer expectations and national laws. The process of product return in one country might include returning the product to the local store where the consumer purchased it whereas in another country it might include shipping the product to a centralized warehouse with prepaid packaging. In some countries more innovation in these processes might be warranted. Japan is unique in that many products—automobiles, financial products and tailored suits!—used to be sold door to door, whether at someone's house or at an office. Even though this trend is slowly disappearing and as a strategy is not utilized as often, it is still acceptable in that culture (Englade, 1985; Lund, 2016).

Customer-Centric Organization Culture: Education and Change Management

CRM researchers and consultants strongly hold the view that a CRM initiative will be easily derailed if the organization cannot cultivate a customer-centric culture (Karakostas et al., 2005; Rahimi and Gunlu, 2016).

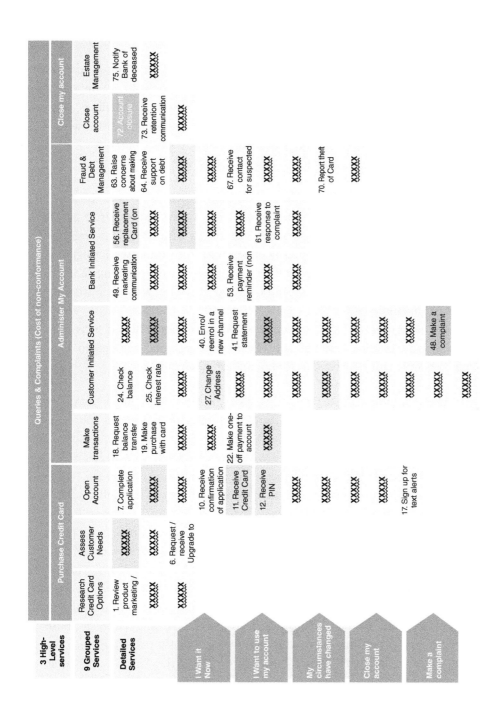

Figure 4.2 Royal Bank of Scotland Credit Card Service Map

Source: Maklan, S., Antonetti, P. and Whitty, S. (2017). "A better way to manage customer experience." *California Management Review*, 59, 2, 92–115.

Customer centricity is at the heart of CRM and supports CRM processes and technology. A customer-centric organization is one where everyone believes that customers are at the center of all organizational operations and where this belief guides customer-oriented behaviors.

However, changing entrenched organizational culture to a customer-centric one is easier said than done. Organizational cultures become entrenched over time and are reinforced through existing roles, responsibilities, and processes. They influence organizational thought processes through both cognitive and emotional pathways, roles become part of organizational identities, and any change is easily rejected.

Two essentials in bringing about a change in culture are:

1   *The involvement of senior leadership* in championing the cause of culture change. Middle-level managers may take a lead in the CRM initiative but senior leadership will also need to walk the talk by adopting the desired behavior themselves. Being regularly exposed to this should send a signal to the rest of the organization about the importance of culture change and create a sense of a shared need. This should have a positive impact on emotional buy-in from employees

2   *Changes to human resources processes and policies* surrounding hiring, incentives, rewards, compensation, and training. These changes should reinforce the cognitive and emotional reasons for buying into the culture change

In global markets change management is trickier because of the impact of different national cultures on organizational culture. Cultural aspects such as collectivism, power distance, uncertainty avoidance, social structure and divisions, religion, and education impact organizational culture and can create different degrees of difficulty in getting buy-in from employees to a customer-centric culture. Types of leadership behaviors and changes to human resource practices and policies that will be impactful will differ to a greater or lesser extent in different countries. In China, compared to the US, the relationship between the leadership and subordinate employees has a stronger and more positive impact on employee satisfaction and leads to a higher commitment to customer service (Kim et al., 2017). This is the impact of higher power distance and lower individualism in China, which requires a more nurturing leadership style. Non-Chinese leadership of international organizations operating in China therefore has to make a strong effort to build a mentoring relationship with subordinates to bring about a culture change where employees take on proactive roles. Cultures and countries vary in the kinds of rewards and incentives (monetary and non-monetary) that motivate them and affect human resource policies.

Technology Needs

Information, communication, and transactions are the lifeblood of a CRM initiative. Their breadth and depth has burgeoned in recent years, creating a challenge. An increase in the diversity and range of operations and decision making because of internationalization and omnichannel consumer behavior have accelerated this trend.

Coming to the rescue is the third arm of CRM: technology. Organizations have at their disposal increasingly sophisticated technology geared towards facilitating organizational processes. For a CRM initiative to be successful organizations need technology to support strategic planning, operations, decision making, communications and interaction, and most crucially management of information, which underlies the effectiveness and efficiencies of all the other processes.

Technology need assessment starts by identifying and then installing or revamping the overarching technology infrastructure such as hardware and software; technology facilitators for data acquisition, storage, transformation and flow such as survey tools, databases, and data analytics; and application technology such as new CRM application software that includes multiple application options for marketing, sales, and customer service.

What follows is a list of the four main types of technology needed for a successful CRM initiative:

1   *Overarching information technology architecture*: The kinds of hardware and software used
2   *Data capture and storage technology*: Data capture technology includes survey and social media tools to obtain data from different touch points, and a dynamic data warehouse contains relevant and high quality data
3   *Data and information analysis technology*: A burgeoning range of sophisticated data analytics software is available to transform data into knowledge that value creation processes can utilize
4   *Application architecture and software*: Software for CRM, enterprise resource planning (ERP), accounting and HR aid in automating processes in marketing, sales, customer service, supply chain, budgeting, and communication

The CRM Automation Software Market

The CRM software market is the biggest software market globally (Syzmczuk, 2019). Organizations have the option of choosing from multiple CRM technology suites that can either be physically incorporated into an organization's systems on its premises or accessed through an online cloud-based system hosted by the vendor. A typical

CRM suite should at the minimum include contact management, marketing automation, sales tracking, and tracking leads from campaign management (Watson and Jolaoso, 2021). Many vendors offer a full suite of supplemental software. Features can be more or less customized for the needs of the organization. Organizations have the choice of selecting different functionalities within these systems and can add on services to the packaged offerings. Most vendors offer CRM as a software and as a service (SaaS) on a subscription model. Large organizations tend to buy large enterprise-level suites whereas small- to medium-sized companies purchase scaled-down versions. More specifics on these alternatives are discussed in Chapters 5 through 7.

It is important to realize that in a CRM program, decisions on processes are made first followed by decisions on technologies that can effectively aid and automate such processes to achieve CRM goals. It is important not to follow fads when making decisions on which technologies to utilize. Keeping in mind CRM goals it is important to carefully evaluate the 1) functionalities of technologies (existing and potential), 2) the extent to which they facilitate CRM processes and 3) the extent to which potential CRM software aligns and integrates with existing software (e.g. HR or supply-chain software).

Given the stage of technology development of a country, technologies may need to be customized to facilitate customer experience—for example, making sure websites work properly on both PC and mobile platforms. In many developing countries a majority of Internet access happens through mobile phones.

TECH BOX: AI CHATBOTS

Source: Oleksandr Panasovskyi / Shutterstock

An AI chatbot is a piece of artificial intelligence software that uses machine learning to answer basic questions in customer service. This automated system simulates an actual conversation through natural language. It is used by companies in both B2C and B2B industries to manage customer interactions and customer service across different channels and languages. According to Forbes magazine, 80 percent of marketers utilize chatbots and an increasing number of customers are more willing to receive immediate help from a chatbot rather than wait a few minutes for a human interaction.

Major benefits of using AI chatbots include:

- Shorter wait time, reduces bounce rate, and increases conversion rate through instant resolution and 24/7 availability
- Increases customer satisfaction by providing more relevant and customized answers by applying learning from previous conversations
- Aids customer service agents to solve problems and quality of support by collecting and interpreting customer information

Table 4.6 provides information on some of the highly rated AI chatbots with different functionalities to suit different business scenarios and industries.

Table 4.6 Chatbots

ChatBot	All-in-one platform that offers tailored support and personalized recommendations without any need for coding
ManyChat	Provides interactive and tailored experience to Facebook Messenger and SMS users by combining both. Seamlessly integrates with the following tools: Shopify, Google Sheets, MailChimp, Hubspot, ConvertKit, and Zapier
Acquire	Built for more human-like conversations. Allows for customer self-service, and improvements in performance by providing chatbot analytics. Seamlessly integrates with commonly used business chatbot software such as IBM Watson, Azure QnA, and Dialogflow
Amelia	Conversational and cognitive chatbot with enhanced human conversation and continuous learning capabilities to creatively engage customers in complex scenarios
SAP Conversational AI	Leverages natural language processing capabilities to have human-like conversations in any language
Nuance	Analyzes past interactions to enhance customer experience across web, mobile and voice channels

Business Case for CRM

A business case for a CRM initiative includes a cost–benefit analysis of adopting and implementing a CRM strategy. This step in development of a CRM strategy is crucial for a couple of reasons. It concretely lays down short- and long-term financial and non-financial returns from the CRM system and underscores the different costs of implementation. It also presents a practical and thorough analysis of the feasibility of implementing CRM. This sends a signal to senior management regarding the resources required to implement CRM and convince them of the importance of securing the same. Table 4.7 highlights some of the benefit areas that are commonly highlighted when making a business case for implementing CRM.

Table 4.7 Organizational Benefits of CRM

Improved leads	Higher sales	Decreased customer acquisition costs
Increased customer conversion rates	Higher customer satisfaction	Decreased customer retention costs
Increased customer retention rates	Higher levels and impacts of word of mouth	Decreased customer service and management costs

These benefits must be weighed against the costs of implementing CRM, which are incurred because of necessary changes in the physical and technological infrastructure, process revisions, change management, project management, and the acquisition of software. Given the broad reach of CRM implementation, total costs can quickly add up.

CRM Implementation

Once the CRM strategy has been developed it is time for implementation. This involves the operations and activities needed to put into motion the elements of the strategy. These include transforming the culture, processes, and technology to ready the organization, determining specific CRM projects and the sequence of implementation, selecting channels for communication and distribution, and choosing alliance partners. Fig 4.3 highlights the 4 strategic activities that an organization needs to work through and align as part of implementation of CRM

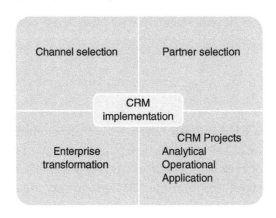

Figure 4.3   CRM Implementation

Enterprise Transformation

Getting an enterprise ready for CRM implementation is no easy task. It is first important to address the people issues to get the organization's people on the same page. To get employees motivated and capable of adopting the changed processes and technologies it is important to create a shared culture of customer orientation, engage in training to develop the requisite skills and tie compensation to CRM objectives. This process of change is often top down and with a sense of urgency created by senior leaders. Other times it is a combination of bottom-up and top-down processes where rank and file management take ownership of the change initiative with active support from top leadership.

Once the CRM mindset and human resource skills are established the actual work of revamping processes and installing new technologies start taking shape. It is also important at this stage to adjust physical location-based assets such as manufacturing facilities and retail stores to facilitate the implementation.

CRM Projects

CRM implementation happens as a series of smaller related projects. Some of the projects happen simultaneously and some sequentially. CRM projects are categorized as operational and analytical.

Before the projects can be put into motion it is crucial to form a CRM project team which will be responsible for overseeing the CRM projects, making key decisions for these projects, and sharing the progress of CRM implementation with the entire organization. To remain true to the organization-spanning nature of CRM, the project team needs to have representation from multiple organizational functions. A CRM project team should consist of members from the following areas (Haines, 2019):

- Senior management to champion the project
- Managers to manage the project
- Representatives from marketing, sales, customer service, logistics, manufacturing, IT, and finance

Local environmental realities vary from country to country. Hence, for global CRM project implementation an effort should be made to include local representatives from the functional areas, an outside consultant and an important customer.

Operational Projects

Operational projects help the organization get the technology ready and facilitate the process and people components of CRM. These projects include establishing the IT infrastructure and the data management technology, and automating aspects of functional and cross-functional processes such as sales, customer service, order fulfillment, and training. Specific operational projects are tied to the automated applications of the core CRM processes of marketing, sales, and customer service such as return of products and refunds, customization of product offerings through co-creation, and tracking so that the customer has more knowledge and control of delivery.

Analytical Projects

These projects utilize the technology-ready organization to transform data into market knowledge for better decision making. Analytical projects, also called CRM analytics, are about gathering, storing, transforming, and analyzing consumer, competitor, and international business environment data and then interpreting the outputs to develop knowledge. This knowledge helps organizations develop effective strategies and tactics for enhancing customer value provision and experiences. Given the volatile nature of global markets, analytical projects are continuously implemented in global CRM initiatives.

Channel Selection

A channel refers to both a mode of communication with customers and a mode of distribution and fulfillment of value proposition through the marketing value chain (Kumar and Reinartz, 2018). Channels thus directly impact the quality of customer experiences, customer satisfaction, and loyalty and are crucial for building and sustaining customer relationships. Increasing omnichannel consumer behavior has pushed organizations to create strategies that sync multiple-channel customer touch points for communicating with the customer in a holistic way, enhancing customer experiences and capturing more diverse customer data (Palmatier et al., 2016). Organizations need to consider issues of both offline/online as well direct/indirect modes of communication and distribution before determining the optimum channels. The optimum choice will likely vary from country to country depending on multiple environmental realities. The stage of technology acceptance and usage, the transportation and logistics infrastructure, legal restrictions on promotions, the availability and security of payment systems, and of course consumer preferences are some of the considerations important in channel selection for global CRM (Adesoga and James, 2019).

Partner Selection

An organization on its own will usually not have all the resources needed to provide the desired and proposed customer value, and it would be unduly burdensome, inefficient, and ineffective to try to do so. Thus, CRM initiatives need to step outside the organization and actively engage external stakeholders such as value-chain partners. Strategic alliance partners that share knowledge and resources for new product development, distributing, retailing, logistical solutions, technology, and consultants are some of the external partners that can help deliver the value proposition (Kodama, 2005; Ku and Fan, 2009). Involving partners in the CRM effort creates a win–win situation for all stakeholders. Organizations should create a clear partner strategy that includes determining areas of operations partners would add value to, identifying ideal partner profiles, and selecting and managing ongoing partner relationships. Strategic partners might include the national government of the country. The availability of skills and resources of partners, as well as their own expectations of an alliance and their business objectives will likely vary across countries, which complicates partner selections for global CRM.

Case Study

Change Management at ING for a New Way of Working

In late 2014, ING, the Dutch multinational banking and financial organization, decided to overhaul its organization and establish a redesign for omnichannel (RIO) structure and usher in a new way of working (NWoW). This approach was in response to the necessity of being more nimble to address the demands of a rapidly evolving world of omnichannel consumer behavior. The three objectives of RIO were: higher employee and customer engagement, shorter time to market, and increased efficiency.

The company decided to shed its rigid top-down, strictly protocoled structure to a bottom-up people oriented organizational structure that came with a culture of more flexibility, openness, and collaboration in decision making.

The New Organizational Structure

The core of the new organizational structure consists of the "squad." These are autonomous multidisciplinary teams of approximately nine people. A squad has autonomy and needs to have the capabilities to determine a customer-oriented project and the value drivers that will be most helpful to fulfill it. Within each squad is a product owner (PO), the person responsible for enhancing the value of the team's work and a customer journey expert (CJE), the designer of a customer journey. About ten squads with related missions form a tribe. A tribe lead (TL) runs a tribe. A tribe's mission includes both customer acquisition and customer retention. To reflect the breakdown of silos and the creation of a flexible structure, people who perform similar functions, such as product experts, form chapters and are placed in specific squads. Each chapter is headed by a chapter lead (CL), a regular member of a squad. The architecture of the new way of working also includes one additional role—agile coaches (ACs), who help three to four squads adopt agile methods. Figure 4.4 illustrates ING's organizational structure for one tribe.

(Continued)

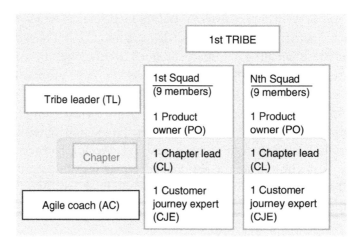

Figure 4.4 ING's Agile Organizational Structure

To facilitate agility within and coordination across tribes, and to constantly reinforce the roles and structures, several weekly and bimonthly structured meetings are held with the POs, CLs, TLs and groups of area experts.

Establishing the New Way of Working: Hiring, Culture, and Tools

Hiring: A fresh start started with brand new hiring. All existing employees had to apply anew for a job at the organization. Hiring was done by a team which was created by tribe leads and chapter leads with input from human resources. Substantial investment was made on training the hires in their new roles with a focus on craftsmanship.

Culture: To garner employee engagement and buy-in with the new way of working ING allowed new hires freedom to selectively adopt the global Orange Code of behaviors. The Orange Code which had been established by ING prior to this transformation consists of three behaviors that are foundational to the new agile way of working:

- "Take it on and make it happen"
- "Help others to be successful"
- "Always be a step ahead"

To reinforce this culture, informal sessions were held where employees identified and discussed values that best help achieve RIO objectives. Collaboration, courage, responsibility, trust and challenge were the values identified collectively in these sessions. Beyond face-to-face meetings regular communication through other media such as videos, films, online, and social outings were also utilized to allow the culture to further sink in.

To facilitate the new way of working culture, the physical structure of the workplace was also revamped. To encourage more casual encounters and informal meetings, barriers were torn down to create open spaces, stairs were created to connect different floors, white boards were put up everywhere, and gardens and cafeterias were created.

Metrics: To measure the effectiveness of this new organizational culture and structure the board required:

- Each tribe to submit a quarterly business review which highlighted its priorities and results. To ensure transparency TLs could view the reviews of other tribes
- Each squad to submit goals and chart progress from the daily stand-up meetings on a tracking software platform

Outcome and Challenges

The change management paid off. This was shown through surveys that tracked objectives and squads' successes, continuous increases in "Best places to work for" rankings, increases in net promotor scores (NPS) as indicative of increased customer satisfaction and improvements in financial performance.

At the same time ING realized that not all was perfect. Challenges still remained. These pertained to coordination and collaboration across tribes, within squads, and between the board and tribes. They also related to implementation of this new way of working in RIO across its global locations given cultural differences.

Sources:

Del Carpio, L., Yvez, D., and Guadalupe, M. (2017). "Embracing digital: ING's journey to a new way of working Part 2: The blueprint for change." ID: 417-0106-1B. INSEAD Business School, distributed by thecasecentre.org

Del Carpio, L., Yvez, D., and Guadalupe, M. (2017). "Embracing digital: ING's journey to a new way of working Part 3: Becoming agile." ID: 417-0106-1C. INSEAD Business School, Distributed by thecasecentre.org

Summary

This chapter discusses a customer-centric approach to developing a CRM strategic plan and implemention. It discusses the steps that go into developing the CRM strategy and implementation. Developing a CRM strategy needs to be an organization-wide effort with explicit support from leadership. The overall intent is to revise and align the people–process–technology arms of the organization in a way that facilitates effective information management and develops capabilities to create and provide superior and profitable customer value and experiences. The steps involved in creating a CRM strategy follows the following sequence. Analysis of the environmental situation shapes the overarching CRM vision and specific objectives. The core of the CRM strategy: development of a value proposition and customer strategy is developed next. Organizational transformation plans follow and they include process revisions, change management, and identification of technology needs. The final step is making a business case for the CRM initiative through a cost–benefit analysis. Implementation follows CRM strategy development. Enterprise transformation is initiated, operational and analytical CRM projects are set in motion, and channels of communication and distribution and value-chain partners are identified and selected.

References

Adesoga, A.D. and James, A.A. (2019). "Channel strategy and marketing performance of selected consumer goods firms in Lagos State, Nigeria." *Academy of Marketing Studies Journal*, 23, 1, 1–18.

Aliyev, R. (2021). "Facing challenges in an omnichannel world." *Varazdin*, www.proquest.com/conference-papers-proceedings/facing-challenges-omnichannel-world/docview/2556845726/se-2?accountid=14982

Becker, J.U., Greve, G. and Albers, S. (2009). "The impact of technological and organizational implementation of CRM on customer acquisition, maintenance, and retention." *International Journal of Research in Marketing*, 26(3), 207.

Englade, K. (1985). "A sales pitch on the front porch." *Chicago Tribune*, August 15, www.chicagotribune.com/news/ct-xpm-1985-08-15-8502230375-story.html

Finnegan, D.J. and Currie, W.L. (2010). "A multi-layered approach to CRM implementation: An integration perspective." *European Management Journal*, 28, 2, 153.

Frow, P., Payne, A., Wilkinson, I.F., and Young, L. (2011). "Customer management and CRM: addressing the dark side." *Journal of Services Marketing*, 25, 2, 79–89.

Frow, P. and Payne, A. (2009). "Customer relationship management: A strategic perspective." *Journal of Business Management*, 3, 1, 7–27.

Haines, D. (2019). "The CRM implementation process: A six step plan for success", Discover CRM, May 15, www.discovercrm.com/crm-implementation-process.html

Karakostas, B., Kardaras, D., and Papathanassiou, E. (2005). "The state of CRM adoption by the financial services in the UK: An empirical investigation." *Information and Management*, 42, 6, 853–63.

Kim, M., Choi, L., Knutson, B.J., and Borchgrevink, C.P. (2017). "Hotel employees' organizational behaviors from cross-national perspectives." *International Journal of Contemporary Hospitality Management*, 29, 12, 3082–100.

Kim, H. and Kim, Y. (2009). "A CRM performance measurement framework: Its development process and application." *Industrial Marketing Management*, 38, 4, 477.

Kodama, M. (2005). "How two Japanese high-tech companies achieved rapid innovation via strategic community networks." *Strategy & Leadership*, 33, 6, 39–47.

Ku, E.C.S. and Fan, Y.W. (2009). "Knowledge sharing and customer relationship management in the travel service alliances." *Total Quality Management & Business Excellence*, 20, 12, 1407.

Kumar, V. and Reinartz, W. (2018). *Customer Relationship Management: Concept, Strategy and Tools*, 3rd edn. Berlin: Springer.

Lambert, D.M. (2010). "Customer relationship management as a business process." *The Journal of Business & Industrial Marketing*, 25, 1, 4–17.

Lund, E. (2016). "Almost half of Japanese people hide when door bell rings: Survey." *Japan Today*, May 15, https://japantoday.com/category/features/lifestyle/almost-half-of-japanese-people-hide-when-doorbell-rings-survey?comment-order=popular

Nguyen, B. and Mutum, D.S. (2012). "A review of customer relationship management: Successes, advances, pitfalls and futures." *Business Process Management Journal*, 18, 3, 400–19.

Palmatier, R.W., Stern, L.W., El-Ansary, A.I., and Anderson, E. (2016). *Marketing Channel Strategy*, 8th edn. New York: Routledge.

Pombriant, D. (2016, 04). "Journey maps: The secret to our customer success: CRM." *Customer Relationship Management*, 20, 4.

Rababa, K., Mohd, H., and Ibrahim H. (2011). "Customer relationship management (CRM) processes from theory to practice: The pre-implementation plan of CRM system." *International Journal of e-Education, e-Business, e-Management, and e-Learning*, 1, 1, 22–7.

Rahimi, R. and Gunlu, E. (2016). "Implementing customer relationship management (CRM) in hotel industry from organisational culture perspective." *International Journal of Contemporary Hospitality Management*, 28, 1, 89–112.

Rigby, D.K. and Bilodeau, B. (2013). *Management Tools and Trends 2013, Boston, MA: Bain & Company*, accessed at https://www.bain.com/insights/management-tools-and-trends-2013

Rigby, D.K. and Bilodeau, B. (2009). *Management Tools and Trends 2009*. Boston, MA: Bain & Company. accessed at https://www.bain.com/insights/management-tools-and-trends-2009/

Santouridis, I. and Tsachtani, E. (2015). "Investigating the impact of CRM resources on CRM processes: A customer life-cycle based approach in the case of a Greek bank." *Procedia Economics and Finance*, 19, 304–13.

Steel, M., Dubelaar, C., and Ewing, M.T. (2013). "Developing customised CRM projects: The role of industry norms, organisational context and customer expectations on CRM implementation." *Industrial Marketing Management*, 42, 8, 1328–44.

Syzmczuk. M. (2019). "5 types of CRM software and how to choose one." Software Hut, Dec. 12, https://softwarehut.com/blog/business/5-types-of-crm-software

Watson, Z. and Jolaoso, C. (2021). "How to choose a CRM system." *U.S. News and World Report* (May 20), www.usnews.com/360-reviews/crm/how-to-choose-crm

5
ANALYTICAL CRM

Measuring Customer Happiness at Hubspot

In 2009, Hubspot, a well known Web startup company that offers marketing and CRM tools to companies, realized that their customer churn rate (the rate at which customers stop purchasing) had increased by almost 100 percent and for April of the same year had climbed to more than three times. The company needed to understand why the churn rate had increased, bring it down, and bolster Hubspot's relationships with their customers.

Hubspot's Market Offering

Hubspot utilizes a software as a service (SaaS) business model to offer subscriptions for marketing and CRM tools to companies. These tools are based on the concept of the "inbound" methodology of marketing. Inbound marketing is about utilizing a pull strategy by creating and targeting customers through websites, blogs, and webinars with compelling and customized content. The easy to use subscription-based software allows Hubspot's customers to create customized content, provide visitor access to such content through search engine optimization or promotion on social media, measure the impact of this content to attract potential customers, and analyze leads to recommend which ones to follow.

Hubspot's products are customized with different functionalities and pricing for small, medium, and large companies. The products include a content management system (CMS), a website management system, and a system for integrating the CMS with the customer's website.

Developing Customer Relationships

Marketing phase: To generate leads Hubspot regularly published contents across different online media.

Selling phase: The leads generated were qualified on a points-based system and Hubspot communicated with the qualified prospects via an online demonstration. The newness of the

(Continued)

technology made the sales process long and complex. It included evaluating customer needs, recommending appropriate products, and educating the prospect on product usage and benefits.

Onboarding phase: This phase began after a sale was completed. Hubspot charged an initial fee for providing a few hours of consulting where consultants integrated the product with the customer's existing system and educated the customer on what the software could do for the customer's business. Customers who had attended all onboarding sessions were provided with the Hubspot Certified Professionals certificate.

Ongoing phase: The ongoing relationship phase between Hubspot and its customers was relatively passive. If the customers faced problems they had multiple options. A customer could log into a free site that offered more training, call the support team, attend a free webinar, or purchase additional consulting.

Understanding Churn and Bolstering Customer Relationships

Hubspot found that the churn rate had increased over time for the following reasons:

- Later adopters were less forgiving than early adopters and left more easily. Early adopters had more personal contact with the founders of the company
- Customers faced marginal benefits from the search engine optimization (SEO) tool over time and did not renew subscriptions
- The economy crashed in 2008
- Email communication to remind customers to renew their subscriptions had the unintended consequence of reminding customers to cancel their subscriptions

Hubspot discovered some patterns with its churn phenomenon:

- Smaller sized customers cancelled their contracts earlier than larger ones
- B2C customers were less loyal than B2B customers
- Customers who stayed longer were less likely to churn
- Customers who used more features were less likely to churn

Churn rate was regarded as a lagging measure and did not allow Hubspot to preemptively identify and correct a problem with customer satisfaction before the customer left. In order to better solidify relationships with customers and lower the churn rate Hubspot realized it had to come up with a leading measure for churn.

Developing the Customer Happiness Index (CHI)

Research on churn rate had shown Hubspot that customers who used more features were likely to stay longer and would be less likely to churn. Thus, the CHI was fundamentally based on the frequency and extent of feature usage. Some of the features which were found to be more "sticky" were analytics, lead tracking and the blogging package. In the development of the CHI, therefore, higher weights were given to features that were more likely to engage customers as well as likely to drive sales leads.

The CHI measure, which was constrained in a scale from 0 to 100, aimed to provide an overall snapshot of the health of customer relationships. After fine tuning the measure over time Hubspot found that it correlated highly with the churn rate. Hubspot had a reliable and effective leading indicator for churn.

Putting CHI into Action for Customer Satisfaction

Hubspot put into action several strategies to reduce customer churn and increase satisfaction:

- Salespeople had to give up their commission for customers who churned in less than four months to positively impact lead qualification
- Medium and large customers had to sign a 12-month mandatory contract
- Additional customer support was provided for customers with low CHI and for those whose CHI had dropped sharply

Hubspot's job was not done yet. To convince venture capitalists to fund their venture they had to make a connection between CHI and the "magic number," the measure venture capitalists use to evaluate Hubspot against its peers. The "magic number" is calculated as follows:

$$\text{Magic number} = \frac{\text{Annualized quarter over quarter recurring revenue growth}}{\text{Sales and marketing expense from previous quarter}}$$

Venture Capitalists considered a "magic number" of 0.75 or higher as potentially valuable investments. Hubspot had to make sure the CHI would keep them one step ahead of churn and help increase satisfaction, loyalty, and in turn revenues that would lead to a higher "magic number."

Source: Martinez-Jeres, F.A., Steenburgh, T., Avery J., and Brem, L. (2013). "Hubspot: Lower churn through greater CHI." ID: 9-110-052. Harvard Business School Publishing. Distributed by www.thecasecentre.org

Introduction

Effective management of customer relationships rests on judicious allocation of resources. Determination of optimum allocation of resources requires knowledge of the current and potential value of the customer and how the company is performing in terms of developing a profitable relationship with the customer. In order to gain this knowledge the organization needs to measure and then analyze different aspects of a customer's profile, from demographics, to attitude and purchase and non-purchase behavior.

CRM metrics: Measures of multiple items that highlight the state of the organization's performance in effectively managing customer relationships. They help to answer the "what" of performance and customer behavior.

CRM analytics: Technology-based tools which collect, organize, analyze and synthesize data to facilitate decision making for enhancing customer experiences and relationships (Gartner, n.d.). They help to answer the "so what" and "what next" of decision making.

CRM Metrics

In today's global market increasing sophistication of technologies have allowed marketers to capture a vast amount of information about customers and competitors. This has allowed usage of a rich mix of traditional and non-traditional social-media-based metrics that provide a broad and deep view into customer attitudes, purchase and non-purchase behaviors, cost and rate of customer acquisition and retention, and overall value that customers provide to organizations.

Table 5.1 shows the different metric categories and individual metrics that are covered in this chapter.

Table 5.1 List of Customer-Based Metrics

Metric Category	Metrics
Customer acquisition	Cost of acquisition
	Acquisition rate
Customer activity and behaviour	Purchase probability
	Purchase frequency
	Retention and churn rate
	Lifetime duration
Customer value	Size of wallet
	Share of wallet
	RFM
	Past customer value
	Customer lifetime value
	Customer brand value
	Customer referral value
Customer satisfaction	Willingness to recommend
	Net promotor score

Acquisition Metrics

One of the core goals of customer relationship management is to grow through customer acquisition. The two metrics that are relevant to marketers across countries are acquisition cost and acquisition rate.

Acquisition Cost and Acquisition Rate

Marketing costs incurred in acquiring new customers have a direct impact on customer value and organizational profit. Acquisition cost is calculated by dividing the total spending on a marketing campaign by the total number of leads converted. It indicates how efficient the campaign has been. It is expressed in monetary terms:

$$\text{Acquisition cost per lead converted} = \frac{\text{Money spent on acquisition}}{\text{Number of leads converted}}$$

Acquisition cost does not, however, provide information on how effective the acquisition campaign was. For that you need to calculate the acquisition rate. Acquisition rate calculates the number of leads that were acquired as a percentage of the total number of leads that were targeted.

$$\text{Acquisition rate}(\%) = \frac{\text{No. of leads converted}}{\text{No. of leads targeted}}$$

For example, you would like to acquire some customers for your wine shop in South Africa. You decide to spend 15,000 South African Rands over the next few months to run a campaign to achieve this objective. You spent 10,000 of this money on sending direct mail to 3000 leads with an attractive offer. A thousand of these leads responded to the direct mail by visiting your store and converted to a customer. To complement the direct mailing campaign you decided to spend the rest of the budget on advertising in local newspapers, local TV, and several wine blogs and websites. What will your acquisition cost and acquisition rate be?

For the direct mailing campaign both are straightforward to calculate. Here are the calculations:

Acquisition cost per lead converted = 10000/1000 = 10 rands

Acquisition rate = (1000/3000) *100 = 33.33%

The calculations get more challenging, however, for the rest of the money that you spent on advertising because it would be difficult to determine who watches your ad (a certain estimate can be arrived at from published readership and viewership information), and consumers who purchase from your store during and after your campaign may or may not have seen your ad or be there because of the ad (you can always do a short survey at the store level to determine that). So the determination of the acquisition cost and acquisition rate in the second scenario will always be approximate.

Global Applicability of Acquisition Metrics

These two metrics are globally relevant because they help marketers to understand how efficient or effective marketing campaigns are. However, differing country environments, consumer characteristics, and consumption-related factors will impact what is feasible and realistic in terms of cost and rate of acquisition. This should then impact acquisition objectives, adequate allocation of resources, and standards for the efficiency and effectiveness of campaigns.

Acquisition costs are impacted by advertising costs, the kind of incentives that would be effective in attracting leads, consumption trends of the product category (e.g. coffee in a tea-drinking country), availability and access to the media, and laws. In any country an achievable acquisition rate should take into consideration consumer characteristics. The size of the segment, willingness and ability to respond, and preferences are all impacted by culture, the economy, and the media utilized, and can vary across countries (de Leeuw et al., 2018). A campaign for condensed soup will tend to have a larger response from Americans compared to Europeans where soup is purchased more commonly in dehydrated form.

Customer Activity and Behavior Metrics

Customer activity metrics collectively inform marketers about the purchase-related status of the customer and facilitate appropriate marketing interventions. Data to calculate these metrics will be found within the organization in transaction, sales, or customer databases.

Probability of Purchase

This metric indicates the probability of a customer purchasing again within a specified period of time. A high probability indicates that a customer is likely to remain active. The equation to calculate this probability is as follows:

Probability of purchase (PP) =

(Time of last purchase as a fraction of a period) ^{Number of purchases in a given period}

Example: Here are the specifics of two customers A and B of an electronic store in Argentina and Vietnam respectively. For a 12-month period customer A had already purchased three times in the first eight months. Customer B in Vietnam had purchased four times in the same eight-month period. What will their probability of future purchase be at the end of this 12-month period?

PP (Customer A) = $(8/12)^3$ = 0.3

PP (Customer B) = $(8/12)^4$ = 0.2

Customer B who has purchased more times than customer A has a lower probability of purchasing again in the near future. This is because customers do not really change their purchase frequency that much. Customer B has already purchased four times and is going to push back her purchase further into the future than customer A, making customer B less likely to be active.

Purchase Frequency

Purchase frequency measures intervals in time during which a customer purchases.

Purchase frequency = Number of purchases made during a time period

Purchase frequency also shows the time lapse between two purchases and indicates how active customers are in a time period or in their lifetime. This is particularly helpful in industries and countries where consumer purchases tend to be more frequent. Data for calculating this metric could be found in a company's sales and transaction database.

Retention Rate and Churn Rate

Retention and churn rates together indicate the overall health of an organization by showing whether customers are purchasing or not purchasing. Retention and churn are opposite sides of the same phenomenon. Retention rate is calculated per time period as the number of customers who are likely to purchase in the current time period as a percentage of the number of customers who bought in the previous time period given that the set of customers in consideration have purchased in the previous time period. It is usually calculated as an average for a segment or for individual customers. The churn rate, which essentially indicates the percentage of customers dropping off, is calculated by subtracting the retention rate from 100.

$$\text{Retention rate} = 100 \times \frac{\substack{\text{Number of customers buying in current time period} \\ \text{who also bought in the previous time period}}}{\substack{\text{Total number of customers} \\ \text{who bought in the previous time period}}}$$

If an organization acquires 100 customers in time period 1 and out of these 75 make purchases in time period 2 the retention rate is 75 percent.

Retention rate = $100 \times (75/100) = 75\%$
Churn rate = $100 - 75 = 25\%$

In calculations for multiple time periods retention rates are sometimes assumed to be stable so an average retention rate is used. However, in reality retention rates tend to increase over periods at a decreasing rate as non-loyal customers drop off.

What counts as a reasonable time period will also vary by organization and industry. It can be a month, or multiple years. It is also important for the organization to determine criteria for measuring retention. Should purchase be the only basis? In many cases customers enter a dormant stage where they are not actively purchasing in every time period. They may keep on using the product/service, however, and have not technically defected from the intention to make future purchases. This means it is important to understand the difference between retention and loyalty. Retention on average simply shows if customers are repeatedly purchasing. Loyalty, however, contains underlying deeper positive attitudes towards the brand (Kumar and Reinartz, 2018).

Lifetime Duration

How long a customer or a customer segment has remained with a brand provides a view of how fast the company needs to replace a customer base. Knowledge of lifetime duration is also important for understanding and determining customer loyalty and profitability.

Assuming the retention rate to be constant from period to period, calculating the average lifetime duration is relatively straightforward.

$$\text{Average lifetime duration for constant retention rate} = \frac{1}{(1 - \text{Retention rate})}$$

If the retention rate for an auto mechanic shop is 50 percent in a time period of one year then,

Average lifetime duration = $1/(1-0.5) = 2$ years

However, if retention rates are not assumed constant, which is the case in many non-contractual relationships, the calculation of lifetime duration is more complex. It is calculated as the ratio of the summation over the total observation period (n) of retained customers for each time period (t), where each time period t could be, for example, of six months duration and the overall observation period (n) could be, for example, six years in total.

$$\text{Average lifetime duration (varying retention rates)} \quad \frac{\sum_{t=1}^{n}\left[\left(t \times \text{Retained customers in t}\right)\right]}{\text{Number of customers in segment}}$$

Data for calculating lifetime duration come from sales and customer databases. Given the importance of lifetime duration to loyalty and profitability, this metric should be complemented by determining the type and pattern of customer purchase and consumption.

Global Applicability of Customer Activity Metrics

Purchase and consumption show similarities and differences across countries impacting the values of customer activity metrics. The combined impact of economy, cultural aspects of consumption (e.g. having coffee at home vs. being served one in a coffee shop) and competition, create both similar and different consumer expectations and perceptions across countries, impacting customer activities. For example, in many developing countries purchasing for grocery and non-durable consumer products such as toothpaste and shampoo on average happens in small quantities and more frequently than in many developed countries because of lower affordability and smaller storage space. However, things are changing in some developed countries too. Many in the UK are now shopping more frequently in order to reduce waste and in Japan too because many consumers live in a household of one (Bennett, 2019). The opposite is true for purchase of home appliances between developing and developed countries. The frequency of purchase of home appliances (even small ones) in developing countries on average is very low compared to developed countries. This is a combined effect of economy and culture. In many developing economies there exists an informal economy of repairs and parts where sellers have ingenious ways of repairing seemingly irrepairable items. Coupled with the tendency of consumers in many of these countries to save money, this has provided consumers with the opportunity to repeatedly repair their appliances and put off purchasing a new one. These purchase patterns should caution marketers to be realistic about their observation time period for calculating the metrics. Covid-19 has added to the dynamic nature of consumer behavior by significantly changing it across the world. Here too there are differences across countries. Whereas in many countries consumers have constrained spending on discretionary items, Chinese and Indian consumers are spending on a broad range of discretionary product categories such as travel and clothing (Charm et al., 2020).

Customer Value Metrics

Beyond assessing the propensity of the customer to keep on purchasing, it is important to know which customers generate high profits for the organization or exhibit the potential to. This knowledge helps channel adequate marketing resources.

The following metrics include both strategic and popular metrics. It is important for organizations to utilize multiple value metrics. Together, they provide a broad-based and holistic picture of the value of a customer. To make sure decisions are reliable, marketers should cross-check across metrics to look for strong correlations.

Size and Share of Wallet

Size of the wallet is the amount of money a customer spends on a particular product category such as grocery or home appliances in a particular time period across all stores and brands.

Share of the wallet on the other hand is the percentage of the above purchase a customer spends at a particular organization such as a particular grocery or appliance store or on a particular grocery or appliance brand. These two metrics together indicate how profitable and loyal a customer is or could be.

$$\text{Size of the wallet} = \text{Total spending in a product category across all stores and brands}$$

$$\text{Share of the wallet} = 100 \times \frac{\text{Spending within a product category in a particular store or on a brand}}{\text{Total spending within a product category across all stores or brands}}$$

If a consumer spends 300 dollars on cosmetics every month across all stores or brands and spends 100 dollars of that in Sephora (a beauty store) then the customer's size of wallet is 300 and the share of the wallet that Sephora gets is 100 x (100/300) = 33.33%.

Data to calculate these two metrics can be sourced through a combination of sales and customer databases and customer surveys.

RFM Value

RFM stands for recency, frequency and monetary value. Here three separate metrics are combined to arrive at a composite score for the value of a customer.

- Recency = Time of last purchase
- Frequency = Number of times a customer purchases in a given observation period
- Monetary value = Average amount spent per purchase over the observation period

The RFM metric categorizes customers into separate value groups and allows marketing expenditures to be spent on the customers with the highest return potential. Data needed to calculate RFM value can be found in sales, customer, and transaction databases.

The process of calculating RFM starts with assigning codes individually for R, F, and M based on a scale (e.g. from 1 to 5, where 1= highest R, F, and M and 5 = lowest R, F, and M) for a representative sample of customers and placing them in highest (1) to lowest (5) category groups. This is done sequentially starting with any one of the measures and ending with the third. The process finally creates a three-digit RFM coded value (e.g. 345) for each customer. Each customer is then grouped with other customers with the same code. The final RFM scores are then calculated by taking an average of the three coded values (e.g. (3+4+5)/3 = 4). Given the scale we have selected for this example (1 being the highest and 5 being the lowest) the lower the RFM value the higher the customer value. Table 5.2 provides a snapshot of the process and the system of coming up with the RFM values. After the final RFM scores are determined, customers are grouped based on RFM values. It is worth noting that in the table customers 4 and 8 have the same final RFM scores but different composite coded values. These customers could be considered of equal value to the organization but exhibit different behaviors for recency, frequency, and monetary value which necessitates different CRM initiatives.

Table 5.2   RFM Value

Customer No.	Coded Recency Value	Coded Frequency Value	Coded Monetary Value	Composite Coded Value	RFM Score (Average of 3 individual scores)
1	4	2	3	423	3
2	3	5	5	355	4.3
3	4	1	1	411	2
4	1	3	3	133	2.3
5	2	4	4	244	3.3

(Continued)

Table 5.2 (Continued)

Customer No.	Coded Recency Value	Coded Frequency Value	Coded Monetary Value	Composite Coded Value	RFM Score (Average of 3 individual scores)
6	5	3	2	532	3.3
7	4	2	3	423	3
8	2	2	3	223	2.3
9	3	5	5	355	4.3
10	5	1	3	513	3

The relative importance of the three measures is an important consideration. The measure for which customer response has dropped the most should be the starting point (Kumar and Reinartz, 2018). This is because the metric with the largest change would likely be the best predictor for future activities and value.

Past Customer Value

This metric shows a customer's current value based on past transactions. Past purchases are good predictors of future purchases and indicate how profitable customers can be in the future. The past customer value metric takes past profit contribution (in monetary terms) from customers and discounts that value forward to the current period. The calculation involves summing up discounted profit contributions of past purchases from individual time periods (e.g. every month) that fall within a specified observation period (e.g. two years) leading up to the current period. Since the value of money changes with time and the purchases happened in the past, discounting the past profit contribution is necessary to get an accurate current estimate of past customer value in the current period.

Past customer value= Σ (for all t's within T) [(Profit contribution in one time period) x $(1+\delta)^t$]

Where δ = the discount rate needed to adjust the time value of money

t = individual time period of purchase

T = observation period

Table 5.3 below shows the profit contribution from customer X for three time periods (month) in a specified observation period in the past (January through March) leading up to the current time period.

Table 5.3   Customer X Purchasing Pattern

	Time period 1 (Jan.)	Time period 2 (Feb.)	Time period 3 (Mar.)
Profit contribution in money terms	240	50	100

If 1.3 percent is the monthly discount rate at which money is discounted to the present,

Past customer value of $X = 240 \times (1 + 0.013)^1 + 50 \times (1 + 0.013)^2 + 100 \times (1 + 0.013)^3$

$= 243.12 + 51.31 + 103.95 = 398.38$

It is important to check if the discount rate provided is for the same duration as the time period being used. In this example both are one month so the given discount rate can be used as is. If a yearly discount rate is provided but the time period of purchase is one month then the discount rate needs to be divided by 12 before it can be used in the calculations. Data needed to calculate past customer value can be found in sales and transaction databases of the organization.

Customer Lifetime Value (CLV/LTV)

For organizational growth and judicious allocation of resources it is not enough to simply know a customer's behavior in the past. It is crucial to evaluate the long-term economic value of the customer by predicting their purchasing behavior in the future. This future value of the customer is known as customer lifetime value (CLV) or simply lifetime value (LTV).

Table 5.4 shows the basic information needed to determine the lifetime value of an individual customer or segment.

Table 5.4   Components of Customer Lifetime Value Determination

Costs (in money terms)	Recurring revenues	Retention rates (in case of a segment)	Contribution margins of individual purchases	Duration and number of purchase time periods (t)	Discount rate (δ)
• Acquisition costs • Recurring retention costs					

Costs incurred in acquiring and retaining a customer over their lifetime (e.g. three years) and projected revenues over the lifetime together determine lifetime profit contribution. The lifetime duration is based on previous purchasing history but for newly acquired customers could be more challenging to determine. For the calculation of lifetime value, lifetime duration is broken down into smaller purchase time periods (e.g. months) based on predictions from past purchase frequencies. Finally, a discount rate is needed to get an accurate picture of the lifetime value of the customer. Money loses value over time and thus future profit contributions in each time period need to be discounted back to the present with the help of the discount rate. The impact of time on money is felt more and more for time periods further into the future.

Thus, CLV calculation principally consists of three steps:

1   Determine profit contributions for each time period (t) in the lifetime duration of the customer by subtracting costs from revenues. (Note: when calculating for segments you will need to multiply the profit contribution for each period by the cumulative retention rate because some customers may have dropped off in that period)
2   Discount the profit contribution for each time period back to the current period to get the present value of future contributions
3   Add up the discounted profit contributions for each time period to arrive at the CLV

Customer lifetime value = Σ (for all t's within T) [(Profit contribution in one time period) x $(1/(1+ \delta))^t$]

Where,

Σ = Summation of

δ = The discount rate needed to adjust for the time value of money

t = Time period of purchase

T = Lifetime duration

Table 5.5 shows the predicted costs and revenues from customer X for her lifetime duration which is predicted to be three months (May through July) with each month being a time period. The scenario also assumes that the customer was acquired in April of the same year.

Table 5.5   Customer X Cost and Revenue Predictions

Costs and Revenues in Money Terms	Current Period (April)	Time Period 1 (May)	Time Period 2 (June)	Time Period 3 (July)
Acquisition cost (customer acquired in current period April)	100	0	0	0
Predicted retention costs	0	10	30	40
Predicted revenues in currencies	Not applicable	200	250	300
Predicted profit contribution (predicted revenues—costs)	Not applicable	200 – (10 +100) = 90	250 – 30 = 220	300 – 40 = 260

If 1.3 percent is the monthly rate at which money is discounted back to the present,

Customer lifetime value of customer X = $[90 \times (1/(1+ 0.013))^1] + [220 \times (1/(1+.013))^2] + [260 \times (1/(1+.013))^3] = 88.84 + 214.39 + 250.12 = 553.35$

Note: The acquisition cost of 100 is considered in the calculation of profit contribution only for time period 1.

Data for calculating customer lifetime value can be sourced from a combination of sales, transactions, and customer- or segment-specific non-transaction information such as demographics and psychographics.

Brand-Customer Value

As consumers we buy brands and not simply products and services. If you think of your favorite brand you know that you have a connection to it. The emotional and cognitive connections we have towards brands have significance for customer value and loyalty. It is thus important to improve and leverage this connection and preference to maximize customer lifetime duration and value.

Brand–customer brand value is the brand-impacted value the customer provides to the organization based on her perception of the brand, preference for it and behavior towards it (Reinartz and Kumar, 2018). It thus can be seen as a complementary metric to CLV. A brand–customer value includes multiple components, information on which can be collected through customer surveys. The relative impact of these components can then be estimated by utilizing estimation techniques such as regression analysis to arrive at a composite score for brand–customer value. Figure 5.1 highlights the component areas of brand–customer value (Kumar and Reinartz, 2018).

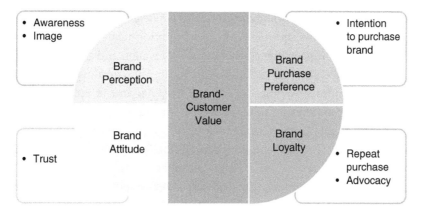

Figure 5.1 Components of Brand–Customer Value

Customer Recommendation Value (CRV)

This metric calculates the indirect value of the customer. This indirect value is reflected in the profit contributions of new customers who join based on recommendations made by a current customer. Customer A is motivated by a direct marketing campaign (e.g. a commonly used refer-a-friend offer) to recommend the focal brand to consumers X, Y, and Z who ultimately purchase from the organization because of recommendations from A. Thus the profits from X, Y, and Z should accrue to A because the former three would not have purchased if not for the recommendations. Hence the customer recommendation value of A should be a sum of lifetime values of customers X, Y, and Z. This can be expressed as:

CRV of Customer A = CLV of customer X + CLV of customer Y + CLV of customer Z

We saw before how CLVs of a customer can be calculated.

The customer recommendation value metric provides a true reflection of the value of customer A and is a complement to the customer's lifetime value and brand–customer value.

To calculate CRV it is important to determine the time period of the campaign and how many new customers were acquired in that time period. The CRV of a particular customer in that time period will then include the CLVs of customers who were acquired in that time period. If the three new customers decided to become customers a year after the campaign was run then the CLVs of these three new customers should be used to determine the CRV for customer A for that year. Data needed for calculating the CRV will come from sales transaction databases, customer databases, and customer surveys.

Global Applicability of Customer Value Metrics

Even though customer value metrics are equally applicable across countries, country-level macro environments, business, and consumption-related factors impact these values. The economy impacts the consumer's size of wallet, and the nature and extent of competition impact the share of wallet. Purchasing and consumption trends impact past and future customer values, and culture, lifestyle, and interests impact brand–customer values and tendencies to recommend. For example, in many countries consumers prefer to purchase from local stores and local or national brands because of nationalistic feelings. Thus, a brand positioned as foreign is likely to face tougher challenges to attract customers, grab a significant share of their wallets, and motivate them to recommend consumers. Covid-19 has also brought about varying degrees of changes in consumption behavior across the world which will have an impact on value metrics. The changes are more stark in large developing countries compared to smaller developed countries. Consumers across multiple countries have become more price sensitive, exhibiting different shopping behaviors. They are concentrating on "value, convenience and availability" when selecting retail and "quality and purpose" when choosing new brands (Charm et al., 2020). It is thus important to get a good understanding of the country-level environments and their impacts on customer consumption. This helps marketers to be realistic about the relevancy and implications of the outputs of customer value metrics for effective decision making.

Customer Satisfaction Metrics

Metrics that help gauge how satisfied customers are are helpful because satisfaction indicates future customer behavior. These measures are thus considered precursors or indicators for both customer activity and customer value metrics. The two measures that capture customer satisfaction are willingness to recommend and net promotor score (Farris et al., 2010).

Willingness to Recommend

This metric indicates the strength of the attitude customers have towards the brand and how loyal they are. The metric is based on a single survey question on whether customers would be willing to recommend the focal brand to others. It is calculated for a customer segment as the percentage of customers who indicated that they would recommend a brand to others such as friends.

$$\text{Willingness to Recommend}: 100 \times \frac{\text{Number of customers who indicated that they would recommend a brand to others}}{\text{Total number of customers surveyed}}$$

If 150 customers are surveyed with this one question and 40 stated they would be willing to recommend the brand to others, then

Willingness to Recommend: $100 \times (40/150) = 26.66\,\%$

Net Promoter Score

Net promotor score (NPS) is a registered trademark of Frederick R. Reichheld, Bain & Company, and Satmetrix. This metric is based on the percentage of customers who are willing to recommend the brand to others. However, the metric is more focused and granular because 1) it divides the customers surveyed into three groups of promotors, passives, and detractors based on a question on the extent of their willingness to recommend and cut-off points on the rating scale for the three groups, and 2) it does not include the passives and subtracts the detractors from the promotors to arrive at the net part of the NPS. Promotors are customers who are willing to recommend, passives are neutral to recommending and detractors are unwilling to recommend.

Net promotor score = Percentage of promotors – Percentage of detractors.

If out of 150 customers, 50 are promotors, 60 are passives and 40 are detractors, then

NPS = 100 × (50/150) – 100 × (40/150) = 33.33% – 26.66% = 6.67

Social Media CRM Metrics

Consumers across the world have significantly changed how they search and shop. Whether on PC or mobile there has been a sharp increase in usage of Internet-based social media for searching, securing recommendations, sharing reviews, and purchasing (Charm et al., 2020). Omnichannel consumer behavior is now the global norm where purchase experience and satisfaction with brand consumption shape the customer's tendencies to recommend a brand. Social media has introduced interactivities, complexities, and volatilities in consumer behavior that can have far-reaching consequences for customer experiences and customer relationships. It is thus important for marketers to complement their traditional marketing metrics with social media metrics. Based on the objectives for social CRM, marketers have a range of metrics they can use to determine customer behavior and organizational performance. Table 5.6 provides a quick view into commonly used metrics for social media CRM (Farris et al., 2010; Garrison, 2012). Social media metrics will be covered in more detail in Chapter 7.

Table 5.6 Social Media CRM Metrics

Metric	Description
Number of impressions	Number of times an online advertisement is seen
Clickthrough rate	Number of click throughs as a fraction of the number of impressions =
Page views	Number of times a Web page is served
Visits	Number of unique viewings of a website
Visitors	Number of unique website viewers in a time period
Bounce rate	Fraction of website visitors that leave without viewing additional pages

Metric	Description
Abandonment rate	Number of abandoned purchases on a website as a fraction of number of finished purchases
Downloads	Number of times an application or file is downloaded
Network size	Number of individuals joining a social network
Conversation buzz	Amount of discussion and responses in social media
Conversation revenue	Share of revenue from a particular conversation across channels
Share of voice	Amount of discussion of a brand as a fraction of discussion of competing brands
Topic frequency	Most common themes discussed about a brand
Topic virality	Speed at which a discussion spreads—measured by increase in number of different entries on a discussion topic
Sentiment analysis	Number of positive, negative or neutral expressions about a topic or brand

Global Applicability and Implications of CRM Metrics

Many of the metric values discussed above will vary from country to country because of the impacts of varying country environments. This means that costs and rates of acquisition, customer activities, values, and satisfaction across countries will be more or less different. These differences should dictate the CRM strategies for each country and the kinds of resources to be allocated. For example, it is commonly expected by consumers in many developing countries that sellers of consumer products such as water purification systems or vacuum cleaners will include installation or repair as part of the product offering. Lack of such inclusion will make it harder to acquire customers, to motivate them to repeatedly purchase, impacting customer value and satisfaction. Hence, what is being measured for better CRM (e.g. frequency of customer purchase) will remain the same globally but the calculated value of the metric and implications for it will vary by different degrees from country to country. At the same time not all customers in a country are the same and hence differences and similarities in metric values will depend on the types of segments targeted across countries. For cross-country segments that are quite similar in demographics, lifestyles, interests, behavior and benefit sought, metric values and implications of the same for CRM will show larger overlaps compared to segments targeted across countries that are quite different.

The differences from country to country in values of these metrics and their implications will be less and more subtle for B2B industries than for B2C industries. This is because organizational purchase is governed by objectives that remain relatively similar across countries and is less impacted by country-level environments. In the case on Hubspot, as discussed above, the foundations of its CHI metric will be applicable from country to country and dissatisfaction with their pricing strategy will be less likely to vary significantly across countries.

CRM Analytics

Analytical tools play a critical and complementary role to metrics in analytical CRM. CRM analytics analyze a range of data that also include CRM metric outputs to create knowledge to help the organization make effective decisions in different operations that impact customer relationship management. Through data mining, online analytical processing (OLAP), and predictive modelling CRM analytics analyze and anticipate customer behavior and recommend appropriate strategies for marketing communication and channels, sales, and customer service (Sirk, n.d.). Globally, the CRM analytics market is projected to grow by 13 percent between 2022 and 2027. Growth is particularly steep in Asian markets and is most advanced in the North American market (modorintelligence.com, n.d.). The market is competitive and includes established players who are trying to grow their market share and new smaller entrants. Proliferation and competition in this industry have benefited firms in customer relationship management efforts because of the increasing level of customization being offered by CRM analytics vendors. CRM analytics can be hosted either on the premises or in the cloud and are mostly offered in a software as a service (SaaS) model (Modor Intelligence, n.d.).

TECH BOX: CRM ANALYTIC TOOLS

The CRM analytics market can be broken down mostly by type of analysis and what it does. Table 5.7 provides a view of the types of CRM analytics tools, and names of highly rated providers (Sirk, n.d.).

Table 5.7 Analytical CRM Types and Tools

Type of Analytics	Features	Providers
Descriptive analytical tool	• Marketing campaigns analysis • Sales analysis • Customer service analysis • Profitability analysis	• Hubspot • Creatio
Diagnostic analytical tool	• Trend recognition • Sales pipeline determination • Anomaly detection	• Zoho • Tableau
Predictive analytical tool	• Probability analysis • Forecasting	• SAP • Salesforce
Prescriptive analytical tool	• Machine learning simulations • Artificial intelligence developers • Network analysis	• IBM Prescriptive Analytics • Salesforce

Success Stories

How Uber Uses CRM Analytics

Uber Inc. is a ride hailing service that started in San Francisco, CA, USA and is the leading ride sharing service in the world, operating in over 80 countries (Uber Countries, 2021). Consumers hail a ride through the Uber app. To provide a good customer ride experience Uber collects massive amounts of anonymized and aggregated forms of data on consumers and drivers, as well as on transportation realities and changes in the areas it serves. All this data is analyzed to connect drivers with consumers, develop demand-based pricing, segment customers on the right attributes for targeting purposes, and run effective marketing campaigns to convert consumers into customers.

How has Uber been able to analyze such vast amounts of information and glean actionable insights? Given the complexity in the data and the analysis needed, Uber had to develop its own in-house tools. These include the following (Jacob, n.d.) :

- *Argos*: Monitors and analyzes millions of GPS locations, interactions, events and metrics to notify the company of irregularities
- *Gurafu*: Analyzes transportation issues and recommends better and safer routes to drivers
- *Data visualization systems*: Collates and analyzes transportation information for mapping, developing, and recommending frameworks for operations, and showing distribution of real-time drop offs to consumers

It is worth noting that Uber's success worldwide has been based on its realization that actionable insights gleaned from data analysis for any specific location cannot be lumped onto another location and that data for each location needs to be analyzed separately.

Sources:

1 "Uber countries 2021." https://worldpopulationreview.com/country-rankings/uber-countries
2 Jacob, S. (n.d.). "How Uber uses data to improve their service and create the new wave of mobility" Accessed at https://neilpatel.com/blog/how-uber-uses-data/.

Case Study

Sales Force Technologies for Facilitating CRM in the Pharmaceutical Industry in India

In 2017 Laurs & Bridz Pharmaceuticals Pvt. Ltd. in India was planning to expand its territories to the whole of the Indian market.

Laurs and Bridz is a state of the art generic pharmaceutical company which specializes in providing combination drugs to customers. The company's marketing strategy in India is

(Continued)

to build relationships with customers by offering high-quality products at competitive prices. The company's customers are physicians who prescribe their products and the stockists and pharmacists who hold and distribute the product. The company's sales force implements this strategy and builds and sustains customer relationships through effective targeting, sales call efficiencies, and developing new businesses. Convincing both physicians and retailers depends upon sound product knowledge and a capability to convince. Sales presentations (aka detailing) allow salespeople to share features, benefits, and risks of the product and handle objections.

Challenges in Sales and CRM

A combined effect of changes happening in the Indian pharmaceutical industry and existing data handling systems at Laurs and Bridz raised challenges to effective development of customer relationships.

Strong competition, regulatory changes, and the increasing importance of relationship selling had changed sales and relationship-building approaches. Government drug price control had reduced profitability for pharmaceutical companies. This and strong competition were forcing Indian pharmaceutical companies to massively increase their sales force to increase market share. The increase in the number of salespeople in the market meant less time available for detailing to physicians and building relationships. To overcome this disadvantage and find a solution companies started taking advantage of technologies to create sophisticated and impactful detailing pitches to make the most of the shorter time and to generate more prescriptions.

Traditional ways of developing and sustaining relationships with major physicians which relied on gifts were being banned by the government. To stay relevant and strengthen relationships with physicians, pharmaceutical companies were augmenting their face-to-face contact with online contact. Usage of such technology was seeing gains in client acquisition.

In its effort to overcome these environmental challenges and manage large volumes of customer data, Laurs and Bridz decided it was time to invest in a CRM solution to support the sales process and capability and build better customer relationships.

CRM and SFA Solutions

CRM and SFA (sales force automation) solutions through automation and integration allow companies to increase efficiency and effectiveness in time spent with clients (physicians, healthcare providers, stockists and retailers), track their activities, and map their preferences.

SFA solutions are a core part of many CRM solutions. These tools allow opportunity analysis, sales forecasting, presentations, and collaboration. After looking at the features of several CRM solutions Laurs and Bridz shortlisted the following CRM packages that offered multiple options at different prices.

CRM Solution	Option Levels	Overview
CRMNext	Small office Home office Small and medium business Large enterprise	Includes marketing, sales, and service modules with varying access to one or more modules for the different option levels
Prophet CRM	Contact manager Team Enterprise	Targeted towards sales teams that want a diverse set of functionalities for the management of contacts, an integrated CRM approach, or functionalities that optimize interdepartmental interactions
Adami CRM	Professional Enterprise Unlimited	Includes tools that facilitate management of clients, and additional features such as analytics for the more expensive options
Veeva CRM		Life sciences-specific CRM solution that includes features such as multichannel execution, guided interactions, actionable insights, and a mobile version

Source: Puri, S., Khanna, A., and Sen, A. (2020). "Laurs & Bridz: Implementation of a customer relationship management solution." ID: 9B18A004. Ivey Business School Foundation. Distributed by www.thecasecentre.org

Summary

This chapter introduced and discussed specific metrics that are useful in developing and sustaining customer relationships. The metrics together facilitate judicious allocation of resources to customer relationship management. The chapter discussed both traditional and non-traditional social-media-based CRM metrics and their application in global CRM. These cover multiple areas such as performance of acquisition-related activities, nature and facets of customer activities and behavior, values that customers provide to the firm, and extent of customer satisfaction. There followed a discussion of CRM analytics and tools that complement CRM metrics for decision making.

References

Bennett, P. (2019). "10 grocery shopping habits from around the world that could save time and get you fresher food." *Insider.com*, www.insider.com/grocery-shopping-habits-from-around-the-world-to-try-2018-11

Charm, T., Grimmelt, A., Kim, H., Lu, N., Mayank, Ortega, M., Staack, Y., and Yamakawa, N. (2020). "Consumer sentiment and behavior continue to reflect the uncertainty of the Covid-19 crisis." *McKinsey & Company*, www.mckinsey.com/capabilities/growth-marketing-and-sales/our-insights/a-global-view-of-how-consumer-behavior-is-changing-amid-covid-19

de Leeuw, E., Hox J., and Luiten, A. (2018). "International nonresponse trends across countries and years: An analysis of 36 years of labour force survey data." *Survey Methods: Insights from the Field*, pp: 1–11, https://surveyinsights.org/?p=10452

Farris, P.W., Bendle, N.T., Pfeifer, P.E., and Reibstein, D.J. (2010). *Marketing Metrics: The Definitive Guide to Measuring Marketing Performance*, 2nd edn. Upper Saddle River, NJ: Pearson Education.

Garrison, L. (2012). "Measuring the value of social CRM: 10 metrics to watch." *Your CRM Team*, www.yourcrmteam.com/blog/2012/09/measuring-the-value-of-social-crm-10-metrics-to-watch

Gartner (n.d.). Gartner glossary: Customer relationship management (CRM) analytics. *Gartner*, www.gartner.com/en/information-technology/glossary/crm-analytics

Kumar, V. and Reinartz, W. (2018). *Customer Relationship Management: Concept, Strategy and Tools*, 3rd edn. Berlin: Springer.

Modor Intelligence. (n.d.). "CRM analytics Market—Growth, Trends, Covid-19 impact and forecasts (2022–2027)", www.mordorintelligence.com/industry-reports/crm-analytics-market

Sirk, C. (n.d.). "What is analytical CRM? (& 10 best CRM analytics tools examples)." crm.org, https://crm.org/crmland/analytical-crm

6
STRATEGIC AND OPERATIONAL CRM

Managing Global Value Co-Creation

After seeing almost a decade of business growth since its launch in 2009, Shoes of Prey (SOP), the Australian e-commerce fashion brand, decided to halt its business because it had hit a major roadblock in capturing the mass market.

SOP's Business Model

SOP's business model was founded on the concept of value co-creation. In value co-creation the customer plays a central role in constructing a customized product and service (Pieters and Jansen, 2017; Prahalad and Ramaswamy, 2000). SOP allowed complete customization of their shoes by the customer. Each customer received a "co-created, customized, and monogrammed pair of shoes" that was stylishly packaged and hand delivered. This created a differentiated perception of the brand in customers' minds.

The success of SOP's business model was dependent on technology and software that allowed the customer to customize the shoes online and submit an order, and on on-demand manufacturing technology. The company developed its website in-house because of a lack of such ready-made capability in the software market. It also integrated backward into manufacturing after a short period of outsourcing it. The company realized that in order to scale up customization it was necessary to be able to manufacture its products itself.

Challenges of the Mass Market Customized Co-Creation Process

Despite consumers' desire for mass market customized fashion, SOP faced implementation challenges in the following operations for which the company was able to find solutions:

(Continued)

- *Manufacturing and delivery*: SOP's solution involved refining the manufacturing process to shorten the time to create and deliver customized shoes. Tracking software expedited handover of the shoe from one phase to the next and a 3D printer printed the shoe mold for every order.
- *Customer–product interaction*: Market research showed that SOP's customer segment wanted to try out the shoes before purchasing them. To meet this desire SOP implemented a store-within-a-store strategy in collaboration with high-end retailers such as David Jones in Australia and Nordstrom in the US. Customers could also design their products at the store level. To establish effective working relationships with foreign retailers SOP had to adapt to cultural aspects of customer service and negotiations.
- *Pricing*: Given the relatively high price (US$250–450) SOP engaged in multilevel pricing where the price started at a low base level and increased as options for customizations were added.
- *Positioning*: SOP made a switch from positioning the brand as a novelty based on customization to positioning it on fashion and style. A marketing campaign was run in collaboration with micro-influencers each of whom designed a collection dedicated to people that inspired them.

Failure in Mass Market Customized Co-Creation

Despite sufficient funding, early promise of profits, and changes in manufacturing, retailing, and positioning that engaged a global group of customized shoe enthusiasts, by 2018 SOP was unable to attract sufficient numbers of mass market customers and had to stop production and sales. The company realized that the two-pronged strategy that might help it achieve mass market adoption was 1) to increase awareness and a positive perception among consumers of the value of co-creation and 2) to develop a pricing strategy that would enhance the value of the product in the eyes of mass market consumers.

Source: Roy, S.K. and Singh, G. (2021). "Shoes of Prey: Managing the dark side of value co-Creation." ID: 9B20A022. Ivey Business School Foundation. Distributed by www.thecasecentre.org

Introduction

The Shoes of Prey case highlights the importance of a CRM strategy that combines effective processes supported by automation. Strategic CRM is a collection of organizational processes that facilitate CRM and operational CRM is its automated version that helps put strategic CRM into operation. Automation of one or more of these value-enhancing processes includes utilizing computer and mobile technologies to simplify them, improve their quality, and reduce the cost of implementation (en.wikepedia.org, 2021).

Analytical CRM will help you find out that customer X always visits the same Italian restaurant to celebrate her birthday and that she likes cooking Italian food. It is strategic and operational CRM, however, that will then help develop attractive products for her, interact and engage her with attractive offers, facilitate her purchase and consumption, solicit feedback from her to understand if she is satisfied, and resolve any problems or complaints she may have.

CRM Processes and Process Automation

Core Strategic CRM processes include customer-facing and customer-connecting processes. These include marketing, sales, and customer service, and those that benefit from customer contribution such as product development. Outside this core it also includes non-customer-facing organizational processes that support fulfillment of CRM objectives. These include knowledge management processes, human resource processes such as training, and collaboration processes that help relationship development with value-chain partners, manufacturing, and R&D processes. Processes are workflows that consist of a series of interconnected steps. Automating some of these steps helps create value for the customer and allows the company to compete more effectively. If the process of new product development includes an automated step of sourcing ideas from a select set of customers via a webpage form that links back to a product idea repository, the organization creates customer value through engaging the customer and benefits by having a wider pool of new product ideas. Process automation facilitates the people component of CRM by allowing them—particularly employees in marketing, sales and customer service—time to do what people do best: creatively enhance customer experiences. Together, strategic and operational CRM facilitate value creation and value co-creation through impacting customer awareness, interaction and experiences. Figure 6.1 illustrates the core aspects of operational CRM.

It is important to realize that to get maximum benefits from automation the processes themselves need to be effective and efficient in facilitating the customer journey and in achieving CRM goals. Automating suboptimum processes only makes things worse (Chung et al., 2021). The following steps are recommended when implementing process automation (Bangia et al., 2020).

1   Determine and quantify the potential for automation across processes and subprocesses. Manual, time-consuming and repetitive tasks are good candidates as well as those where automation will positively impact the buyer's journey.

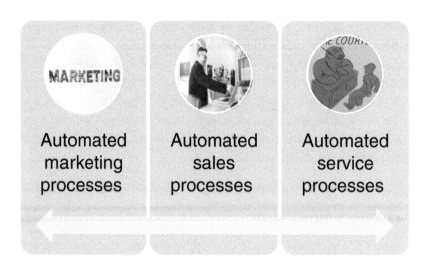

Figure 6.1   Core Operational CRM

Photo by Merakist on Unsplash
Photo by LinkedIn Sales Solutions on Unsplash
Photo by Library of Congress on Unsplash

2   Review the processes and sub-processes prioritized for automation, remapping them to make sure that they are efficient, effective, and add value, and standardize them
3   Implement automation

Marketing, Sales, and Customer Service Processes and Automation

The core CRM processes belong in marketing, sales, and customer service. Together, value-creating marketing, sales, and customer service processes cover marketing research, market segmentation and management of product, marketing communication, distribution, retailing, and purchase and post purchase services such as returns and product usage. These processes together facilitate customer acquisition, retention, and growth by targeting profitable segments, developing products and services that have meaningful benefits, promoting and interacting with customers to create engagement, providing access to products and services, and facilitating consumption and post-consumption interactions in ways that create desirable experiences. Tracy and Wiersema (1995) identified product leadership, operational excellence, and customer intimacy as value drivers for successful companies. Nokia developed smart phones (with long-lasting batteries) that can double as flashlights for the Indian market where extended power failures are common (Knowledge at Wharton, 2007). GlaxoSmithKline provided exceptional value in the same market by promoting their health and energy drink Horlicks as an overall "family nour-isher" for family members with different lifestyles (MBA Skool Team, 2017). And Apple opened an Apple store in the 1990s when it had a small market share to improve customer awareness and engagement.

Examples of operational CRM in marketing, sales, and customer service include automa-tion of: customer input for new product development processes; website browsing for customer convenience and ease; sales presentations and product demonstrations; sequences of activities for online service access for businesses like banking; email campaigns; and purchase and post-purchase customer communications. Table 6.1 adds to this list by high-lighting various areas of marketing, sales force and customer service automation that benefits CRM. The table also mentions popular software products that make the automa-tion possible (Bangia et al., 2020; Buttle, 2009; Gel, 2021; Trujillo, 2021).

The next three subsections discuss some core strategic CRM processes in marketing, sales, and customer service, and their automation. These sections detail the process work-flows, automation details, and global issues that impact the processes and automation.

Marketing Processes and Automation
New Product Development

New products and services tend to provide fresh and updated value to customers and thus facilitate customer acquisition, retention, and growth. For example, when Campbell came out with healthier versions of their regular soups or when a home insurance com-pany added a new product that allows access to funds for college education, they both extended their product offerings to provide additional value (Wassnik, 2021).

Product development is a cross-functional process in which the marketing function plays a crucial and leading role. Besides marketing, the product development team is usually represented by finance, manufacturing, R&D, and sometimes even includes value-chain partners and customers. The process of developing new products can be broken down into four sequential steps. These are 1) generation, screening, and testing of new product concepts, 2) determination of the market potential of the new product concepts, 3) design and development of the new product prototype, and 4) Beta testing of the product and test marketing (Iacobucci, 2021). Figure 6.2 illustrates this sequence of activities in product development.

Table 6.1 Marketing, Sales and Customer Service Process Automation

Process	Automation	Software Tools*
Marketing		
Market research	Audience definition, surveys and reporting. Panelist feedback to identify trends and make recommendations	• Qualtrics • Discuss.io • Alchemer • CheckMarket • Nextiva
Market segmentation	Create segments. Uses analytical tools such as cluster analysis, key driver analysis, conjoint analysis	• Hubspot • Experian • SproutSocial • Qualtrics • Mailchimp
Marketing resource management	Marketing resource allocation and collaboration. Multiple marketing processes such as planning, product launch, campaigns, digital assets, media purchase and expense	• Mavenlink • Monday.com • Float • Forecast • ProjectManager.com
Product management	Collaboration, product development (design and launch), product portfolios and product lifecycle	• Jira • Wrike • Monday.com • Asana • Clickup
Lead management	Campaigns, events, seminars and other tactics to generate attention and interest in prospects	• Pipedrive • Hubspot Marketing Hub • Monday.com • Bitrix 24 (free) • ClickFunnels
Campaign management	Campaign modelling and design, selection of segments, execution, measurement, analysis, and reporting	• Wrike • SharpSpring from Constant Contact • ActiveCampaign • SmartSheet • Marketing360

Process	Automation	Software Tools*
Marketing		
Event-based trigger management	Customer communication or offer based on customer behavior	• Wrike • RSVPify • monday.com • Whova • Cvent
Loyalty management	Customer segmentation, communication, provision of loyalty rewards, and fulfillment	• TapMango • Yotpo • FiveStars • Tango Card • Higher Logic
Customer data privacy management	Customer notice and consent, and compliance with privacy regulations	• OneTrust • DataGrail • TrustArc • Osano
Digital marketing management	Content development, customer experience, keyword and search engine optimization, online advertisements and campaigns	• Hubspot • Campaigner • Salesforce Pardot • Sendinblue • Constant Contact

(Continued)

Table 6.1 (Continued)

Process	Automation	Software Tools*
Sales		
Record creation	Administrative tasks performed in the sales cycle–data: sales calls, website forms and email	Sales force automation
Outreach and communications	Communication and recording across channels and across customers and prospects	• Salesforce Sales Cloud • Pipedrive
Lead qualification	Lead evaluation	• Capsule
Negotiations	Optimum pricing, proposal generation, objections and solutions, configuration of technical solutions	• Pipeliner • VanillaSoft
Order management	Billing, inventory management and other order-related service handling	Hubspot Sales Hub
Onboarding	Customer onboarding process with follow-up and after-sales service	• Salesmate • Nutshell
Post sales	Customer journey optimization: cross- and upselling, repair request, renewal, and new product activation	Sales forecasting
Churn prevention	Identification of customers, and sales and marketing interventions	• Gong.io • Outreach
Training	Access and customization of multiple training (e.g. sales scripts for best handling objections)	Sales enablement • Mindtickle • 360 Learning
		Sales content management • Paperflite • Outreach
		Sales training and coaching • Dialpad • Mindtickle

Process	Automation	Software Tools*
Customer Service		
Self-service	Knowledge base and consolidated FAQ (frequently asked questions) that provides answers and solutions to customers	• Zendesk • Front • Livechat • Freshdesk • Zoho Desk
Integrated support	Centralization and organization of all customer conversations in all-inclusive support hub Identification of ownership of conversations and assigning targeted responsibilities for support	
Live chat	Real time and instant customer service for quick, customized solutions Assignment to appropriate support agent	
Canned responses	Preset email response to all customer service requests and tickets	
Interactive voice responses	Call forwarding by phone receptionist based on keywords to appropriate support	
Artificial intelligence and chatbots	Cognitive and artificial intelligence agents such as chatbots handle one-on-one customer conversations, create tickets, and direct customers towards self-help knowledge guides	

*Sources:

Marketing:

Baker, C. (2021). "The ultimate guide to customer segmentation: How to organize your customers to grow Better," July 27, https://blog.hubspot.com/service/customer-segmentation

capterra.com (2021). "Market research software," www.capterra.com/market-research-software

Capterra.com (2021). "Resource management software," www.capterra.com/resource-management-software/?sortOrder=sponsored

Capterra.com (2021). "Product management software," www.capterra.com/product-management-software/#shortlist

Capterra.com (2021). "Lead management software," www.capterra.com/lead-generation-software

Capterra.com (2021). "Campaign management software," https://www.capterra.com/campaign-management-software

Capterra.com (2021). "Event management software," www.capterra.com/event-management-software

Capterra.com (2021). "Customer loyalty software," www.capterra.com/customer-loyalty-software

G2 (2021). "Best data privacy management software," www.g2.com/categories/data-privacy-management

Sevilla G. (2021). "The best marketing automation software for 2021," www.pcmag.com/picks/the-best-marketing-automation-software

Sales:

Capterra.com (2021). "Sales force automation software," www.capterra.com/sales-force-automation-software

Capterra.com (2021). "Sales forecasting software," www.capterra.com/sales-forecasting-software

Capterra.com (2021). "Sales enablement software," www.capterra.com/sales-enablement-software

Capterra.com (2021). "Sales content management software," www.capterra.com/sales-content-management-software

Capterra.com (2021). "Sales coaching software," www.capterra.com/sales-coaching-software

Customer service:

Capterra.com (2021). "Customer service software," www.capterra.com/customer-service-software

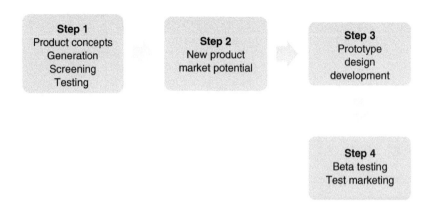

Figure 6.2 New Product Development Process

Step 1: Generation, screening and testing of new product concepts: Employees, consumers, and marketing channel members are valuable sources for product ideas. Strong product ideas contain customer desires, are differentiated, complement the existing product portfolio, and utilize existing competencies. Product ideas need to be screened against specific criteria and then tested with consumers and channel members.

Step 2: Determination of market potential of the new product concepts: This involves calculating potential sales and revenues for screened product ideas to narrow them down to one final product concept.

Step 3: Design and development of the new product prototype: The product development team designs the product (features and look). Conjoint analysis is an analytical research tool that helps the team with the design by determining the most attractive combination of features. Once the design is finalized a prototype of the physical product is created in collaboration with R&D and manufacturing.

Step 4: Beta testing of the product and test marketing: In the beta testing stage physical products are offered to a select set of customers for consumption. Marketing communication materials are developed to facilitate awareness, persuasion, and consumption. If the beta testing is satisfactory the product is test marketed in a limited geographic location.

Global Considerations in Product Development for CRM

Market-perceived quality is culture specific and determines what customers value. Successfully diffusing a new product across multiple international markets requires aligning value creation with cultural aspects of consumption and overcoming regulatory hurdles. Ability to innovate based on deep knowledge of similarities and differences in consumption culture across markets is key. Disney's ultimate success in both Europe and China came only after the company offered culturally adapted versions of the Disney experience, different for each country (Cateora et al., 2011).

Every step of the new product development process will need to consider the impact of country environments—and particularly culture—on consumption. Attractiveness and market potential of product ideas, distribution, and promotional considerations during test marketing will be impacted by country environments. Culturally aligned product development is facilitated by collaboration with product, marketing, and sales managers from multiple country subsidiaries, and outside stakeholders such as customers, channel members, and other alliance partners such as advertising agencies, marketing research firms, and suppliers (Pisharodi et al., 2019). Google collaborated with consumers in India (btw a movie-crazed country) to come up with an update where reviews of TV shows and movies would be available right within the search results (Cook et al., 2019). Figure 6.3 illustrates the structure of collaboration in the international product development process.

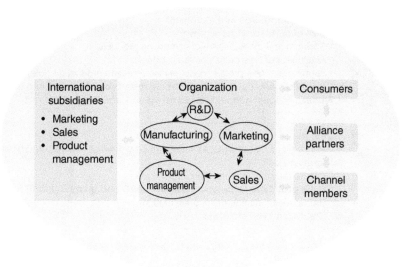

Figure 6.3 International Product Development Collaboration Structure

Automation in Product Development

Automation of the product development process for global CRM involves creating and streamlining a sequence of particular tasks and activities for each step of the process, assigning these tasks to particular teams in the new product collaboration structure, and making progress visible to all through the entire workflow in the process. Automation streamlines and standardizes documentation, access to information, communication across and within task groups, and task reallocation, and creates seamless integration in cross-functional and cross-organizational systems (integrify.com, 2021; toddherman.com, 2002).

Figure 6.4 shows a breakdown of automation areas and activities in a new product development process.

STEP 1:
NEW CONCEPT
GENERATION &
EVALUATION

Concept generation
  Do market research
  Create report of findings (fill form)
  Create presentation for product development team
Concept evaluation
  Determine criteria for new product idea evaluation (fill form)
  Evaluate product ideas and create report (fill form)
Concept testing
  Conduct focus groups to test product ideas
  Create report of findings (form)

STEP 2:
MARKET
POTENTIAL
DETERMINATION

Collect information and document
  Size of potential target segments
  Strength and market share of competing products
  Availability of type of distribution channels
  Alignment of new product concepts with existing product portfolio
Calculate market potential and create report (create report and fill in form)
Finalize product concept based on steps 1 and 2 (create report)

STEP 3:
PROTOTYPE
DESIGN &
DEVELOPMENT

Design
  Perform conjoint analysis to determine best product feature combination, form and look
  Create report of findings (fill form)
Create prototype in collaboration with R&D and manufacturing functions
  Set up meetings and make presentation
  Create report on prototype

STEP 4: BETA
TESTING &
LAUNCH

Beta testing
  Recruit customers for beta testing (communication forms)
  Manufacture new product
  Distribute new product to customers (transportation and delivery forms)
  Create report of findings (fill form)
Launch
  Select test markets
  Recruit customers for electronic or simulated test marketing (communication forms)
  Distribute new product to retailers (contract agreement, transportation and delivery forms)
  Create report from test marketing and present (fill form)
  Commercialize

Figure 6.4 New Product Development Process Automation Areas

Marketing Campaigns

Marketing campaigns are essential components of marketing communications, and through creating awareness and persuasion play a central role in customer relationship management. A marketing campaign is a series of organized, strategic, and interconnected marketing projects that help achieve a particular goal in customer relationship management (Kumar and Reinartz, 2018).

Process of Campaign Management

The process of managing a successful marketing campaign consists of planning the campaign activities, executing and monitoring them, and evaluating their effectiveness (oracle.com, 2021). Figure 6.5 illustrates the steps in a marketing campaign.

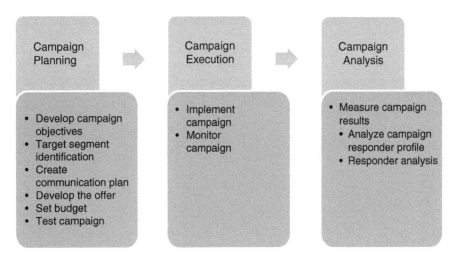

Figure 6.5 Campaign Management Process

Campaign Planning

Planning involves developing the following activities:

- *Campaign objectives*: This describes what the campaign is trying to achieve, such as increasing awareness, image, sales, and rewarding customers. Objectives should be aligned with marketing objectives.
- *Target segment*: Selection of a segment is based on criteria of 1) past purchase and 2) profile information that contains demographics, lifestyle, interests, and non-purchase behavior such as activities on social media and media viewing habits.
- *Communication contents and channels*: Communication content includes type of message, unique selling proposition, and the style of execution. Channels are

media tools used to convey the message to the target segment. Both will depend upon campaign objectives, segment characteristics, and media characteristics and complementarity. Table 6.2 identifies commonly used message strategies, executional styles, and digital media tools that are increasingly used by marketers beyond the traditional offline ones in running global campaigns.

Table 6.2 Commonly Used Message Strategies, Execution Styles and Digital Media

Message Strategies**	Execution Styles**	Digital Media Tool*
Generic: Emphasizes category rather than brand	*Lifestyle*: Depicts enhancement or fit with consumer's lifestyle	Social networking
Unique selling proposition: Emphasizes brand differentiation factor	*Slice-of-life*: Depicts consumers enjoying brand in a particular lifestyle setting	Social media
Positioning: Creates brand perception based on one particular aspect—e.g. price/quality, product user, or competitor	*Fantasy*: Creates a fantasy around brand usage	Search engines
Brand image: Creates a psychological connection to the brand	*Endorsement*: Has celebrities and experts explain the brand	E-commerce
Pre-emptive: First to claim superiority of brand	*Mood*: Creates a particular mood around the brand	Digital TV and video
Emotional: Creates an emotional connection to the brand	*Musical*: Depicts characters or people singing about the brand	Mobile
Cognitive/Logical: Provides rational information to convince	*Scientific evidence*: Presents evidence about the superiority of the brand	Augmented reality

*Sources:

Bump, P. (2021). "The marketing trends of 2022," Hubspot Blog, https://blog.hubspot.com/marketing/marketing-trends

McCarthy, J. (2021). "The top global media consumption trends of 2021", Oct. 23, www.thedrum.com/news/2021/10/22/the-top-global-media-consumption-trends-2021

**Sources:

Bigbuzzinc.com (2021). "6 messaging strategies for 2021," www.bigbuzzinc.com/6-messaging-strategies-to-market-your-practice

Definition.com (2021). "Execution style," https://the-definition.com/term/execution-style

DMA Solutions Team (2021). "5 types of marketing appeals to use to captivate your audience," Dec. 7, >www.dma-solutions.com/thecoreblog/marketing-101-5-types-of-marketing-appeals

Pack, S. (2017). "Types of advertising appeals and execution styles—what sells," April 14, https://skywestmedia.com/types-of-advertising-appeal-and-execution-style-what-sells

Vasiliev, A. (2019). "Great marketing message strategies for successful campaigns," May 20, www.apifonica.com/en/blog/marketing-message

- *Campaign offers*: A campaign offer includes the incentive to motivate the target segment to respond to the campaign. This should be relevant and attractive to the segment and at the core needs to include the promise of the brand (Stone and Jacobs, 2008). Other aspects of the offer such as positioning of the brand, price, period of commitment, payment terms, and guarantees and warranties also impact the effectiveness of the offer. Table 6.3 lists the most commonly used types of offers in marketing campaigns.

Table 6.3 Types of Campaign Offers

Type of Offer	Characteristics
Buy one get one free	Used by larger organizations such as supermarkets and department store chains for low-cost products. More effective than 50% off
Competitions	Used for higher-priced products. The higher the reward the higher participation tends to be—e.g. travel companies giving away free holidays
Free deliveries	Used by organizations such as supermarkets and furniture stores that provide delivery
Gift vouchers	Vouchers can be used to claim discounts or free items
10%-off discount	Used to speed up sales for slow-moving items
Loyalty cards	Cards come with different perks
Free workshops, webinars, e-books, podcasts, videos, reports	Used to create brand awareness, education, and interest
Student discounts	Used by high street brands that attract students—e.g. fashion and food discounts
Free item or service if you buy before "date"	Used by companies offering paid membership services such as movie streaming
Free trial	Used by companies selling expensive items or services to provide knowledge and gain trust in the brand
Cash back	Used by high street stores to provide an incentive
Gift cards	Used by high street stores to get customers in
Package deals	Combines multiple complementary (e.g. lodging and food) offers to provide extra incentives
Guarantees	Provides assurance and incentives for higher-priced complex products such as automobiles
Better payment terms	Used by expensive consumer brands or B2B brands

Source: Williamson, W. (2021). "20 special offer ideas for marketing my business", jdr Group, Oct 26, https://blog.jdrgroup.co.uk/digital-prosperity-blog/special-offer-marketing-ideas

- *Campaign budget*: Developing a campaign budget involves determining the cost of all marketing activities for the campaign. Rigorous cost estimates for both easily measurable (e.g. a direct mail offer) and less easily measurable activities (e.g. blog posts) help to make a business case for the campaign. Table 6.4 provides a list of different budgeting methods.

Table 6.4 Campaign Budgeting Methods

Budget Method	Characteristics
Percentage of sales	Based on previous year's sales
Competitive parity	Based on competitors' budgets
Objective and task	Based on costs of campaign tasks needed to achieve campaign objectives
Key performance indicators	Based on costs of achieving key performance indicators such as conversion rate

Source: Kumar, V. and Reinartz, W. (2018). *Customer Relationship Management: Concept, Strategy and Tools*, 3rd edn. Berlin: Springer. Used with permission of Springer Nature.

- *Campaign testing*: Testing helps marketers come up with the most effective campaign by comparing the results of different small-scale versions of a campaign where each version has one unique campaign element (e.g. price). This helps tie campaign effectiveness to individual campaign elements. Any element of the campaign, such as the price, the type of offer, the media, or message can be tested.

Campaign Execution

This involves implementing the campaign, monitoring, and tweaking it if necessary. Implementation includes the following actions:

- Creation of a task list with specific deadlines
- Task assignment to teams
- Selection of offers
- Selection of media
- Description of all marketing materials including formats
- Creation of a campaign timetable—list of planned events with completion time frames for each

It is important to monitor the results on an ongoing basis and make necessary changes to the offer, media or messages.

Campaign Analysis

Analysis measures the impacts of the campaign. It includes the following two activities:

1 *Analyzing different key campaign performance indicators (KPIs).* Table 6.5 highlights commonly used campaign KPIs.

Table 6.5 Campaign KPIs

KPI	Description
Number of impressions	Number of views of campaign ad in a time period
Number of clicks	Number of times the campaign offer and ad were clicked on
Click-through rate (CTR)	Number of clicks/number of impressions
Cost per response	Campaign cost/number of responses
Cost per click (CPC)	Campaign cost/number of clicks
Cost per sale (CPS)	Campaign cost/(total orders and returns)
Conversion rate	(Number of buyers/number of responders) x 100
Return on investment (ROI)	Sales revenues/campaign cost

Source: Used with permission of Springer Nature

2 *Analyzing and profiling responders*: Analyzing the impact of multiple responder characteristics such as demographics and psychographics on campaign response, and creating a typical profile of a campaign responder.

Global Considerations in Campaign Management

Cultural, economic, and market realities become particularly important when running campaigns in international markets. Economic development, culture, and laws lay down the conditions for feasibility of campaign objectives, determine which target segment would be appropriate for the campaign, and impact the effectiveness of message strategy, media tool set, and offer type. Whereas fairness is an important desired benefit from cosmetic products among a significant percentage of women in South Asia and in many parts of South America, that desire is largely unsought among developed-country white women, many of whom on the other hand desire achieving a skin tan through usage of cosmetics (Bhatt, 2014). This difference in consumer desires and cultural traits may force a beauty brand running campaigns for a fairness beauty product across countries to adapt multiple elements of the campaign. At the same time as national culture, associated consumption culture and ethical values change, organizations will also have to walk a fine line between catering to cultural traits and being aligned to changing value. Recent backlash from women consumers in India led to the repositioning and rebranding of Hindustan Lever's long-standing brand Fair and Lovely (now Glow and Lovely), which had ran successful campaigns in India over decades catering to this cultural trend among South Asian women (McEvoy, 2020). Unilever, the parent company of Hindustan Lever, on the other hand ran a successful global campaign called Dove's Real Beauty that targeted global consumer concerns and desires (Dove.com, n.d.). Whether a country-specific message or a global message with country-specific tweaks would be more effective will depend on the relative strength of the brand in the market, culture, economy, and on consumption trends.

Media consumption habits too vary from country to country and from segment to segment, impacting choice of media for campaigns. In Germany early adopters of the Internet used mobile platforms significantly more than the rest of the population (Reith et al., 2019). In many developing countries there is a stark divide between rural and urban areas in media viewing habits. Whereas young urban consumers get on the Internet regularly with their smartphones (unlike their counterparts in the developed world where PCs are still the more common platform), consumers (particularly older people) in rural areas may still be listening to the radio or TV and only a small handful of consumers there have access to smartphones and the Internet.

Automation in Campaign Management

Automation in campaign management streamlines the workflow, collaboration, and documentation in campaign management. Campaign workflow establishes the order in which tasks have to be performed, who performs these tasks and what forms need to be filled. The primary campaign areas suited for automation are (Buttle, 2009):

- *Target segment selection*: Creating subsets of customers based on particular campaign criteria
- *Campaign budget*: Financial analysis and extraction of information on sales and marketing expenses from previous campaigns
- *Offer and message*: Tailoring of messages and offers for different segment members based on a set criteria such as type of previous purchases
- *Campaign execution*: Setting timetable and communication of messages and offers through multiple channels based on the timetable
- *Campaign analysis*: Measuring and interpreting campaign results, and creating responder profiles

Loyalty Programs

Loyalty programs are incentive-based marketing intervention tools aimed at customers. The objective is to increase repeat purchase and revenues, and strengthen customer relationships and referrals through enhancing value (Capizzi et al., 2004; Kumar et al., 2010; Plazibat et al., 2016; Vesel and Zabkar, 2009). A longitudinal study of loyalty programs of 322 listed companies have shown that loyalty programs do work and add to sales and profits (Chaudhuri et al., 2019).

To be effective a loyalty program needs to be both attractive and provide value (Ruzeviciute and Kamleitner, 2017). This helps create a rational and emotional customer–brand connection (Tanford et al., 2011). To achieve both objectives the organization has to carefully consider the value-added benefits built into the loyalty program structure (Melancon et al., 2011) and the segment of customers it is being targeted to (Tanford and Malek, 2015).

Loyalty Program Mechanism Process

Successfully developing and implementing a loyalty program requires the organization to follow the basic sequence of activities as stated below.

1   *Customer selection*: Selection should be based primarily on customer profitability and profit potential and to some extent on profile information such as demographics, lifestyle, and behaviors
2   *Nature of rewards*: Determination of type of reward. Rewards can be hard or soft. Examples of hard rewards are point accumulations or free meals whereas soft rewards are more experiential in nature, such as free special services. Soft rewards tend to generate more emotional value. Best practices recommends, i) offering flexibility in reward redemption across multiple product categories, ii) offering customization in rewards to build more emotional attachment to the brand (Tanford et al., 2016), iii) offering multiple tiered rewards which are tied to different spending levels or patterns, or to other criteria, iv) tying value of the reward to purchase value or volume. This drives program popularity but also reins in program costs, and v) offering reward redemption frequencies based on program goal. Shorter intervals create more program value whereas longer terms create more loyalty (Hu et al., 2010)
3   *Program communication*: Use of appropriate channels to communicate the program and its benefits
4   *Enrollment*: Determination of criteria of enrollment and creation of a system that allows customers to enroll in the loyalty program
5   *Reward credit acquisition*: Determination of criteria for earning rewards (e.g. purchase or non-purchase behavior such as sharing videos on social media or posting a review). Multi-tier reward programs need to identify specific criteria for each tier that differentiate the tiers and help to increase attraction for the next

higher tier. This stage also involves creation of a system that allows customers to acquire reward credits

6   *Reward credit redemption*: Determination of criteria for redeeming rewards and creation of a system that allows customers to redeem reward credits

Figure 6.6 visualizes this process.

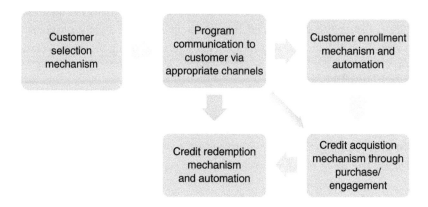

Figure 6.6 Loyalty Program Process Mechanism

The hospitality industry has been at the forefront of innovation in loyalty programs. Table 6.6 summarizes some of the common elements of loyalty programs in the hotel sector. Availability of these elements varies across tiers.

Table 6.6 Hotel Industry Loyalty Program Elements

Points earned per dollar	Free Internet
Points bonus	Free breakfast
Redeem points for rooms	Car rental point accrual
Redeem points for food and beverages	Credit card point accrual
Redeem points for merchandise, giftcards, spas, donations	Points purchase
Redeem points for experiential rewards (concerts, sporting events, and shows)	Upgrades
Free health club access	Exchange points between hotel and partner airlines
Gift on arrival	Rollover nights
Mobile app	No blackout dates
Separate and early check-in	Guaranteed room availability
Late check-out	Dedicated customer service
Lounge access	Executive concierge
Luggage tags	Preference profile for customized benefits

Source: Tanford, S., Shoemaker, S., and Dinca, A. (2016). "Back to the future: Progress and trends in hotel loyalty marketing," *International Journal of Contemporary Hospitality*, 28, 9, 1937–67. Used with permission of Emerald Publishing.

Global Issues in Loyalty Program Management

Economy and culture impact the extent of customer loyalty towards brands and determine what will help secure it. Different levels of income, awareness, perceptions, and expectations of customers across countries will thus impact the effectiveness of a loyalty program. For example the loyalty program benefits that microwave customers in countries with different histories of usage of microwave ovens and different consumption trends will look for will likely be different. Countries in which microwave oven use is established will be more interested in perks that go beyond the product whereas countries new to microwave ovens (many developing countries) may be more interested in perks that are connected with the product itself, such as free microwave recipe books (Thompson and Chmura, 2015). Consumers in a country are, however, not homogeneous and segments may be very local, global, or somewhere in between. So, based on the segments being targeted, some aspects of a loyalty program can be tweaked across some countries but for others the programs may need to be significantly adapted. Whereas in developed countries efficient service and rewards are more desirable than price discounts, in developing countries price discounts are much more sought after as are different payment options (Koncar et al., 2019). Research done across countries shows that some elements of a loyalty program remain equally desirable. These are price discounts, efficient service and rewards, better information provision on program benefits and perks, and additional benefits (Koncar et al., 2019).

Automation in Loyalty Program Management

Given the widespread availability of competing loyalty programs, effective loyalty program management needs regular member engagement. This is inefficient to do manually for a wide variety of customers. Automation in management of a loyalty program takes care of this by automating delivery of customized in-app messages, texts, and emails that highlight the benefits of the program during onboarding, and contain incentives such as coupons or reminders to boost engagement for active members or reengagement for inactive ones (Ahuja, 2021). Examples include messages that promise incentives to customers to complete their profile or remind them about achieving a target points goal needed to claim a reward. These messages are based on automated triggers determined in the loyalty program structure. Both customization and triggers are automated and are based on customer activity within the loyalty program and profile information, such as encouraging a customer to purchase particular desired items that may not be in stock for very long to accumulate points, or to use points to secure a much wanted reward on the customer's birthday. Loyalty program automation is usually tied to a broader CRM system which provides the information needed for customization for the message and triggers.

Best Practices in Loyalty Programs

The following loyalty programs have helped these brands differentiate themselves from the pack.

Brand	Characteristics
Sephora Beauty INSIDER	Points-based reward program
	Customers have flexibility in reward choice (gift cards, discounts, limited editions products and experiences such as in-store beauty tutorials)
DSW Shoes	Points-based tiered reward program based on purchase
	Automatic enrollment
	No loyalty card
	Personalized and timely reminder emails to inform customers about:
	• Number of points needed to get discounts
	• Deals the customer is eligible for
	• Snapshot of the customer's interaction with the brand
Starbucks	Reward system operated on the Starbucks app
	Provides customer behavior data for future personalized perks and communication
Amazon Prime	For an annual fee prime members get access to:
	• Unlimited two-day shipping on millions of items
	• Amazon's streaming services
	• Prime day sales
The North Face	Points-based system that curates experiential redemption options
	Points-based reward program based on
	• Every purchase
	• Unique activities (e.g. Checking in at certain locations, attending North Face events, and downloading the app)
	Customers have flexibility in redemption of points (travel experiences, early access to limited edition collections, opportunities to wear test products)

Source: Peacock, L. (2021). "Keep them coming back: 7 innovative customer loyalty programs (and how to start yours)," Shopify Blog, Apr 29, www.shopify.com/blog/loyalty-program

Sales Processes and Automation

An effective CRM initiative needs a sales function that is aligned with the marketing and customer service functions. The sales function performs a number of different activities that go from acquiring customers to building and sustaining customer relationships. Successful salespeople follow a structured sales process that coordinates all the primary sales activities into several sequential interconnected steps (Andzulis et al., 2012; D'Haen and Van den Poel, 2013). Figure 6.7 illustrates the relationship between the steps in the sales process and Table 6.7 highlights and describes these steps (Altschuler, 2021; Freshworks.com, 2021).

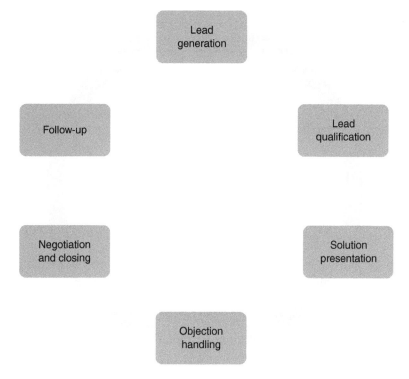

Figure 6.7 The Sales Process

The sales process is supported by several support processes that are necessary for its execution. These support processes help with keeping records of visits, order management activities such as creating proposals and contracts, delivery and returns, communication pre-, during and post-purchase, and training of salespeople. Doing these processes manually is very time consuming and diverts the skills of the salespeople from selling creatively and building customer relationships. That is where sales automation has helped.

Table 6.7 The Sales Process

Steps	Activities
Lead generation/ prospecting	Searching for new potential customers (leads) that match with current buyer persona. CRM database, cold calls, cold emails, social media activities and webinars are ways to find leads
Lead qualification	Making an initial contact to know more about the lead and determine if the lead has a problem that the salesperson can solve. If yes, the salesperson needs to determine whether the lead has a reasonable time frame to implement the solution, a budget, willingness, and authority to make decisions
Solution presentation	Presenting and demonstrating the solution to the prospect. The solution needs to highlight differentiated benefits of the offering and tie those in to the particular needs and problems of the prospect. Deep product and prospect knowledge is critical to gain attention and consideration
Question and objection handling	Satisfactorily addressing concerns and overcoming objections surrounding quality, product usage, price, delivery, service, etc. Customer orientation, knowledge about the customer's business, and empathy are desired qualities
Negotiation and closing	Negotiating the terms of the sale happen, transmitting a contract proposal, and closing the sale
Follow-up	Nurturing customers for repeat purchase, profitability, and loyalty. Asking for feedback on usage, consumption, and satisfaction with the solution and for serving better

Sales Process Automation

Sales automation has made both the primary sales process and the support processes more efficient and effective, including basic automation such as following up emails and advanced automation such as machine learning and cognitive agents for cross-selling. A significant percentage of the steps in a sales process can benefit from automation, including (Bangia et al., 2020):

- *Lead generation and qualification*:
  - Customer intelligence development and distribution
  - Customer profile development
  - Interactions among marketing, sales, and customer service
  - Lead evaluation and prioritization based on criteria
  - Lead probing through artificial intelligence
- *Solution presentation and handling of objections*:
  - Training (pre-presentation) based on salesperson knowledge level and customer needs
  - Presentation and demonstration
  - Real-time tips on better objection handling
  - Cognitive agent-facilitated distribution of knowledge materials to prospects based on type of query

- *Negotiation and closing*:
  - Pricing analysis and discount management based on inputs
  - Natural language processing-based inquiry resolution
  - Draft proposal generation and distribution
  - Order management—billing, payment, inventory
- *Follow up*:
  - Cross-selling and upselling recommendations
  - Contract renewal generation and distribution
  - Reminder-based communication

Customer Service Processes and Automation

Customer service plays a complementary role to marketing and sales in a CRM initiative. Through solving customer problems in product consumption and usage, answering product and service-related queries, and facilitating access to information, services, and products, customer service function enhances the consumption experience and helps solidify relationships.

The customer service process begins when the customer makes contact with the company and ends when the reason for the customer's call is resolved to the satisfaction of the customer. Depending on the complexity of the customer query, resolution of the process may include more or fewer steps (DaSilva, 2021; Heflo.com, 2022). Table 6.8 highlights and describes the steps in a customer service process.

Table 6.8 Customer Service Process

Process Step	Description
Initial customer contact	• Customer contacts the company in order to complain, ask a question, request information
	• Agent collects necessary information to provide the service
Service ticket	• Agent issues a service ticket to register the request
Analysis	• Agent accesses a knowledge base to determine resolution (if knowledge base lacks resolution information and if needed)
	• Agent reaches back to the customer for more information
	• Agent elevates the problem to area expert within the organization for resolution
Resolution	• The agent communicates with the customer about resolution
Closure	• If resolved, agent submits a closure notice and adds the resolution to the knowledge database for future reference
Survey	• Agent sends a survey to the customer for gauging satisfaction and for feedback for improvements

For a customer service process to run smoothly and be consistently high quality it is important to have standardized protocols for communication and collaboration both among agents and between agents and the customer.

The Covid-19 pandemic has significantly changed consumer behavior and expectations from customer service. It has forced organizations to elevate the internal and external aspects of the customer service process (McAllister et al., 2022). To create better customer experiences through the customer service function organizations are:

- *Improving automation*:
  - Incorporating more flexible technology that allows customers to seamlessly switch between communication channels
  - Unifying communication and contact centers that allows 1) customers more options to get connected to customer service agents through texting or calling a local office and 2) customer service agents to dip into a deep organizational expert knowledge pool to solve customer problems
- *Activating "dark" unstructured data for improving the customer experience:*
  - Bringing together offline and online internal (agent–agent) and external (agent–customer) conversations from across all functions to develop rich data
  - Facilitating cross-functional collaboration on artificial intelligence (AI) initiatives for customer service
  - Facilitating human–AI collaboration for smoother resolution of customer problems
- *Humanizing the contact center—increasing empathy in communications and customer service and reducing customer service agent burnout by*:
  - Changing performance metrics (from efficiency based to customer satisfaction based) and
  - Improving customer service agent relationship management (see Chapter 10)

Customer Service Process Automation

The ultimate goal of customer service in CRM is to create a high-quality customer experience by satisfactorily addressing customers' inquiries and resolving their problems. Keeping this in mind the following areas of customer service benefit from automation (Trujillo, 2021):

- *Artificial intelligence and agent collaboration*: Chatbots initiate the customer service process and if needed, and based on specific criteria, elevate the inquiry to a human customer service agent
- *Self-service*: Provision of a self-service online knowledge base with intuitive search functionality that helps customers to find answers

- *Communication centralization*: Centralization of both internal (agent–agent) and external (agent–customer) communication and conversations in one hub allows for easier access to a deeper knowledge pool and if needed elevation of problem resolution to area experts
- *Channel integration*: Integration of channels within the contact center system allows customers more options to reach customer service (e.g. by text, calling, emailing)
- *Record keeping*: Collection and logging of information on customer service issues (ticket) and solutions into a database
- *Standardized templates*: Editable standardized templates with pre-built responses speed up communication and delivery of documents (e.g. service issue ticket, customer satisfaction surveys, knowledge manual) to customers

Global Issues in Sales and Customer Service Management

Sales and customer service are two of the most important customer-facing functions in an organization and hence can make or mar customer relationships. National culture, economy, and laws together play a significant role in shaping consumption and communications. It is therefore critical to understand them in order to adapt sales and customer service for global CRM initiatives. The foundational processes for sales and customer service, as discussed in the previous sections, can be standardized across countries. However, the methods and techniques utilized will likely need to be adapted to be effective. Two technical and more obvious areas that create a need for adaptation in some countries are 1) the language used for written and verbal communication and 2) the extent of automation and technology. Consumers in some cultures may not find the concept of chatting with an artificial intelligence entity (e.g. a chatbot) palatable because of perceptions of trust and quality, may predominantly use different communication technology such as telephones rather than email, and may use mobile platforms for accessing the Internet. Other areas that demand adaptations have to do with overall cultural behavioral patterns and are less obvious, such as acceptable modes of expression. Some cultures trust direct, straightforward, and objective communication but others may find that objectionable and prefer a more sociable and friendly style. For example, use and perception of the word "no" are different across countries and need to be adapted accordingly in presentations, negotiations, objection handling and complaint resolution. Non-verbal expressions and gestures which have significance vary across cultures and if not adapted to the culture will likely create misunderstandings and dissatisfaction. Additionally, consumers have different expectations and goals from a particular consumption (e.g. enjoying a picnic with friends). Some of these differences are culture based, as in the example of microwave ovens used earlier in this chapter. These differences may also impact the type of customer service needed and resolutions to consumption problems leading to needed adaptations to sales presentations and customer service communications. Finally the buyer's journey across countries might be different for the same product category. This will impact the frequency and timeline of completion of sales and customer service processes and the length of each step of the process, necessitating some adaptations.

Case Study

CRM Application Software for Omnichannel Customer Service at a US Airline

In 2007 JetBlue Airlines, one of the low-cost airlines operating in the United States faced a public relations crisis that prompted it to concentrate on improving its customer service, a differentiating factor in an industry seen by most consumers as uncaring and unhelpful.

JetBlue has been consistently rated highly by JD Power and Associates. Its revenues and profits have increased since 2006 (except for the year 2020) (Macrotrends.com, 2021; WSJ.com, 2021). The airline's business model was grounded in low cost and differentiation by providing amenities other low-cost airlines in the US do not provide.

Multi-Channel Customer Service Efforts

In response to the 2007 crisis JetBlue founder took to YouTube to apologize to consumers and to promise improvements in customer service. The main tactics JetBlue implemented to improve were:

- Creating customer communication goals to respond within ten minutes on Twitter and within two to four hours on Facebook
- Removing restrictive customer service policies
- Hiring "empathetic, caring and fun" customer service employees, training them and empowering them to be "creative and responsive" in providing solutions to customers
- Embracing social media channels, particularly Facebook and Twitter, for 24/7 monitoring, promotion, and communication with customers
- Creating a dedicated "social care team" to manage social media interactions and to support the company's mission "To Inspire Humanity."

Omnichannel Customer Service Challenge

Despite these multi-channel efforts, the level and quality of service did not reach optimal levels because of the lack of alignment in systems used across channels that did not allow seamless sharing of information. To be truly omnichannel in its operations JetBlue had to look for a technological solution that would align all channels so that all customer conversations were consolidated and customer service employees interacting with customers would have a complete view of them.

Gladly—the Customer Service Technology Platform

JetBlue formed a partnership with Gladly. Gladly is a Web-based customer service technology platform that connects and consolidates all conversations a customer has across multiple communication channels (offline and online) with multiple customer service agents. All customer service agents have access to this information so that answers to questions and solutions to problems can be provided efficiently and effectively. The customer is central to Gladly's system and they are seen as more than a numbered enquiry ticket. Customer not tickets were routed. Based on the customer need, enquiries and problems are routed for effective resolution.

Gladly tested and refined its app with a pilot group of customers including those from 2016 and in 2017. JetBlue implemented a phased roll-out of the app over 12 to 18 months. The question that now remains to be answered is will Gladly enhance the distinctive customer-service focus of JetBlue or will increasing reliance on customer relationship management technology erase the differentiation from other airlines that also use CRM software.

Source: Youngdahl, W.E. (2017). "JetBlue and Gladly: Omnichannel customer service." ID: A04-17-0013. Thunderbird School of Global Management. Distributed by www.thecasecentre.org

Summary

Chapter 6 introduced strategic and operational CRM. Strategic CRM is a set of strategic organizational processes that help to achieve CRM objectives. The core strategic CRM consists of marketing, sales, and customer service processes. Operational CRM is the automated version of these processes and also includes a multitude of software that can be "added on" to these automated CRM processes. The rest of the chapter was devoted to a discussion of marketing (product development, campaign management and loyalty programs), sales and customer-service processes that are crucial for CRM, their automation, and the global considerations for each of them.

References

Ahuja, K. (2021). "Drive your customer loyalty program with automated campaigns." *Oracle*, July 12, https://blogs.oracle.com/marketingcloud/post/improve-your-customer-loyalty-program-with-automated-campaigns

Altschuler, M. (2021). "Everything you need to know about building & scaling your sales process." Sales Hacker, Feb. 12, www.saleshacker.com/sales-process

Andzulis, J.M., Panagopoulos, N.G., and Rapp, A. (2012). "A review of social media and implications for the sales process." *Journal of Personal Selling & Sales Management*, 32, 305–16.

Bangia, M., Cruz, G., Huber, I, Landauer, P., and Sunku, V. (2020). "Sales automation: The key to boosting revenue and reducing costs." McKinsey & Company Insights Article, May 13, www.mckinsey.com/business-functions/growth-marketing-and-sales/our-insights/sales-automation-the-key-to-boosting-revenue-and-reducing-costs

Bhatt, S. (2014). "Journey of fairness creams' advertising in India." *Economic Times of India*, Feb. 26, https://economictimes.indiatimes.com/journey-of-fairness-creams-advertising-in-india/articleshow/30997189.cms?from=mdr

Buttle, F. (2009). *Customer Relationship Management: Concepts and Technologies*, 2nd edn. Amsterdam: Elsevier.

Capizzi, M., Ferguson, R., and Cuthbertson, R. (2004). "Loyalty trends for the 21st century." *Journal of Targeting, Measurement & Analysis for Marketing*, 12, 3, 199–212.

Cateora, P., Gilly, M.C., and Graham, J.L. (2011). *International Marketing*, 15th edn. New York: McGraw-Hill Irwin.

Chaudhuri, M., Voorhees, C.M., and Beck, J.M. (2019). "The effects of loyalty program introduction and design on short- and long-term sales and gross profits." *Journal of the Academy of Marketing Science*, 47, 4, 640–58.

Chung, D.J., Huber, I., Kayacan, C., Landauer, P., and Sunku, V. (2021). "What's your sales automation strategy?" *Harvard Business Review*, Jun 2, https://hbr.org/2021/06/whats-your-sales-automation-strategy

Cook, L.A., Northington, W., and Hiler, J. (2019). "Consumers who collaborate with the firm, but against each other: An abstract", in P. Rossi and N. Krey (eds), *Finding New Ways to Engage and Satisfy Global Customers: Proceedings of the 2018 Academy of Marketing Science (AMS) World Marketing Congress (WMC)*. Cham, Switzerland: Springer, p. 29.

DaSilva, D. (2021). "Customer service flowchart: Find out what it is, what it is for, and how to make one." Zendesk Blog, June 22, www.zendesk.co.uk/blog/customer-service-flowchart-find-make-one

D'Haen, J. and Van den Poel, D. (2013). "Model-supported business-to-business prospect prediction based on an iterative customer acquisition framework." *Industrial Marketing Management*, 42, 544–51.

Dove.com (n.d.). *Dove Campaigns*, www.dove.com/us/en/stories/campaigns.html

en.wikepedia.org (2021). "Business process automation." https://en.wikipedia.org/wiki/Business_process_automation

Freshworks.com (2021). "The ultimate guide to sales process." Freshsales, www.freshworks.com/crm/sales/sales-process

Gel, C. (2021). "What is sales automation? A guide for successful deployment." Dialpad, Aug. 3, www.dialpad.com/blog/sales-automation

Heflo.com (2022). "Customer service process flow chart." www.heflo.com/blog/workflow/customer-service-process-flow-chart

Hu, H., Huang, C., and Chen, P. (2010). "Do reward programs truly build loyalty for lodging industry? *International Journal of Hospitality Management*, 29, 1, 128–35.

Iacobucci, D. (2021). *Marketing Management*, 6th edn. Boston, MA: Cengage.

Integrify.com (2021). "Product development process." www.integrify.com/landing-pages/product-development-process

Knowledge at Wharton (2007). "How did Nokia succeed in the Indian mobile market, while its rivals got hung up?" https://knowledge.wharton.upenn.edu/article/how-did-nokia-succeed-in-the-indian-mobile-market-while-its-rivals-got-hung-up

Koncar, J., Maric, R., and Vukmirovic, G. (2019). "Analysis of key indicators that affect the expected benefit of customers when using loyalty cards." *Journal of Business Economics and Management*, 20, 5, 821–40.

Kumar, V. and Reinartz, W. (2018). *Customer Relationship Management: Concept, Strategy and Tools*, 3rd edn. Berlin: Springer.

Kumar, V., Aksoy, L., Donkers, B., Venkatesan, R., Wiesel, T., and Tillmanns, S. (2010). "Undervalued or overvalued customers: Capturing total customer engagement value." *Journal of Service Research*, 13, 297–310.

Macrotrends.com (2021). "JetBlue Airways revenue 2006–2021 JBLU." www.macrotrends.net/stocks/charts/JBLU/jetblue-airways/revenue

MBA Skool Team (2017). "Horlicks marketing strategy & marketing mix (4Ps)." mbaSKOOL.*com*, www.mbaskool.com/marketing-mix/products/16996-horlicks.html

McAllister, C., Ball, M., and Bellomo, E. (2022). "Forrester: The three customer service megatrends in 2022." Forrester, www.forrester.com/report/the-three-customer-service-megatrends-in-2022/RES177174

McEvoy, J. (2020), "Critics slam Unilever rebrand of 'Fair & Lovely' skin lightener as 'Glow & Lovely'", *Forbes*, July 2, www.forbes.com/sites/jemimamcevoy/2020/07/02/critics-slam-unilever-rebrand-of-fair--lovely-skin-lightener-as-glow--lovely/?sh=345067ab4b7a

Melancon, J.P., Noble, S.M., and Noble, C.H. (2011). "Managing rewards to enhance relational worth." *Journal of the Academy of Marketing Science*, 39, 341–62.

Oracle.com (2021). "What is campaign management." www.oracle.com/cx/marketing/campaign-management/what-is-campaign-management

Pieters, M. and Jansen, S. (2017). *The 7 Principles of Complete Co-creation*. Amsterdam: BIS Publishers.

Pisharodi, R.M., Parameswaran, R., and Henke Jr, J.W. (2019). "OEM Pressure to Innovate and Buyer-Supplier Relationship: An Abstract", in P. Rossi and N. Krey (eds), *Finding New Ways to Engage and Satisfy Global Customers: Proceedings of the 2018 Academy of Marketing Science (AMS) World Marketing Congress (WMC)*. Cham, Switzerland: Springer, p. 29.

Plazibat, I., Šušak, T., and Šarić, T. (2016). "Functionality of customer loyalty programs in retail." *Ekonomska misao i praksa*, 1, 303–18.

Prahalad, C.K. and Ramaswamy, V. (2000). "Co-opting customer competence." *Harvard Business Review*, Jan.–Feb., https://hbr.org/2000/01/co-opting-customer-competence

Reith, R., Fischer, M., and Lis, B. (2019). "How to Reach Early Adopters: An Empirical Analysis of Early Adopters' Internet Usage Behavior: An Abstract", in P. Rossi and N. Krey (eds), *Finding New Ways to Engage and Satisfy Global Customers: Proceedings of the 2018 Academy of Marketing Science (AMS) World Marketing Congress (WMC)*. Cham, Switzerland: Springer, p. 29.

Ruzeviciute, R. and Kamleitner, B. (2017). "Attracting new customers to loyalty programs: The effectiveness of monetary versus nonmonetary loyalty programs." *Journal of Consumer Behaviour*, 16, 6, 113–24.

Stone, B. and Jacobs, R. (2008). *Successful Direct Marketing Methods*, 8th edn. New York: McGraw-Hill.

Tanford, S., Shoemaker, S., and Dinca, A. (2016). "Back to the future: Progress and trends in hotel loyalty marketing." *International Journal of Contemporary Hospitality*, 28, 9, 1937–67.

Tanford, S. and Malek, K. (2015). "Segmentation of reward program members to increase customer loyalty: The role of attitudes towards green hotel practices." *Journal of Hospitality Marketing & Management*, 24, 3, 314–43.

Tanford, S., Raab, C., and Kim, Y.S. (2011). "The influence of reward program membership and commitment on hotel loyalty." *Journal of Hospitality & Tourism Research*, 35, 279–307.

Thompson, F.M. and Chmura, T. (2015). "Loyalty programs in emerging and developed markets: The impact of cultural values on loyalty program choice." *Journal of International Marketing*, 23, 3, 87–103.

Toddherman.com (2002). "Using workflow automation to redefine product development." www.toddherman.com/case-study/archive/workflow-automation-product-development

Tracy, M. and Wiersema, F. (1995). *The Discipline of Market Leaders*. London: Harper Collins.

Tujillo, E. (2021). "What is automated customer service? A guide for growth that helps people do more, not less." www.groovehq.com/blog/automated-customer-service

Vesel, P. and Zabkar, V. (2009). "Managing customer loyalty through the mediating role of satisfaction in the DIY retail loyalty program." *Journal of Retailing and Consumer Services*, 16, 5, 396–406.

Wassnik, B.K. (2021). "How can insurance protect the customers who need it most?" *EY, 21 Sept*, www.ey.com/en_us/insurance/how-can-insurance-protect-the-customers-who-need-it-most

WSJ.com (2021). "WSJ markets: JetBlue Airways Corp." www.wsj.com/market-data/quotes/JBLU/Financials/Annual/Income-Statement

7

SOCIAL CRM

FNB's Digital Marketing Innovation in South Africa

After almost two centuries of operations, in 2011 FNB (First National Bank), one of South Africa's largest national banks, faced pressures resulting from rapid advancements in technology. To differentiate itself, acquire customers, build stronger relationships, and live up to its positioning of "How can we help you?" FNB decided to engage in innovations with a particular emphasis on digital marketing and social media.

FNB's Digital and Social Media Innovation

As part of its digital innovation, FNB decided to concentrate on a dual-pronged strategy of developing innovative products and offering them through diverse channels, notably on social media. FNB also realized that to truly grow, they also had to educate and entertain consumers with respect to these innovations.

FNB introduced the following as part of its new digital innovation strategy:

- Online dotFNB banking
- Mobile handset and innovative mobile banking platform
- "EasyPlan" infrastructure
- Facebook transactional capabilities
- Rewards program
- Online cross-channel advertisements

FNB's Social Media Customer Relationship Management

FNB felt that social media would allow them to develop and enhance customer relationships through more effective campaigns for awareness, education, sales, and support. It wanted to implement social media as a "holistic channel rather than just as a marketing tool."

(Continued)

FNB decided to concentrate only on Facebook, Twitter, and LinkedIn based on their popularity and quality of communication. FNB created separate plans for each channel and interactions had to be customized to align with the channel's "intent and mood." This included analysis of competitor actions, identification of the strengths of each channel, decisions on when to activate each channel, creation of visual branding elements, marketing messages, and putting into place processes and people.

To humanize the brand promise of "How can we help?" a social media persona was developed. R.B. Jacobs was created with a particular tone of voice and look to match the helpfulness image FNB was trying to create. This persona would help disseminate brand stories and create engagement and trust. For timely dissemination of information on new products and campaigns the social media team also had to be in sync with marketing, public relations, and new product development functions. To deepen the alignment of social media with its digital strategy, FNB started incorporating social media into other online channels by using application program interfaces for different platforms.

Organizational Changes

To effectively support its digital and social media strategy FNB had to bring in a few changes to its organizational processes, structure, and culture.

To attract new talent and buy-in from different levels of the organization, FNB promoted itself as the "cool, hi-tech" company, created an innovative organizational culture by giving free rein to employees to be innovative, developed an "Innovators" Initiative Award for beneficial and trend-setting ideas, and even had the CEO personally respond to many consumer queries. In addition, agreements for social media service levels were made with all business unit heads and processes were put in place for sharing real-time feedback from customers with all these business units as well as with senior executives.

Financial Impact

The impact of the innovation-led digital and social media strategy was positive. Even though advertising expenses had moderately increased to implement the new strategy, pre-tax profits, return on equity, customer acquisition, and sales volumes also moderately increased.

Source: Mazinter, L., Kleyn, N., Goldman, M.M., and Lindsey-Renton, J. (2015). "Banking on social media (A)." ID: 9B14A070. Ivey Business School Foundation. Distributed by www.thecasecentre.org

---

Introduction

The global spread of the Internet and the rise of PCs and mobile devices have made social media ubiquitous. More than 90 percent of 5 billion global Internet users and 85 percent of 5 billion mobile phone users are active on social media (Dean, 2021). Social media has diversified into multiple types such as social networking, review sites, and ecommerce sites and each type has honed in on areas of specialization such as images for Pinterest and videos for YouTube. Companies have jumped on this trend with increasing spending on global social media advertisements standing at US$132 billion in 2020 (Statista Research Department, 2021b). Table 7.1 highlights different types of social media and examples of popular software platforms for each type.

Table 7.1 Social Media Types

Social Media Type	Characteristics	Popular Software Platform
Social networking service (SNS)	• Build personal connections and relationships among consumers who share similarities • Build professional connections among people • Build connections between businesses and consumers	• Facebook • Instagram • LinkedIn
Blogs and micro blogs	Websites that publish objective information on a topic in text format authored either by a single person or multiple people	• Tumblr • Twitter • Medium • WordPress
Media sharing	Applications that can share multimedia files such as audio, images, videos (short and long form)	• YouTube • Vimeo • Snapchat • Instagram • TikTok • Pinterest
Review sites	Websites where reviews about businesses, brands, products, and services can be posted and shared	• TripAdvisor (Travel) • Yelp
Discussion forums	Websites that allow contributions and discussions on topics and consumers can get answers to questions	• Reddit • Quora
E-commerce and social shopping networks	Websites that allow product sales (business2consumer and consumer2consumer) and sharing of recommendations	• Amazon • T-Mall (China) • Taobao (China) • LetGo • Etsy (unique products) • Faveable (Fashion)
Sharing economy networks	These communities allow sharing of products and services instead of selling them. Usually special interest based	• Uber/Lyft (ride sharing) • Airbnb (Lodging)

(Continued)

Table 7.1 (Continued)

Social Media Type	Characteristics	Popular Software Platform
Messaging apps	Mobile-based applications that allow sharing of information among consumers and from businesses to consumers	• WhatsApp • Messenger • WeChat
Social network gaming	Website that allows gaming within a social network	• Reddit • Steam • Twitch • RevHolics • Raptr • Facebook • Instagram
Virtual world	Computer-simulated environments where avatars (people and businesses) interact, communicate, and sell products and services	• Second Life • World of Warcraft • IMVU • Kaneva

Sources: Bump, P. (2021). "The 5 types of social media and pros & cons of each." Hubspot.com, July 21, https://blog.hubspot.com/marketing/which-social-networks-should-you-focus-on

Shayne. (2021). "13 types of social media you should be using in 2022,", invideo, Dec. 31, https://invideo.io/blog/types-of-social-media

Virtual Reality Society (n.d.). "Top 10 virtual worlds for adults." www.vrs.org.uk/virtual-reality-games/top-10-virtual-worlds-for-adults.html

Wikipedia (n.d.). "Social media." https://en.wikipedia.org/wiki/Social_media

Increasing social media usage has been both a boon and a challenge to companies, as detailed in the opening case. Even though time spent on social media and frequency of usage have been shown to positively impact consumption (Gupta and Aastha, 2019) and a good number of marketers have seen positive impacts of social media on revenues and market learning (Williams, 2019), it is also true that a significant number of companies struggle to prove the positive impact of social media to the broader organization (Williams, 2019). This reflects the complexity and challenge in managing social media's proliferating diversity, depth, and unique capabilities for profitably enhancing customer relationships. This is certainly accentuated when engaging in global CRM.

When deciding to utilize social media for CRM it is important to align it with offline CRM channels, such as sales and offline retail. Social media is uniquely complementary to offline channels, with different impacts on consumers. Research has shown that the impact of complaint resolution through social media on loyalty is stronger compared to offline channels (Sugathan et al., 2018).

The following sections will help us understand the diversity in social media, why it is important for global CRM, and how it can uniquely contribute to customer experiences and value creation.

Diversity in Types and Usage of Social Media

Many social media platforms such as Facebook, Twitter, and YouTube have a global reach. However, the popularity and extent of usage of particular social media platforms vary across countries, impacting availability and effectiveness. Two examples are China and India, which have the largest number of social media users. In China, compared to India, the T-mall e-commerce site is more popular than Amazon, and WeChat and Weibo are far more popular social networks than Facebook. In India the ride-sharing app Ola Share is as popular as UberPool.

Social media: Can be loosely defined as forms of Internet technologies that enable sharing of ideas, information, files and documents, and e-commerce, through virtual interactive networks (Dollarhide, 2021; Merriam-Webster, n.d.; Wikipedia, n.d.).

It is also important to understand why consumers use social media. In general it is to socially connect with other consumers, to gather information, to boost their public profile, and to mobilize around socio-political issues such as obesity and environmentalism (Wikipedia, n.d.). In a 2021 global survey on the usage of social media, almost 50 percent of respondents stated staying in touch with family and friends as their top reason for using social media (Statista Research Department, 2021a). This is not surprising given that humans are social animals. Table 7.2 highlights important reasons for using social media based on survey findings.

Table 7.2 Top Global Reasons for Using Social Media

Staying in touch with family and friends	Catching up with what's being discussed
Filling spare time	Getting ideas for things to do
Reading news and stories	Finding products to buy
Searching for entertaining content	Sharing opinions

Customer Engagement

Customer engagement is core to customer relationship management because it positively impacts consumers' attitudes and behavior towards the brand, in turn generating more trust, satisfaction, referrals, and continuing commitment (Carvalho and Fernandes, 2018).

Customer brand engagement has been defined as "a consumer's positively valenced brand-related cognitive, emotional and behavioral activity during or related to consumer–brand interactions" (Hollebeek et al., 2014: 154).

Social influence theory states that engagement is strengthened when consumers are exposed to information provided in a social context because of its influence on attitudes and behavior (Fulk and Steinfield, 1990). The diversity in the types of social media and the reasons for usage underscore why social media is uniquely engaging.

Social media allows the creation and sharing of user-generated content (UGC), interaction with community circles, and learning about news, entertainment, products, and services. These come together to create and bolster consumer engagement. Figure 7.1 illustrates the impacts of these social media behaviors on engagement.

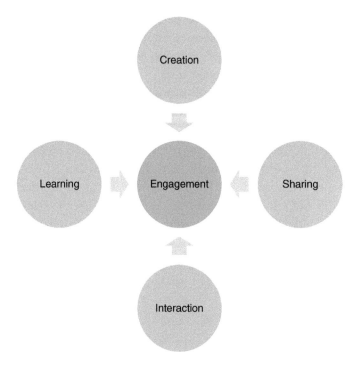

Figure 7.1 Social Media Behaviors

Research has shown that strategic social media CRM initiatives facilitate these behaviors (Demir and Selçuk, 2021).

Consumer engagement behaviors on social media are a multidimensional phenomenon with cognitive, emotional, and behavioral attributes (Hollebeek et al., 2014). Research on social networking site (SNS) Facebook has shown that there are three related factors that give rise to and impact these three attributes (Carvalho and Fernandes, 2018; Kujur and Singh, 2019). These are:

1   Content related factors (information and entertainment)
2   Social factors (group norms, social identity, involvement, brand representative and consumer interaction, interactivity, flow experience, and enjoyment)
3   Perceptual factors (perceived value of products and services, perceived credibility of information source)

The relative importance and impacts of these factors will vary based on a combination of country and the kind of product or service. Economy, culture, and demographic factors have significant impacts on social interactions, and individual consumer perceptions and consumption (Kanje et al., 2020).

Electronic Word of Mouth (e-WOM)

Engagement in social media is significantly impacted by electronic word of mouth and vice versa (Demir and Selçuk, 2021; Man et al., 2021). e-WOM has emerged in social media from the concept of traditional word of mouth where consumers share information and opinions face to face within their physical social network (Lis & Neßler, 2014).

e-WOM in social media can be broken down into four types (Chu and Kim, 2011):

1   *Opinion seeking*: Engaging in searching for more information
2   *Opinion giving*: Engaging in providing recommendations and advice
3   *Opinion passing*: Multidirectional sharing of information
4   *Endorsements*: Liking products, comments, and promotions and posts

More endorsement behaviors and opinion-seeking behaviors are observed in brand-initiated communities and more opinion giving and passing behaviors are seen in consumer-initiated communities. Importantly, opinion giving and opinion passing behaviors tend to grow where there is increasing involvement with and trust in the network.

The viral nature and impact of the spread of e-WOM is a result of the network effect. A social media network is "an enduring, self-selected group of consumers, sharing a system of values, standards and representations, who accept and recognize bonds of membership with each other and with the whole" (Veloutsou and Moutinho, 2009: 316). Taking the form of company promotions and responses, recommendations from influencers and positive comments, e-WOM spreads through different types of network to help generate confidence and trust in the brand (Liang and Yang, 2018; Voicu, 2020). This in turn positively impacts purchase intention, purchase decision, customer experience, satisfaction, and loyalty. The positive impact of e-WOM in social networks has been shown to be true for multiple products and services and across countries (Noor et al., 2021; Ruangkanjanases et al., 2021; Schijns and van Bruggen, 2018; Shih et al., 2018). The impact of e-WOM seems to be globally strong.

So what motivates consumers to engage in e-WOM? According to social exchange and social expectancy theories, e-WOM is regarded as a voluntary social exchange, and a consumer deciding to participate in e-WOM bases their decision on a cost–benefit evaluation of the utility of participation (Fishbein and Ajzen, 1975; Nusair et al., 2010; Kordzadeh et al., 2014). Costs and benefits can be cognitive, emotional, and behavioral. Research finds that this evaluation is centered around the following attributes (Carlson et al., 2018; Gvili and Levy, 2018; Hajli, 2018; Han et al., 2020; Madzunya et al., 2021; Prasad et al., 2017; Rebwar et al., 2020):

- Authenticity and credibility of e-WOM
- Usefulness of e-WOM, which depends on the attitude towards online information and the credibility of online information
- Interactivity
- Emotional ties to the network actors
- Trust in the network

The kind and extent of e-WOM behavior, however, is not uniform and is impacted by country and individual factors. The theory of reasoned action (Fishbein and Ajzen, 2010) helps us understand what factors underlie consumer beliefs and behavior about e-WOM:

- *Socio-cultural*: Education, age, gender, religion, ethnicity, and culture
- *Individual*: Personality, mood, emotion, values, general attitude, perceived risk, and past behavior
- *Information*: Knowledge of the topic, product/brand, media utilized, and type and frequency of e-WOM engaged in

Table 7.3 elaborates on this by highlighting 12 consumer motives for engaging in e-WOM.

Table 7.3 Motives for Engaging in e-WOM on Organizations

Positive e-WOM	Negative e-WOM
Help others	Help other consumers from experiencing problems
Help company	Resolution seeking
Express positive feelings	Express negative feelings
Help employees	Vengeance
Product involvement	Want to be heard by organization
Self-enhancement	Help company make changes

Source: Whiting, A., Williams, D.L., and Hair, J. (2019). "Praise or revenge: Why do consumers post about organizations on social media," *Qualitative Market Research*, 22, 2, 133–60. Used with permission of Emerald Publishing.

Global Issues Affecting Consumer Engagement and the e-WOM Phenomenon

Despite increased participation in e-WOM across the globe and similarities in the most important reasons for doing so, economy, culture, laws, and consumers shape e-WOM behavior across countries.

The stage of a country's economic development determines the extent of access to the Internet and whether it is via PC or mobile phone. A significant percentage of consumers in developing countries utilize mobiles to access the Internet and social media. Engagement and e-WOM vary between the two platforms because of differences in functionality and capability. For example, marketers can take advantage of a host of rapidly developing mobile applications for engaging customers through geofencing or geotargeting. Geofencing is a strategy of restricting communication with consumers within a locational boundary and geotargeting adds a layer of focus by lumping customer-based criteria such as age or specific interests with location. Mobile platform application CRM will allow an icecream shop in a mall to communicate information about coupons with icecream lovers who are already in the mall.

Culture, on the other hand, shapes the type of content that impacts engagement and e-WOM behaviors. What is being created and shared, the types of products being searched, the nature and extent of interactions and conversations, and the types of news, stories, and entertainment being sought are determined by cultural values and norms and vary across countries to some extent. For example, cricket is a popular sport in Australia but it is not in Korea where baseball is popular. This difference in culture will make a difference between the two in the content that will be created, shared, interacted with, and learned from in the sporting world. For a sporting goods manufacturer or retailer operating in both countries, the social media content strategies for engaging customers will be impacted by this difference. Additionally, cultural perceptions about social media usage and engaging with e-WOM, preferences for social media tools, communication patterns such as frequency of communication, usage of text vs. images vs. videos, tone and enthusiasm in e-WOM will also vary at the country level between Korea and Australia. For example, Asia as a whole and the Philippines as a country lead the world in social media usage time. Consumers in the Philippines spend close to 4.5 hours in one day on social media, which is 60 percent higher than the world average (Digital Marketing Institute, 2021). Chinese netizens tend to retweet much more frequently than their counterparts in other countries (Schaffmeister, 2015). In Indonesia, attitudes towards e-WOM and its usefulness impact participation, but in Thailand only attitude is important (Ruangkanjanases et al., 2021).

Even within a country, participation in e-WOM will vary across segments because of differences in consumer and product/brand characteristics and interaction between the two. Consumer demographic factors such as age, gender, and education, and psychological factors such as perceptions, attitudes, and personalities vary from segment to segment and these then interact with product/brand attributes such as complexity, the product's role in the consumer's life, and brand personalities to impact e-WOM participation.

Lastly even if economy, culture, and segment-specific characteristics allow very similar e-WOM behavior to potentially evolve across multiple countries, laws regulating social media activities and marketing could be different in these countries, impacting e-WOM behavior and social CRM strategies and forcing brands to adapt.

Customer Co-creation

The secret of increasing e-WOM engagement lies in the ownership of conversations on social media, which is firmly with consumers and not brands. The brand should not see this lack of control as a negative, however, but learn from it and take advantage of it by involving consumers further through co-creation.

Customer co-creation can be defined as active customer participation in marketing activities. Customers are actively recruited by brands to provide input into the design of products, brands, and packaging, the development of new service offerings, the personalization of product and service offerings, and the creation of new marketing communications (Yadav et al., 2016). Musicians have gone on Twitter to take suggestions from fans about album titles, and football clubs have solicited ideas about rebranding.

Social media creates a virtual eco-system that allows co-creation to happen. Co-creation helps bring companies and consumers closer together through mutually beneficial engagements. Social exchange theory states that consumers engage in co-creation for both internal rewards such as enjoyment, and external rewards such as recognition and monetary and career gains (Yadav et al., 2016).

There is ample evidence of companies increasingly engaging in customer co-creation and reaping benefits. To maximize the benefits of co-creation it is important for companies to incentivize customers in suitable ways.

Table 7.4 highlights a few examples of creative co-creation strategies.

Table 7.4 Examples of Customer Co-Creation Strategies

Company/Brand	Co-Creation Strategy
Pepsi India	"Crash the Pepsi IPL"
	A contest for consumers to create a 30-second YouTube commercial expressing their love of Pepsi and registering it at www.crashthepepsiipl.in. Winner's ad was played during live telecast of Indian Premier Cricket League*
Volkswagon China	To inspire audience to design their own personalized automotive ideas, share and discuss on a dedicated web platform (www.zaoche.en)&

Company/Brand	Co-Creation Strategy
Heineken	"Heineken Open Design Exploration Edition 1: The Club"
	Heineken invited a group of 19 emerging designers to create an innovative club concept in an online creative hub and share with Heineken fans. The end result was the Heineken Concept Club unveiled during Milan Design Week 2012[#]
DHL	DHL Innovation Centers where customers are invited to co-creation sessions to brainstorm new initiatives. One of the innovative outcomes was the "Parcelopter," a delivery drone[&]
Anheuser-Busch	Competition held between brewmasters, and tastings held among 25,000 consumers in 2012 to determine a new craft beer. This resulted in the creation of the golden amber lager "Black Crown"[*#]

Sources: [#] Livescault, J. (n.d.). "Customer co-creation examples: 12 companies doing it right." Braineet, www.braineet.com/blog/co-creation-examples

[&] Schaffmeister, N. (2015). *Brand Building and Marketing in Key Emerging Markets.* Cham, Switzerland: Springer.

[*] Yadav, M., Kamboj, S., and Rahman, Z. (2016). "Customer co-creation through social media: The case of 'Crash the Pepsi IPL 2015'." *Journal of Direct, Data and Digital Marketing Practice,* 17, 259–71.

Influencers

In a social network, e-WOM tends to spread faster with the active participation of a select set of users who create and share valuable information and opinions on topics, products, and brands more than others and whose created content is regularly followed and engaged with. These participants are known as social media influencers. Unlike traditional celebrity brand endorsers, social media influencers are experts in different industries, have made their careers in the social media world, create their own content such as blogs for sharing and are frequently hired as brand endorsers. Influencers regularly publish persuasive informational content that has both educational and entertainment value. Influencers have been shown to positively impact brand attitude, trust and equity, and purchase intentions (Jun and Yi, 2020; Pick, 2021; Taillon et al., 2020). In comparison to celebrity endorsers, they have also been found to have a broader impact on purchase intention relating to a brand (Cowen and Hunt, 2019 Sudha and Sheena, 2017). A study of the Indian tourism industry found that 71 percent of travelers were inclined to consider information, opinions, and recommendations of social media influencers before making a purchase decision (Dutta et al., 2021). The perceived unbiased nature of an influencer's e-WOM, their large following, and positive experiences with previous recommendations from the same influencer, were the reasons provided.

Social media influencers are a unique and interesting phenomenon in the digital world because in contrast to traditional WOM, consumers do not share a personal relationship with influencers but tend to find brand information coming from them as more believable than information coming from the brand itself. One explanation provided for the impact of an influencer lies in parasocial interaction which is a one-sided psychological relationship experienced by someone towards another person they have never physically met and are unlikely to meet (Lueck, 2015). In the case of influencers this phenomenon happens because of the combined impact of the influencer's perceived expertise, interactivity, authenticity, as well as attractiveness and likeability.

Identifying Influencers

Influencers exhibit behaviors differently from regular social network members and this helps marketers identify and recruit them. Influencers tend to score highly on the following six qualities (Agarwal and Mehta, 2020; Kumar and Reinartz, 2018; Myers, 2021):

1   *Connectivity*: Central location in the network. This is characterized by a significant number of connections to other members, other influencers in the network, and other related networks
2   *Activeness*: Characterized by a high frequency of engagement (posts and replies) and what would be reasonably considered long and sizeable postings based on the topic
3   *Spread*: Extensive sharing of e-WOM of an influencer far into a social media network
4   *Temporal*: Relatively long period of time over which the influencer's e-WOM is shared
5   *Clout*: Significant number of network members that follow and engage with the activities of the influencer
6   *Likeability*: High similarities with other members and strong attractiveness and emotional closeness felt by other members towards the influencer

TECH BOX: DIGITAL AVATAR INFLUENCERS ON SOCIAL MEDIA

In 2018, *Time* magazine named Miquela Souza one of the 25 most influential people on the Internet. By 2018 Miquela had acquired more than a million followers and in 2021 that number stood at 3 million. She has accounts on Twitter and Tumblr and is active on YouTube and TikTok. Miquela is not a real person.

Miquela was digitally created in 2016 by Trevor McFredies and Sara DeCou of Brud as an Instagram character with a fictional storyline using computer generated imagery (CGI). Miquela is a teenage Brazilian-American girl from Downey, California. As part of the narrative, in 2020 Miquela disengaged from her "human" boyfriend, another CGI character.

As a social media influencer Miquela has played multiple roles of social activist and music artist, but is most well known for being a fashion influencer. As an influencer in fashion marketing she :

- Collaborated with multiple fashion celebrities such as Diplo, Millie Bobby Brown, Nile Rogers
- Has been interviewed and featured in multiple publications such as *Vogue* and *The Guardian*
- Appeared on the cover of *Highsnobiety* as early as 2018
- Oversaw the Instagram account for Prada for Milan Fashion Week in 2018
- Was featured in a Calvin Klein advertisement with American model Bella Hadid
- Collaborated with Samsung
- Contributed as an arts editor for the British style magazine *Dazed*
- Signed a contract with American talent and sports agency CAA

Even though digital avatars like Miquela have and can be effective in social media marketing, ethical questions have arisen about their rise. These surround 1) how the inability of society to distinguish between what is real and what is fabricated impact the construction of identity and the preservation of social values such as transparency and trust in social media, 2) promotion of a certain beauty standard that may be unrealistic and 3) opportunities for real life fashion model influencers.

Sources: Robinson, B. (2020). "Towards an ontology and ethics of virtual influencers." *Australasian Journal of Information Systems*, 24, 1–7.

Wikipedia (n.d.). "Miquela." https://en.wikipedia.org/wiki/Miquela

Social Media Campaign Strategy

The discussion about Miquela Souza highlights social media's unique suitability to facilitate CRM. Marketers should take advantage of the unique capabilities of social media to empower participants through knowledge, to increase brand appeal and trust by humanizing the brand, and to enhance product experience through engagement, co-creation, access, and customer service (Gashaw et al., 2020). An effective social CRM strategy should rest on a five-pronged approach that needs to include the following critical components 1) engage in social media monitoring, 2) judiciously select social media tools, 3) create relevant, helpful, interactive and enjoyable content, 4) promote this content utilizing the selected social media, reinforced by influencers, and 5) facilitate purchase, consumption, return and recycling of products. Figure 7.2 illustrates the sequence of steps towards building a social CRM strategy.

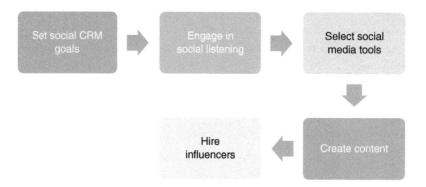

Figure 7.2 Social CRM Strategy Development Sequence

Engage in social listening and select social media tools: To select the most effective set of social media tools with a complementary set of features and capabilities it is important to have knowledge of social media usage patterns and trends. To gather this knowledge needs disciplined monitoring of what is being discussed and shared in social media, where, how much, how, and by whom. This step is crucial not only for determining the choice of tools and content but also for identifying influencers. In India social networking sites (Instagram), blogs, microblogs and YouTube are popular among travelers to seek out information on travel. (Dutta et al., 2021). If you are a hiking footwear brand social media planner you might want to:

- Monitor activities in a broad range of social media sites devoted to hiking and footwear such as blogs, websites, ecommerce and review sites
- Research search engine results and visit associated landing pages
- Follow information that would directly and indirectly be relevant such as opinions, conversations, and sentiments about company and products, and products and brands that are used together, such as hiking apparel and competitive promotions

Create relevant and engaging content: Content marketing plays a significant role in generating consumer engagement and brand trust (Martínez-Navarro and Bigné, 2017; Ramzan and Syed, 2018). Content that engages is enjoyable, credible, and useful (Man et al., 2021). In social media, marketing will depend upon brand and influencer reputation, entertainment value, and incentives provided. Creative and effective use of social media content marketing by India's Bollywood movie industry helped develop an emotional connection with the audience by allowing the audience to be immersed in the movie through identification with the main protagonist. The following types of content have been found to be most effective for engagement:

- Customizable content—e.g. gamification (Meenakshy et al., 2020)
- Customer co-creation—in the areas of product, packaging, logos, colors, jingles, etc. (Man et al., 2021)
- Content linked to the brand's identity and reputation—expertise, values, culture, and achievements (Artha et al., 2019)
- Promotions—"free products or price discounts," "giveaway contests/competitions," "access to the brand's e-shop/e-commerce site" or "publishing casual socialization content" or monetary and non-monetary draws/contests (Artha et al., 2019; Casaló and Romero, 2019)

Table 7.5 provides more examples of creative social media content to drive customer engagement and relationships.

Facilitate Purchase and Consumption—Social Media and Customer Service: Customer service on social media can be described as provision of customer support through social media channels such as social networking sites, blogs, and websites. Seamless online–offline customer service has improved service experiences by reducing time to purchase and consumption problem and solution. Social media automated customer service has created a win–win situation for both high value and lower value customers. It provides a more satisfying service experience by allowing customers to access quick solutions through social conversations with AI systems, which are far superior and more helpful than automated telephone customer service to which lower value customers would traditionally be shuffled to. Social media customer service has also taken an undue load off more expensive traditional customer service agents, allowing them to devote adequate time to high-value customers.

Social media can step in and provide a much cheaper and more engaging purchase and customer service experience in multiple ways. More specifically, social media can:

- Be part of an offline–online purchase and customer service continuum by identifying negative and positive conversations about the brand and taking pre-emptive steps to address them
- Create a separate handle for social media involved in purchase and customer service such as blogs, social networking, and websites
- Utilize intelligent artificial intelligence bots to quickly answer consumer questions and solve problems during and after purchase

While concentrating on social CRM through e-WOM it is important not to lose sight of traditional WOM through offline channels which complement the impacts of e-WOM. Research on 21 leading brands in a broad range of product categories that include technology, beverages, groceries, pain relievers, and beauty has shown that both offline WOM

Table 7.5 Creative Social Media Content Tactics

Content Type	Description	Brand Example
AMA (Ask me anything) session	Q&A sessions that help to share and show off knowledge and insights. This creates additional customer value	US Congresswoman Alexandria Cortez utilized the Instagram Stories' Question Sticker for Q&A on Covid-19
Social media takeover	Allow a client, user, follower, or influencer to showcase themselves through your social media account. This creates more engagement	Food Republic allows popular chefs to take over
Repurposing own content	Reformat and refresh content to highlight particular details such as converting long blog post into bite-sized videos on YouTube. This creates more value	First We Feast brand converts longer YouTube videos into bite-size previews
Spotlight on customers	Highlighting loyal customers' successes and rewarding them to create more loyalty	Sprout Social created and promoted case study on customer Tito's handmade vodka
Spotlight on team brand	Showcasing organizational teams that are behind the brand to create authenticity	Warby Parker creates amusement by sharing videos on office dynamics
Co-branding	Teaming up with another brand for a webinar, e-book, campaign or promotion to create more customer value	Levi's co-branded with Pinterest to offer visualized versions of individualized style experiences
Tutorials	Develop short how-to-do lessons to help create customer knowledge	Go Clean Company's cleaning guide videos
Product in unusual situations	Showcasing surprising situations with your brand to create engagement	Vessi Shoes creates video on TikTok of Starbucks coffee being poured on shoes

Sources: Barnhart, B. (2020). "20 social media ideas to keep your brand's feed fresh." Sproutsocial, August 3, https://sproutsocial.com/insights/social-media-ideas

Bernazzani, S. (n.d.). "21 examples of successful co-branding partnerships (and why they're so effective)." Hubspot, https://blog.hubspot.com/marketing/best-cobranding-partnerships

McLachlan, S. (2021). "29 creative social media content ideas you should try." Hootsuite Strategy, Sept. 13, https://blog.hootsuite.com/content-idea-cheat-sheet

and e-WOM complement each other to positively impact purchase intentions and customer loyalty, but they are different in nature. Traditional word of mouth has often been found to be more impactful (Fay et al., 2019). Nordstrom, the US upscale clothing retailer, faced significant negative e-WOM on social media when in 2017 they dropped Ivanka Trump's clothing line from the store. Ivanka Trump is the daughter of Donald Trump, then president of the US and the negative e-WOM likely stemmed from consumer perceptions of and associations with Donald Trump and his actions as the US President.

However surveys done offline showed stable and fairly positive consumer sentiment about Nordstrom. Nordstrom went on to increase their holiday sales that year by 2.5 percent compared to the previous year. It is thus important for marketers to create and coordinate marketing messages to stimulate both offline and online conversations to maximize the impact of overall word of mouth. This can be done by optimizing both offline and online customer touch points (e.g. in-store display and Facebook page) and determining what will drive conversations in and across both touch points.

Global Issues Affecting Social CRM Strategy

Given that the impact of country-level environmental factors and consumer characteristics creates differences in e-WOM behavior across countries, the type of social media tools that would be impactful, the optimum social tool set and the nature of content that would be effective will also vary to some extent from one country market to another. For example, India's unique cultural context provides strong opportunities for utilizing social media. Unlike teens in many other countries, teens in India tend to spend a large amount of their time at home instead of hanging out with their peers. A significant percentage of teens do not have their own rooms to withdraw into. Thus they tend to use social media heavily to avoid boredom and to mentally log out of their physical surroundings (Schaffmeister, 2015). The popularity of different social media varies across countries. This coupled with the varying capabilities of different media suggests that the optimum set of social media tools will differ to some extent across countries.

Content that informs, involves, and engages consumers will also likely vary from country to country given the differences in culture, consumer segment characteristics, and media capabilities. Young people in China tend to tweet and retweet considerably more than their counterparts in other countries. In both Russia and Brazil, however, blogs have taken on added significance but for different reasons. In Russia, consumers trust blogs more than print publications because of the government's relative lack of control over the Web, and in Brazil consumers use blogs to research products before purchase (Schaffmeister, 2015). Consumer perceptions of content related to languages, colors, and type of images also varies across countries forcing brands to make adaptations. A lot of Chinese consumers prefer to use Baidu (a Chinese search engine company) instead of Google because the former has done a much better job of reflecting the nuances of Mandarin Chinese (Schaffmeister, 2015). Prevalent technology infrastructure also makes a difference in both content and media choice. Videos may be more difficult to stream in some countries because of weak Internet connectivity, meaning that video making and sharing media would not be effective. Video contents thus may need to be replaced with images. This discussion and the examples indicate that global social CRM campaigns will need minor or major tweaks as brands roll them out in different countries.

Table 7.6 highlights a few examples of successful global social media campaigns.

Table 7.6 Social CRM Campaign Examples

Brand	Description
Kraft Bis Chocolate	"The Chocolate Tree" Campaign in Brazil positioned the mini Bis as addictive sweets which can be stolen. Utilizing Orkut social media platform Kraft created a "Happy Harvest" game where virtual cocoa seeds were sent to millions of online farmers who planted the seeds, which then grew into trees with mini Bis hanging fruits. If these were not harvested quickly they could be stolen by other farmers. Over 100 million seeds were planted in four weeks*
Ford India	"One Tank 1500 Kms one Classic Story" to promote the affordability of Ford automobiles. Eleven people were recruited through Facebook and given the new product- Ford Classic Titanium with a full tank of gas to go about and fulfill their dreams. A videographer was sent with each to create videos of their journey. These were then uploaded on social media and voted on for the best videographer[¹]
Dove	"Project#ShowUs": Intended to shatter beauty stereotypes, Dove partnered with Girlgaze, Getty Images to motivate women across the world to create and share a picture library of themselves[&]
Zalando	"Zalando's #styledayfriday": European fashion brand Zalando in combating a drop in fashion clothing sales during the pandemic promoted a weekly "get dolled up" challenge themes such as "Matchy Monochrome" and "Flower Power" and live content[Ω]
Shedd Aquarium Chicago	"WheresWellington": During the pandemic when the aquarium was closed to the public the Penguin caregivers took the penguins on a tour of the aquarium. As the penguins roamed and explored, followers on social media were able to learn about various exhibits[δ]

Sources: [δ]Chen. J. (2020). "Marketing campaigns & social media examples to inspire you in 2021." Sprout Blog, June 24, https://sproutsocial.com/insights/social-media-marketing-examples

[&]Law, T. (2021). "7 epic social media campaign examples you need to learn from." Oberlo, Feb. 18, www.oberlo.com/blog/social-media-campaign-examples

[Ω]Mclachlan, S. (2022). "7 Inspirational social media campaigns." Hootsuite, Jan. 4, https://blog.hootsuite.com/social-media-campaign-strategy

[*]Schaffmeister, N. (2015). *Brand Building and Marketing in Key Emerging Markets*. Cham, Switzerland: Springer.

[¹]Nagpal, P.A. (2012). "'One of our least expensive campaigns but one of the most rewarding': Anurag Mehrotra, Ford." Campaign India, Aug 27, www.campaignindia.in/article/one-of-our-least-expensive-campaigns-but-one-of-the-most-rewarding-anurag-mehr/417082

TECH BOX: SOCIAL NETWORK ANALYSIS TOOL

A social network analysis tool investigates relational structures of networks. It describes the structure of a network as well as analyzes the position of individual members within the network based on centrality metrics. This allows the tool to identify network influencers and to highlight opportunities for developing effective e-WOM strategies for CRM. It has been used in multiple disciplines and has significant benefits for social CRM.

The tool describes a network in terms of the following attributes:

- *Nodes*: Users discussing a particular topic or brand (the more the better)
- *Edge*: Number of separate discussions of a particular topic or brand (the higher the better)
- *Average degree*: Average number of relationships among network members (the higher the better)
- *Diameter*: Maximum distance between nodes in a network (the shorter the better for faster diffusion of information)
- *Average path length*: Average distance between nodes in a network (the shorter the better for faster diffusion of information)

It determines the overall centrality of members by utilizing the following types of centrality measures:

- *Degree centrality*: Measures the number of direct connections each member has with other members in a network
- *Eigenvector centrality*: Measures the degree to which a member with a high degree of centrality is also connected to other members in the network with high degrees of centrality. It essentially measures the direct and indirect importance of individual members through calculation of eigenvalues
- *Between-centrality*: Measures the number of communication paths that run through a particular node to reach other nodes compared to the total number of paths that allow these nodes to connect. In essence it determines if the member takes on a strategic "bridge" position in the flow of communication between networks

A member who is central to the network (high eigenvector centrality) and also has significant links to other networks (high between-centrality) has a high potential to be influential.

(Continued)

There are many software tools that help in performing social network analysis. Table 7.7 highlights some of the common ones.

Table 7.7 Social Network Analytic Software Tools

Gephi	AllegroGraph
Pajek	Social Network Visualizer
NetworkX	Graphstream
Tulip	Graphviz
Commetrix	NodeXL

Sources: Bhatia, R. (2018). "Top 7 network analysis tools for data visualisation." AIM, Nov. 9, https://analyticsindiamag.com/top-7-network-analysis-tools-for-data-visualisation

RankRed (2022). "23 Free social network analysis tools [as of 2022]." RankRed, Jan. 3, www.rankred.com/free-social-network-analysis-tools

Template. (n.d.). "5+ social network analysis tools & softwares." Template.net, www.template.net/business/tools/social-network-analysis

Wikipedia. (n.d.). "Social network analysis software." https://en.wikipedia.org/wiki/Social_network_analysis_software

Sources:

Febrianta, M.Y., Yusditira, Y., and Widianesty, S. (2021). "Application of social network analysis for determining the suitable social media influencers." *International Journal of Research in Business & Social Science*, 10, 6, 349–54.

Litterio, A.M., Nantes, E.A., Larrosa, J.M., and Gómez, L.J., (2017). "Marketing and social networks: A criterion for detecting opinion leaders." *European Journal of Management and Business Economics*, 26, 3, 347–66.

Case Study

Instagram Marketing Campaign in the Indian Market

In 2019 Swiggy decided to launch an Instagram marketing campaign in the Indian on-demand food delivery market. Swiggy, one of the biggest on-demand food delivery companies in India wanted to bolster their relationship with millennials to stay one step ahead of rising competition. Millennials are the primary target segment for on-demand food delivery given their high usage of the Internet and such services.

The goal of the campaign was to make Swiggy the preferred platform for on-demand food delivery among millennials by increasing the number of their Instagram followers through an engaging and memorable experience.

Swiggy named the marketing campaign "#SwiggyVoiceofHunger." The campaign utilized a less used feature of Instagram's messaging system: the voice note. The reason for using this feature was a uniqueness in Instagram's voice note feature. Each Instagram voice note resembles a specific shape. Different voice notes have different shapes and desired shapes can be created by saying particular words and phrases in a certain way. Swiggy was the first company to utilize this particular feature of Instagram in a marketing campaign in India. The company felt that tying in a less well known but unique Instagram feature to a campaign would create a buzz.

The Campaign

The campaign revolved around a series of challenges: to create particular food shapes using the voice note feature of Instagram. The winners would receive a whole year's worth of food vouchers.

Swiggy launched the campaign by sending out a nonsense voice note from its official Twitter handle and tying that to the campaign announcement. This action generated speculation among consumers as to the meaning of the nonsense voice note and helped create a buzz and engagement with the campaign.

In total Swiggy promoted five challenges. These challenges asked consumers to recreate the shapes of kebabs, nachos, shawarma, fish and a stacked-up set of 21 pancakes, with Instagram voice notes. To promote and popularize the campaign Swiggy also partnered with several Instagram influencers.

Impact

The ten-day campaign was successful. It generated over 15 million impressions and over 150,000 voice notes. Swiggy's reach on Instagram increased by 7,700 percent and its food delivery business increased by more than a fifth. Even consumers living beyond India—in Canada, Thailand, Japan and Italy—participated. It also attracted the attention of popular companies such as Netflix and Airtel which voluntarily participated. The "#SwiggyVoiceofHunger" was also honored with several awards at the 2019 Cannes Lions International Festival of Creativity and from Kyoorius.

Source: Nair, J. and Vasudev, B. (2020). "Swiggy's 'Voice of Hunger' Instagram Campaign." ID: 520-0084-1. IBS Center for Management Research. Distributed by www.thecasecentre.org

Summary

This chapter discussed the role of social media in global CRM efforts. The unique benefit of social media to CRM lies in its capability to increase consumer involvement and engagement and spread information and opinions rapidly and far through electronic word of mouth (e-WOM). The chapter described ways to harness this capability through content and influencer marketing. Brands need to create relevant, enjoyable, interactive, and enjoyable content to engage customers. Social media influencers can support the brand's social CRM by endorsing the brand through creation and sharing brand-related information and recommendations. The second part of the chapter discussed the core parts of developing a social CRM strategy. These include monitoring social media extensively to deeply understand types of conversations taking place, selecting an appropriate set of social media tools, and creating relevant and meaningful content.

References

Agarwal, S. and Mehta, S. (2020). "Effective influence estimation in twitter using temporal, profile, structural and interaction characteristics." *Information Processing & Management*, 57 (6), https://doi.org/10.1016/j.ipm.2020.102321

Artha, S.A., Hernández-García, Á., Acquila-Natale, E., & Lamberti, L. (2019). "What makes fashion consumers 'click'? Generation of eWoM engagement in social media." *Asia Pacific Journal of Marketing and Logistics*, 31, 2, 398–418.

Carlson, J., Rahman, M., Voola, R., and De Vries, N. (2018). "Customer engagement behaviours in social media: Capturing innovation opportunities." *Journal of Services Marketing*, 32, 1, 83–94.

Carvalho, A. and Fernandes, T. (2018). "Understanding customer brand engagement with virtual social communities: A comprehensive model of drivers, outcomes and moderators." *Journal of Marketing Theory and Practice*, 26, 1/2, 23–37.

Casaló, L.V. and Romero, J. (2019). "Social media promotions and travelers' value-creating behaviors: The role of perceived support." *International Journal of Contemporary Hospitality Management*, 31, 2, 633–50.

Chu, S.C. and Kim, Y. (2011). "Determinants of consumer engagement in electronic word-of-mouth (eWOM) in social networking sites." *International Journal of Advertising*, 30, 1, 47–75.

Cowen, K. and Hunt, L. (2019). "What Makes Digital Content Influential? A Comparison of Celebrities and Influencers: An Abstract", in P. Rossi and N. Krey (eds), *Finding New Ways to Engage and Satisfy Global Customers: Proceedings of the 2018 Academy of Marketing Science (AMS) World Marketing Congress (WMC)*. Cham, Switzerland: Springer, p. 541.

Dean, B. (2021). "Social network usage & growth statistics: How many people use social media in 2022?" BackLinko, Oct. 10, https://backlinko.com/social-media-users

Demir, D. and Selçuk, Y.Y. (2021). "The mediating role of consumer engagement in the effect of social media marketing on electronic word-of-mouth intention." *Business & Management Studies: An International Journal*, 9, 2, 649–61.

Digital Marketing Institute (2021). "Social media: What countries use it most & what are they using?" Nov. 2, https://digitalmarketinginstitute.com/blog/social-media-what-countries-use-it-most-and-what-are-they-using

Dollarhide, M. (2021). "Social media: Definition, Effects, and List of Top Apps." *Investopedia*, August 31, www.investopedia.com/terms/s/social-media.asp

Dutta, K., Sharma, K., and Goyal, T. (2021). "Customer's digital advocacy: The impact of reviews and influencers in building trust for tourism and hospitality services." *Worldwide Hospitality and Tourism Themes*, 13, 2, 260–74.

Fay, B., Keller, E., Larkin, R., and Pauwels, K. (2019). "Deriving value from conversations about your brand." *MIT Sloan Management Review*, Winter, 72–7.

Fishbein, M. andAjzen, I. (2010). *Predicting and changing behavior: The reasoned action approach*. Psychology Press.

Fishbein, M. and Ajzen, I. (1975). *Belief, Attitude, Intention, and Behavior: An Introduction to Theory and Research*. Reading, MA: Addison-Wesley.

Fulk, J. and Steinfield, C.W. (1990). *Organizations and Communication Technology*, Vol. 1. Thousand Oaks, CA: Sage.

Gashaw, A., O'Reilly, N., Finch, D., Séguin, B., and Nadeau, J. (2020). "The role of social media in the co-creation of value in relationship marketing: A multi-domain study." *Journal of Strategic Marketing*, 28, 6, 472–93.

Gupta, G. and Aastha, V.V. (2019). "Social media usage intensity: Impact assessment on buyers' behavioural traits." *FIIB Business Review*, 8, 2, 161–71.

Gvili, Y. and Levy, S. (2018). "Consumer engagement with eWOM on social media: The role of social capital." *Online Information Review*, 42, 4, 482–505.

Hajli, N. (2018). "Ethical environment in the online communities by information credibility: A social media perspective." *Journal of Business Ethics*, 149, 4, 799–810.

Han, J.A., Feit, E.M., and Srinivasan, S. (2020). "Can negative buzz increase awareness and purchase intent?" *Marketing Letters*, 31, 1, 89–104.

Hollebeek, L.D., Glynn, M.S., and Brodie, R.J. (2014). "Consumer brand engagement in social media: Conceptualization, scale development and validation." *Journal of Interactive Marketing*, 28, 2, 149–65.

Jun, S. and Yi, J. (2020). "What makes followers loyal? The role of influencer interactivity in building influencer brand equity." *The Journal of Product and Brand Management*, 29, 6, 803–14.

Kanje, P., Goodluck, C., Tumsifu, E., Mossberg, L., and Andersson, T. (2020). "Customer engagement and eWOM in tourism." *Journal of Hospitality and Tourism Insights*, 3, 3, 273–89.

Kordzadeh, N., Liu, C. Z., Au, Y. A., and Jan, G. C. (2014). "A multilevel investigation of participation within virtual health communities." *Communications of the Association for Information Systems*, 34, (Article 26), 493–512.

Kujur, F. and Singh, S. (2019). "Antecedents of relationship between customer and organization developed through social networking sites." *Management Research Review*, 42, 1, 2–24.

Kumar, V. and Reinartz, W. (2018). *Customer Relationship Management: Concept, Strategy and Tools*, 3rd edn, Springer, Germany.

Liang, X. and Yang, Y. (2018). "An experimental study of Chinese tourists using a company-hosted WeChat official account." *Electronic Commerce Research and Applications*, 27, 83–9.

Lis, B. and Neßler, C. (2014). "Electronic word of mouth." *Business & Information Systems Engineering*, 6, 1, 63–5.

Lueck, J. (2015). "Friend zone benefits: The parasocial advertising of Kim Kardashian." *Journal of Marketing Communications*, 21, 2, 91–109.

Madzunya, N., Viljoen, K., and Cilliers, L. (2021). "The effect of Instagram conspicuous consumptive behaviour on the intention to purchase luxury goods: A developing country's perspective." *South African Journal of Information Management*, 23, 1, 1267.

Man, L.C., Pires, G., Rosenberger, P.J., Wilson, K.S.L., and Chang, M.K. (2021). "The role of social media elements in driving co-creation and engagement." *Asia Pacific Journal of Marketing and Logistics*, 33, 10, 1994–2018.

Martínez-Navarro, J. and Bigné, E. (2017). "The value of marketer generated content on social network sites: Media antecedents and behavioral responses." *Journal of Electronic Commerce Research*, 18, 1, 52–72.

Meenakshy, M., Saxena, R., and Srivastava, M. (2020). "Gamification: Increasing electronic word of mouth in tourism." *SCMS Journal of Indian Management*, 17, 4, 51–62.

Merriam-Webster (n.d.). "Social media." www.merriam-webster.com/dictionary/social%20media

Myers, S. (2021). "Instagram source effects: The impact of familiarity and likeability on influencer outcomes." *Journal of Marketing Development and Competitiveness*, 15, 3, 50–5.

Noor, U., Kamal, N., and Rabbani, S. (2021). "Discovering the mediating role of electronic-word of mouth between consumers' attitude and purchase behaviors." *City University Research Journal*, 11, 3, 427–48.

Nusair, K., Hae, J.Y., Naipaul, S., and Parsa, H.G. (2010). "Effect of price discount frames and levels on consumers' perceptions in low-end service industries." *International Journal of Contemporary Hospitality Management*, 22, 6, 814–35.

Pick, M. (2021). "Psychological ownership in social media influencer marketing." *European Business Review*, 33, 1, 9–30.

Prasad, S., Gupta, I.C., and Totala, N.K. (2017). "Social media usage, electronic word of mouth and purchase-decision involvement." *Asia-Pacific Journal of Business Administration*, 9, 2, 134–45.

Ramzan, U. and Syed, A.R. (2018). "Role of content based social media marketing in building customer loyalty and motivating consumers to forward contents." *Journal of Internet Banking and Commerce*, 23, 3, 1–20.

Rebwar, K.G., Garcia-Perez, A., Dibb, S., and Iskoujina, Z. (2020). "Trust and reciprocity effect on electronic word-of-mouth in online review communities." *Journal of Enterprise Information Management*, 34, 1, 120–38.

Ruangkanjanases, A., Jeebjong, P., Natalia, N., and Sanny, L. (2021). "E-WOM and its impacts on purchasing behavior: A comparative study between Thai and Indonesian millennials." *International Journal of Electronic Commerce Studies*, 12, 1, 65–83.

Schaffmeister, N. (2015). *Brand Building and Marketing in Key Emerging Markets*. Cham, Switzerland: Springer.

Schijns, J.M.C. and van Bruggen, N. (2018). "The tower of eWOM through social networking sites." *Journal of Marketing Development and Competitiveness*, 12, 3, 95–101.

Shih, K-H., Sresteesang, W., Dao, N.T., and Wu, G-L. (2018). "Assessing the relationship among online word-of-Mouth, product knowledge, and purchase intention in chain restaurant." *Journal of Accounting, Finance & Management Strategy*, 13, 1, 57–75.

Statista Research Department (2021a). "Leading social media usage reasons worldwide 2021." Statista.com, Nov. 16, www.statista.com/statistics/715449/social-media-usage-reasons-worldwide

Statista Research Department (2021b). "Social media marketing worldwide—statistics & facts." Statista.com, Nov. 15, www.statista.com/topics/1538/social-media-marketing/#dossierKeyfigures

Sugathan, P., Rossmann, A., and Kumar, R.R. (2018). "Toward a conceptualization of perceived complaint handling quality in social media and traditional service channels." *European Journal of Marketing*, 52, 5/6, 973–1006.

Sudha, M. and Sheena, K. (2017). "Impact of influencers in consumer decision process: The fashion industry." *SCMS Journal of Indian Management*, 14, 3, 14–30.

Taillon, B.J., Mueller, S.M., Kowalczyk, C.M., and Jones, D.N. (2020). "Understanding the relationships between social media influencers and their followers: The moderating role of closeness." *The Journal of Product and Brand Management*, 29, 6, 767–82.

Veloutsou, C. and Moutinho, L. (2009). "Brand relationships through brand reputation and brand tribalism." *Journal of Business Research*, 62, 3, 314–22.

Voicu, M.C. (2020). "Research on the impact of social media on consumer trust." *Global Economic Observer*, 8, 1, 120–32.

Wikipedia (n.d.). "Social media." https://en.wikipedia.org/wiki/Social_media

Williams, R. (2019). "90% of marketers see revenue impact from social media, survey says." *MarketingDive*, May 7, www.marketingdive.com/news/90-of-marketers-see-revenue-impact-from-social-media-survey-says/554204

Yadav, M., Kamboj, S., and Rahman, Z. (2016). "Customer co-creation through social media: The case of 'Crash the Pepsi IPL 2015'." *Journal of Direct, Data and Digital Marketing Practice*, 17, 259–71.

8

CRM IN SMALL- AND MEDIUM-SIZED ENTERPRISES

Case Study

A Small Business Handles Digital Change in Germany

Since 2016 the advent of digital retailing in Germany forced many of the traditional smaller-sized independent specialized stores to close because of pressures on margins. Those that survived were located in the urban, highly populated areas in the country.

HKS-Dessous is such an independent retailer. The store was founded in Dusseldorf, Germany in 2000 and sells fashion lingerie and beachwear to women. The owner Nicole Busch was able to deftly adapt to the onslaught of digital commerce. HKS-Dessous was repeatedly voted in the top 10 lingerie stores in Germany and in 2015 was awarded the prestigious Star of Lingerie award.

Fashion Lingerie Consumer Behavior

According to Busch, women in Germany love to buy fashion lingerie and beachwear and are not willing to compromise even in financially hard times. This was reflected in stable sales of the category for over a decade. For such purchases women tend to prefer small and intimate stores. Lingerie and beachwear categories are considered the most personal of all fashion products and a significant percentage of women lack a strong body image, suffering from insecurities about it. Small retailers are thus better able to provide a desired user experience.

(Continued)

Transformation of the Fashion Lingerie and Beachwear Retail Industry

Changes in the fashion industry in 2016 brought about the increased presence of offline and online competition and a downward pressure on prices. More specifically:

- Fast fashion companies such as H&M and Zara as well as mid-tier fashion chains such as Esprit made major investments in the lingerie category
- The number of outlet malls that sold lingerie at vastly discounted prices increased
- Lingerie brands started to sell directly to the consumer through company-owned offline and online retail
- There was an increasing presence of online-only small independent brands selling fashion lingerie using e-commerce hubs such as Amazon, which introduced a lingerie category
- Online members-only shopping clubs such as brands4brands and Amazon's BuyVIP emerged, selling premium lingerie at discount prices
- The product life cycle of lingerie started speeding up because customers were demanding more and faster changes to collections. This created excess stock, increased costs, and uncertainty around sales

Beyond the impact of costs and prices, another reason for the demise of many small independent retailers was the inability to differentiate themselves. Differentiation demanded updates to store design and product presentations, maintenance of product quality, and training of sales and service staff to provide professional advice and care.

HKS-Dessous's Competitive Strategy

In order to compete effectively and grow in this changed competitive environment Busch utilized the following four-pronged strategy that helped her to control costs, increase sales, and differentiate her brand from the bigger mainstream competitors.

1. *Physical store location*: To be cost effective Busch chose a side street location of a premium part of Dusseldorf. Her premium value proposition meant she needed to be in the right part of town. Lingerie purchase is, however, intimate and pre-planned and thus a side street location not only preserved the intimacy of purchase but also saved Busch from the higher costs of a main street location.
2. *Products and services*: Understanding that her target segment consists of middle- and upper-class quality-conscious women, Busch made sure her value proposition differentiated her brand from others. The store was large and included spacious changing rooms, a waiting area, and a children's play area. Busch also hired and trained salespeople who were knowledgeable enough to provide adequate advice and care. A large assortment of products and outstanding and intimate customer service helped HKS-Dessous to gain the loyalty of her customers who were regular repeat buyers.

3   *Purchasing, stocking and merchandising*: The large assortment of styles, sizes, and combinations HKS-Dessous stocked forced Busch to be strategic about purchasing and stock keeping to maximize sales and minimize extra inventory which would then have to be sold at a discount. This needed a good understanding of customer preferences and purchasing skills. Busch carefully studied new collections and designs from catalogues and attended trade fairs in France and Germany. This not only allowed for the necessary touch and feel and comparisons, but also provided an opportunity to network with sales reps and designers to streamline her purchase and optimize stocks.

4   *Cross-channel selling*: Busch understood the importance of growing sales through the Internet and opened the HKS-Dessous website right from the beginning of her business in 2000. She also realized that her value proposition and target segment behavior made foot traffic into an actual store necessary for differentiation and customer loyalty. At the store the company could more effectively engage in both cross-selling and upselling, enhance customer experiences and increase sales. Busch thus decided to integrate the two channels. She kept on improving her company website to a full-fledged online store with additional service information. Her purpose was to convert higher online traffic into higher foot traffic. To extend online access Busch also started selling complementary products on two different ebay stores.

This combination of strategic moves allowed HKS-Dessous to compete based on access, quality, and customer purchase experience. Knowing she could not compete just on price with heavyweight competitors, Busch had to carve out a niche for her business and she was successfully able to do so.

Source: Tiemer, J., Kleyn, N., Guderian, C.C., and Bicam, P.M. (2017). "DKH-Dessous: A main street entrepreneur handling digital change." ID: 9B17M090. Ivey Business School Foundation. Distributed by www.thecasecentre.org

Introduction

In most countries small- and medium-sized enterprises (SMEs) comprise more than 90 percent of all businesses and make a significant contribution to economies, particularly in emerging and less developed countries. SMEs have also been increasing their presence in international business (Morais and Ferreira, 2020) and are a very important element of the global economy (Genc et al., 2019).

Despite their widespread existence, SMEs face multiple internal shortcomings different from their large counterparts that make it challenging for them to adequately meet increasing omnichannel consumer behavior and strong competition. The case of HKS-Dessous highlights some of these but also shows how SMEs can overcome these challenges by identifying opportunities for differentiation in value creation and by developing creative CRM strategies.

What defines an SME?

SMEs are small- and medium-sized businesses that have revenues and employees below a certain threshold. This threshold is not clearly stated in many countries, including the United States. In the European Union (EU), however, a company is considered a small-sized enterprise if it has fewer than 50 employees or a medium-sized enterprise if it has fewer than 250 employees, and annual revenues of less than €50 million (Liberto, 2020; Morteza and Nader, 2018). In many countries the SME category also includes micro organizations with up to ten employees.

Terms for designating small and medium sized companies are also different across countries. In the EU, and by the World Trade Organization they are termed SMEs but in the US these companies are called small- and medium-sized businesses (SMBs). In Kenya, however, they are called micro-, small- and medium-sized enterprises (MSME) and in India micro-, small- and medium-enterprise developments (MSMED) (Liberto, 2020). For the rest of the chapter the term SME will be utilized to refer to this category.

Unique CRM Challenges and Opportunities for SMEs

In many countries SMEs fail to compete adequately with large organizations because of a lack of strong market and customer orientation (Appiah-Adu, 1998; Konstantopoulou et al., 2019). The underlying reasons for this deficiency lie in characteristics of SMEs that are common across economies and that collectively act as barriers to developing market and customer focus (Elliot and Boshoff, 2007; Muhammad et al., 2019; Smith, 1997). These characteristics are highlighted in Table 8.1.

Table 8.1 SME Characteristics

Strategic Orientations	Knowledge and Skills
Orientation towards short-term sales instead of long-term customer retention	Inadequate managerial and technical skills
Lack of strategic marketing approach that includes segmentation, targeting, and utilization of the 4Ps of marketing for customer acquisition and retention	Inadequate marketing education
Lack of formal processes, structures, and reporting in running business operations	Inadequate data analysis
Lack of high degree of interest in utilizing technology for purposes of market data analysis and customer relationship development	Inadequate market knowledge

At the same time their relatively small size compared to large organizations can give SMEs the potential advantages of higher agility and flexibility to adapt to market forces. Once SMEs make a concerted effort to overcome the challenges stated above, their higher agility in making decisions and the higher flexibility to adapt to market changes should provide opportunities to create a more personalized customer experience and build more intimate connections with them.

Market Trends That Impact CRM in SMEs

In today's global world, SMEs face multiple evolving changes in business and consumer markets. It is important to have a good grasp of these so that they can identify opportunities for effective CRM initiatives. The list below outlines four global market trends that are impacting the success of organizations.

1   *Increased impact of technology on consumer behavior*: The rise of diversity in technology usage by global consumers on multiple platforms have made them increasingly comfortable in using technology to search for information, communicate, engage in transactions, and utilize technology-facilitated automation in products and services. This has changed consumers' overall attitude towards, and expectations of, technology

2   *Increased impact of social media on consumers*: Across countries social media has transformed the consumer's world in how they interact, search for information, perceive products and services, and engage in transactions and consumption. Its use is widespread in urban areas in both developed and developing countries. Close to 60 percent of the world population regularly use social media (Chaffey, 2022)

3   *Rising sophistication and expectations of consumers*: Increasing wealth, education and usage of social media has transformed the typical global customer. She is knowledgeable, confident of her desires, comfortable sharing her desires on social media and sophisticated in expectations of products and services, particularly in the experiential aspects of consumption. A global customer wants to be engaged by products and brands and desires a great experience in consumption. It is worth noting that the rise of a global customer segment does not belie the significant differences that exists among other segments and customers across countries

4   *Increased impact of technology on marketing activities*: As digital marketing becomes ever more important for businesses to embrace, the capabilities of technologies that enable and facilitate are becoming more sophisticated, user friendly and cheaper. The primary force behind this trend is the rise of the cloud-based software as a service industry that is fast becoming popular.

Strategic Initiatives for CRM

In their first step towards CRM, SMEs should undertake to develop a set of five strategic CRM initiatives that will address both the challenges and opportunities discussed above.

These initiatives collectively create a foundation to help develop and implement the process, people, and technology imperatives of CRM and achieve CRM goals of acquiring, satisfying, and retaining profitable customers. Figure 8.1 illustrates these strategic initiatives.

Figure 8.1   CRM Strategic Initiatives in SMEs

Before such initiatives can be developed it is important to understand the organizational areas and environmental factors that impact the success of this effort. These include leadership, human resources, marketing, finances, technology, competition, and value-chain relationships (Alshawi et al., 2011; Phayaphrom et al., 2021). Table 8.2 highlights a detailed list of these factors.

Table 8.2　Factors Impacting SMEs Success with CRM

Organization and Environment	Orientation and Capabilities
Size of the organization	Customer orientation and response
Business objectives	Customer knowledge management: data (quality and integration) and software (cost, complexity, and support)
CRM goals	Managerial skills
Technology infrastructure	Marketing, technology, and analytical skills
Supplier relationships	Social media adoption
Competitive pressures	Budget and available financial resources

Even though all of these factors impact CRM efforts across organizations of all sizes, the nature and extent of impact on SMEs tends to be different and more pronounced. For example, the significantly smaller budgets of SMEs and the relative lack of technical skills together tend to more significantly impact the rewards and risks of selecting a particular CRM software.

Entrepreneurial Marketing: CRM Strategic Capability

Two specific organizational orientations and capabilities have been shown to aid in the development of effective CRM strategies and processes. These are:

1　Market orientation and capabilities
2　Entrepreneurial orientation and capabilities

Market orientation helps create an organization-wide customer culture bringing a laser focus on customers and competitors, and developing capabilities to deeply understand customers and satisfy their needs and wants through marketing interventions. Entrepreneurial orientation helps identify hidden opportunities for acquiring and maintaining profitable customers and developing capabilities of innovating in value creation (Hinson, 2011). Together these can help SMEs adopt and implement entrepreneurial marketing (EM) for profitably managing customer relationships.

Entrepreneurial marketing (EM) refers to marketing interventions supported by entrepreneurial activities. EM is particularly applicable and beneficial for SMEs because it allows companies to take advantage of SMEs' higher operational agility and flexibility in decision making and support that by creatively leveraging limited resources for value creation (Hinson, 2011). EM for SMEs relies on more than the traditional 4Ps of marketing. For EM marketing to be successful, product, promotion, pricing, and place (distribution and retail) need to be complemented by purpose, practices, process, and people (Martin, 2009). Research has shown that EM allows SMEs to be "innovative, proactive, opportunist, risk taker and customer oriented," which has a positive and significant impact on market performance (Morteza and Nader, 2018).

Market Knowledge Management

To successfully implement entrepreneurial marketing for CRM, market knowledge is key. Market knowledge is created by capturing, storing, analyzing, and transforming environmental, consumer, and competitor information. This knowledge is essential to developing customer-oriented innovative solutions which are then used for marketing communications and interventions. In today's global world of technology, social media, and omnichannel consumer behavior, effective management of market knowledge requires SMEs to adopt information and communication technologies (ICT).

ICT integrates different forms of communication technologies such as telephone, television, radio, wireless, and computer with different types of enterprise hardware and software that allow storage, access, transmission, analysis, and manipulation of information. Adoption of ICT not only improves CRM performance through better management of knowledge, marketing, and customers but also improves the image of ICT in the eyes of SME leaders and employees (Hassan et al., 2019).

The following are specific requirements in ICT:

- A database to store information
- A CRM software suite that
    - Integrates marketing, sales, and customer service
    - Captures and analyzes customer information from across channels to facilitate the creation of knowledge
    - Facilitates relevant and customized customer communication and interventions

Market knowledge can benefit SMEs in specific ways in their CRM initiatives. Knowledge allows innovation in products and services and customization of marketing offerings, solutions, and communication. These strengthen the relationship with the customer by satisfying the consumer's stated and unstated desires and enhancing consumption experience. Done consistently this leads over time to a more positive perception of the product offering and customer loyalty (Phayaphrom et al., 2021).

Perception of the value of ICT and CRM solutions tends to be less positive in SMEs compared to large organizations. In many SMEs business and customer strategies are directed by owners who for a number of different reasons that are tied to budget, lack of adequate market orientation, and lack of sufficient technical and marketing knowledge, fail to view ICT and CRM solutions positively and are hesitant to implement them. Research has shown that as SMEs develop their innovation orientation their perception of the value of CRM systems also improves, leading to a higher likelihood of SMEs implementing ICT and CRM systems (Hassan et al., 2019; Nguyen and Waring, 2013).

Where a significant percentage of SMEs have adopted ICT systems in their daily operations, the adoption of CRM solutions and integration of the two still lag behind. Even though SMEs regularly collect customer data either through ICT or CRM systems, the lack of integration between different organizational systems and of sufficient knowledge of CRM create barriers in fully utilizing ICTs and CRM solutions to manage and improve customer relationships (Hassan et al., 2019).

Value Creation

The cornerstone of developing and sustaining customer relationships rests in creating superior value. This can be done through a combined effort of helping to create a clear and desirable brand value image through marketing communications, providing differentiated and innovative product and service offerings, and effectively managing customer engagement and consumption experiences. The last is considered the most important because engagement and experiences ultimately determine if customers will be loyal or not.

Value Creation through Engagement Management

An effective strategy that SMEs can use to enhance customer engagement is that of storytelling. Storytelling has become increasingly popular among marketers as a way to connect deeply with customers and differentiate their brands. It includes telling the stories behind the brand, all it stands for, all it does, and all it can be. The content of these stories helps create an emotional and personal connection between the brand and the consumers. Research has shown that personal connection is essential to customer engagement and engagement can lead to increasing revenue directly through repeat purchase and indirectly through referrals (Kemp et al., 2021). SMEs, unlike large organizations, are usually privately owned and operated by individuals and families. Their businesses are always more personal to them and so are their stories. SMEs are thus perfectly suited to take advantage of the power of storytelling. The relatively low cost of e-marketing and social media also makes it cost effective for SMEs. SMEs should however note that brand storytelling is most powerful when these stories are generated and shared by users of the brands rather than by the brand itself. Today's consumers tend to trust information coming from the brand less, and are much more readily moved by user-generated content (UGC) from other consumers, especially influencers. To strengthen and widen the impact of storytelling, however, SMEs should complement their own brand stories with those told by influencers. To engage in influential marketing, SMEs need to identify, hire and collaborate with local and regional influencers to share the brand story to their significant number of followers.

A well-told story has the power to increase the value of what the products offer. What makes a story powerful? It needs to be relevant, useful, relatable, meaningful, and very importantly genuine and unique to create a differentiated perception of the brand and generate memorable emotions. Given the importance of emotions in creating a personal connection between the brand and the consumer it is important to use emotions holistically in the stories. SMEs may not only want to induce positive emotions to fuel interest and excitement but also address negative emotions in terms of pain points or dissatisfaction that customers may have experienced. This helps in many cases to create a perception of genuineness and humility in the brand, to preempt future criticism and to address the challenges to a brand's reputation and image. Research identifies several forms these stories can take (Donotan, 2016; Lim and Childs, 2020):

- Solutions to consumer problems through tying in product benefits
- Ways the brand would address or have addressed ethical, societal, and environmental issues
- Guest posts from influentials
- Consumer criticism and complaints and addressing them

Market knowledge management done well provides material for storytelling.

Value Creation Through Experience Management

Providing a superior consumption experience is a multi-pronged strategy. It depends upon:

- *Brand image*: Increasingly sophisticated consumers are attracted to value-based brand images and so it is imperative for SMEs to determine what their brands stand for and the role the brands want to play in the lives of their customers and society. Even though today the Bath and Body Works company in the US is a large organization, it started off in 1990 in New York State as a stand-alone store with a simple mission of making consumer lives happier with fragrances. That has guided their operations and shaped their brand image in the last 30 years.

- *Innovative products and service offerings*: Products and services should provide solutions to life's problems through unique benefits. A small SME selling its locally manufactured yogurts and frozen desserts through its retail store can provide additional health benefits by adding healthy and tasty ingredients to its yogurts and incorporating events such as health talks and meditation sessions in its offerings.
- *Consistent quality and access to offerings*: Inconsistency in the quality and availability of products and services is the fastest way to detract from superior experiences of an otherwise innovative product. It is important to make sure not to let bad variability seep into product or service components—for example, inconsistent food and table service quality in a restaurant. Equally important is to make sure that popular items are regularly available so that customers are not repeatedly disappointed.
- *Engaging, meaningful and differentiated customer communication and customer service*: Product and service innovation, quality, and access need to be actively and regularly communicated to consumers to increase consumer knowledge and enhance perception. Engaging, meaningful, and customized communication facilitates the start of a personal, cognitive, and emotional connection between the brand and the consumer. This is reinforced over time with superior and empathetic customer service that helps solve customer problems. Together communication and customer service raise the quality of consumption experience.

Value Creation through Loyalty Management

Brand loyalty is the ultimate goal of a CRM initiative. Brand loyalty has been shown to increase purchase, reduce the operational costs of customer maintenance, and promote tolerance for price increases and a willingness to promote the brand (Biscaia et al., 2017).

There are two kinds of loyalty: attitudinal and behavioral. Attitudinal loyalty is characterized by a positive attitude towards the brand and a willingness to promote the brand to others. Behavioral loyalty is exhibited when customers repeatedly purchase a brand. Behavioral loyalty is significantly impacted by attitudinal loyalty (Biscaia et al., 2017).

Both are important for SMEs. The trust and satisfaction that is generated by customer engagement and experience help achieve attitudinal loyalty (Aobakwe et al., 2019). To get from attitudinal loyalty to behavioral loyalty SMEs need to develop and execute responsive and customized strategies that provide incentives to consumers to engage in repeated purchase.

Loyalty programs have been shown to be effective not only in increasing behavioral loyalty through repeat purchase but also in increasing attitudinal loyalty through enhancement of brand image and customer satisfaction. Loyalty programs have the added advantage of keeping customers continuously engaged and provide positive purchase and consumption experience. Behavioral data from the loyalty can be transformed into customer insight which can make future allocation of marketing resources towards marketing interventions more impactful (DeMoulin and Zidda, 2009). Examples would be offering loyalty card members extra quality guarantees for purchases and shorter turnaround times based on card member behavioral information. There is thus a competitive demand for loyalty programs in the SME industry, particularly on the retail side.

To offer a loyalty program, SMEs need to determine the requirements for operating a loyalty program as part of a CRM program. It is important to align firm, product, and consumer characteristics with these requirements. Micro firms with less than ten employees need to keep their loyalty program relatively simpler than medium-sized firms for ease of implementation. Effectively managing a loyalty program requires marketing management and technical skills to analyze market and transaction data, and develop customized communication. To facilitate program

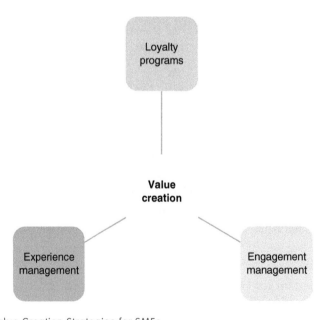

Figure 8.2 Value Creation Strategies for SMEs

implementation for SMEs with few technical resources there is plenty of technology support available in the form of CRM software from vendors (Hutchinson et al., 2015). (See the section on technology later in this chapter and more on loyalty programs in Chapter 6.)

Figure 8.2 illustrates the three related activities through which SMEs can create superior customer value.

Social CRM and E-marketing

A significant proportion of consumer purchase decisions globally are driven by social media. Whether a purchase happens at a physical store or online the decision process is impacted by consumer activity on social media. The establishment of a social CRM and e-marketing is thus an imperative for SMEs because without one these businesses are in the dark and unable to compete effectively (Henschen, 2012). The good news is that given the rapid rise of technology the management of customer relationships using social media is no longer expensive.

E-marketing and social CRM together allow SMEs rich access to consumers throughout their purchase decision process and a wealth of information. This presents multiple opportunities in the following value creation areas:

- Product and service innovations
- Innovation in transactions and interactions
- Customization and personalization of customer communication

Interactivity, the core of e-marketing and social media, can provide opportunities for differentiation and stronger customer relationships. Sharing information, telling stories, and interacting with customers via multiple social media platforms such as social networking, blogs, gaming sites and email, and utilizing banner ads on multiple websites to grab attention and interest, help improve engagement and experiences, and over time positively impact brand image and attitudinal loyalty (Law et al., 2013; Orenga-Roglá and Chalmeta, 2016). When a liked and trusted beauty influencer advertises an SME brand to followers on Instagram, it leads to increased awareness and an intention and willingness to purchase the brand (Konstantopoulou et al., 2019). Enabling transactions online and utilizing the Web for customer service such as AI bots provides convenience in purchase and in resolution of customer problems. This facilitates repeat purchase (Muhammad et al., 2019; Sharma, 2016). Over time effective e-marketing and social CRM help increase brand trust and satisfaction (Marolt et al., 2020).

The challenge here for SMEs is to manage this deluge of information to secure the benefits. Despite the relative ease of access to data on social media and online, integrating such data across media types and with organizational databases, analyzing and acting on them remain a challenge for SMEs given their limited resources (Hassan et al., 2019). This pain has been alleviated in recent years by a plethora of CRM solutions targeted particularly at the specialized needs of SMEs. More on that in the technology section below.

Collaboration

Generating differentiating value for customers in this complex and dynamic global economy forces organizations to consider every aspect of the value chain. Success for many organizations has come from forming alliances with entities in the value chain that can add to customer value: manufacturers offering complementary products and services, distributors, logistics providers, and retailers (Perez and Cambra-Fierro, 2015). Such alliances are particularly beneficial for SMEs given their limited resources. Reasons for SMEs to proactively consider collaboration with value-chain partners include (Perez and Cambra-Fierro, 2015):

- Economic performance, such as increasing flexibility and sales
- Innovating and improving processes
- Access to markets
- Brand positioning and image
- Stability and efficiencies

There are multiple instances of SME collaboration with larger organizations where the growth of SMEs has depended on these alliances (Ariño et al., 2008; Klijn et al., 2010). SMEs should also actively seek collaboration with other SMEs with complementary products and capabilities for mutual gain.

Communication and information exchange among partners is crucial to build and sustain the relationship in the alliance. Also joint projects on technology, product and service innovation, training, and marketing are beneficial. The social ties that result from these activities develop trust and commitment in the alliance. It is important, however, to keep in mind that selection of the right partners is key to gaining advantages from collaboration.

Bespoke Collection

Bespoke Collection's offers include fine wine and art. The US-based company strives to take every opportunity to enhance customer experiences through creating value. They do this by customizing the experience for the customer. According to Paul Leary, president and partner, "Bespoke, in essence is about tailored scenarios."

To be able to do that Bespoke partnered with Salesforce, a cloud-based software company. Salesforce's marketing cloud facilitates identifying, understanding, and attracting the right customers and building relationships with them via loyalty programs and memberships. The sales cloud facilitates customization based on customer activities. For example, it helps to determine whether to use a "welcome" or a "welcome back" greeting based on customer activities. Further, investment in social technology has helped the customization to be more meaningful by allowing it to be based on insights into customer interests rather than just on frequency of visits and purchase amounts.

Source: Salesforce (2021). "Building connections a glass at a time.", Salesforce.com, www.salesforce.com/customer-success-stories/bespoke-collection

Process–Technology–People Requirements

Successfully developing and implementing the CRM strategic initiatives discussed above depends upon the combined strengths of the process–technology–people tools of CRM.

Process

It is important for SMEs to consider the particularities of their strategic initiatives (e.g. What types of values do the organization plan on providing?) and fashion processes to align with them. What follows is a discussion of some core foundational processes that will facilitate implementation of the strategic initiatives. Each of them can be broken down into smaller sub-processes.

Customer value creation processes: These processes provide different ways of creating value for and with the customer, allowing for co-creation and co-production. While developing the different steps in these processes it is important to consider consumer definitions and expectations and how the consumer would like to engage with these processes. The customer not the product should be the focus:

- *Customer communication process*: This allows two-way interactive communication with the customer that facilitates need assessment, co-creation and complaint management. Personalized communication through multiple and desired channels is key.
- *Customer engagement process*: This facilitates sharing of relevant, useful, and engaging content from the brand, influencers, and consumers across multiple channels.
- *Customer complaint management process*: This allows communication and resolution of consumer grievances and complaints, aimed at improving customer consumption experiences, organizational operations, and product offerings.
- *Loyalty program process*: This process includes enrolling the customer into a rewards program, recording the customer's transactions and offering customized rewards based on them.

Marketing innovation processes: Marketing innovation processes support the value creation processes and strengthen customer loyalty and customer profitability. They are about improving ways of doing marketing activities and include adapting 1) the product and service functionalities to cater to customer desires, 2) distribution pathways and retail options and services for more convenient access to the product and service, 3) prices and price-based promotions for a more positive brand image, and 4) promotional channels to satisfy omnichannel consumer behavior. In many cases marketing innovation processes will require collaboration with value-chain partners.

Customer information management processes: The viability and effectiveness of the value creation and marketing innovation processes rely heavily on the quality of market information and its management. The process of customer information management consists of gathering, storing, analyzing, and transforming customer information from across multiple channels of communication and transactions to create actionable knowledge. Such knowledge is then used for customer retention through adaptation and improvements in engagement and customization of communication and offerings, and for customer acquisition by unearthing new segments to target.

Technology

Technology is a critical enabler of CRM processes (Marolt et al., 2020). In order to adequately manage market information, innovation, communications, transactions, and service it is necessary for SMEs to 1) create a relational database that contains and connects information on customers, and related operations such as purchases, returns, and complaints, and 2) implement a CRM software solution with integrated capabilities of marketing, sales, and customer service and align that with the company's database to maximize benefits. Software companies have come with a multitude of customizable offerings tailored to the needs of SMEs. Table 8.3 identifies and describes the top CRM software for SMEs.

Table 8.3   Best CRM Software for SMEs

CRM Software	Benefits
Freshsales	• Lightweight and simple to use • Comprehensive and customizable
Monday.com	• Project management customizable tools • Easy to use
Begin by Zoho	• Developed for SMEs • Sales pipeline based • PC and mobile compatible
Less Annoying CRM	• One of the most affordable • High flexibility and performance
Salesforce Essentials	• Condensed set of features aimed at SME needs

Sources: Rist, O. (2022). "The best small business CRM software for 2022." *PCMag.com*, Feb. 11, www.pcmag.com/picks/the-best-small-business-crm-software

Sirk, C. (n.d.). "12 best small business CRM 2022." CRM.org, https://crm.org/crmland/best-crm-for-small-business

People

One of the most common failures of CRM lies in the "people" prong of CRM. Despite the presence of effective processes and tailored technology, shortcomings in human resources have tripped up CRM initiatives of many companies (Nguyen and Waring, 2013). Despite the flexibility and agility of SMEs because of their smaller size, the "people" problem is particularly challenging for a significant number of SMEs because of the following realities (Hassan et al., 2019; Nguyen and Waring, 2013; O'Dwyer et al., 2009):

- The oversized influence of the owner on decisions
- An informal way of conducting business
- Relying on gut feelings instead of data to make decisions
- Reluctance of the owner to implement CRM processes and technology because of a poor perception of the value of CRM

- Lack of marketing education
- Primarily sales and supply (not customer) focused
- Limited resources

For SMEs to strengthen the people arm of CRM and make it capable and ready to administer CRM processes and technologies, they need to develop the following organizational culture and capabilities (Anderson and Wen-yeh, 2006; Aobakwe et al., 2019; Hotho and Champion, 2011; Hutchinson et al., 2015; Marolt et al., 2020; Nguyen, 2009):

- *Leadership*: Should support innovation and technology and recognize the importance of employees' contribution to the CRM effort
- *Employee engagement*: Leadership should engage employees as participants in the decision to adopt CRM; communicate to employees throughout the organization to create awareness of the CRM initiative and avoid misunderstandings
- *Management structure*: Leadership should establish a management structure that includes formal communication and reporting
- *Use of market information*: Leadership should set an example by accepting and utilizing market data for decision making and disseminating the new data across departments
- *Delegate responsibility*: Leadership should delegate decision-making responsibility to employees
- *Training and knowledge*: Leadership and employees should be trained in technology and marketing

Case Study

Small Business Expansion in the Indian Market

Facing increasing competition after multiple years of growth and popularity, Kapoor— the owner of My Kind of Cakes in Ghaziabad India—wanted to implement a strategy of growth. Based on his research on competitors' strategies, Kapoor had several options at his disposal. He had to decide which option or combination of options was the best strategy moving forward.

When he was 22 years of age Kapoor founded My Kind of Cakes in 2011 in Ghaziabad, India. He decided on the name of the store because he wanted to target the younger generation who were more interested in cakes and pastries than the older generation, and in spending time with friends at eateries. Kapoor hired two chefs and other employees. He trained his staff both on soft skills such as customer service as well as on hard skills such as using the store system and serving. Kapoor himself was also fully involved in specialized tasks such as customizing cake designs and creating unique cakes.

Value Proposition

My Kind of Cakes' value proposition was based on customization and customer service. Kapoor offered customized cakes with unique designs and in smaller sizes that other bakeries would not entertain. These designs were based on storylines provided by the customers. Kapoor carefully took notes of these storylines to best depict them. This made him indispensable during the order-taking process where many customers would not place orders if Kapoor was not present in the store. His presence thus also helped in further differentiating the brand and create brand loyalties.

Kapoor wanted "to create a fantastic experience every time a customer places an order." This included:

- Recognizing and greeting customers by name and remembering their desired customizations
- Offering free samples of specialty items whenever a customer visited
- Making special arrangements for parties
- Offering telephone ordering
- Making home deliveries which, depending on the order value, could be free
- Obtaining feedback from customers using paper or telephone surveys

Marketing Mix

My Kind of Cakes offered customized and standardized cakes in different sizes. Beyond cakes it offered other pastries and savories as well as non-food items such as dishes, candles, and decorative items that customers needed for parties. It was seen as a one-stop-shop for parties. Kapoor also took his love and expertise of photography to his customers by photographing occasions for them. They were happy to pay for this additional service.

My kind of Cakes mostly relied on word of mouth promotion. Products were also promoted through a Facebook page. A placard was sent with every order for events, which helped to promote the brand. At the store level an appealing display and an attractive ambience helped promote the value proposition.

My Kind of Cakes were competitively priced and provided a high-quality product at reasonable prices. Preferring to utilize the freshest of materials, Kapoor only started work on cakes after an order had been placed. The minimum cost for a cake for two people was INR (Indian Rupees) 150.

My Kind of Cakes had only one location in a side street in Ghaziabad. Despite its lack of prominent location it became a landmark in that community and during special holidays, such as Diwali, people would gather at the store to celebrate and socialize.

Customer Relationship Management Efforts

In an effort to develop and sustain strong customer relationships Kapoor maintained a database of customers and regularly communicated with them by email, on Facebook, and

(Continued)

using mobile apps such as WhatsApp, with information on discounts, free coupons, and other forms of promotion. My Kind of Cakes sent greetings to its customers through WhatsApp for special occasions such as birthdays and anniversaries and delivered free cakes to select customers.

Kapoor also took advantage of spreading the brand name around town by collaborating with nearby universities, schools, and large organizations to offer his products through their cafeterias. Kapoor's young age helped him to connect with the students. Faculty and staff also preferred to purchase from My Kind of Cakes for events held at their institutions.

Kapoor's value proposition, marketing strategies, and customer relationship management paid off over time. By 2016, the company's revenues increased three-fold to just under INR 20 million. Kapoor set his eyes on an objective of INR 50 million by 2020.

Competition

Kapoor faced increasing competition from new entrants and a new consumer environment. Consumer preferences for consumption of cakes and desserts were also changing including a heightened concern for health.

Kapoor did an analysis of the offerings of his strongest competitors. His research showed he provided good value from a pricing perspective. However, there were several strategies his competitors were using that gave them an edge over My Kind of Cakes, including:

- Digital and social media platforms for communication and transactions
- Reward programs
- Central locations
- Multiple outlets
- Express delivery
- Specializing in wedding cakes
- Designs based on characters

The Road Ahead

To achieve its growth objective Kapoor knew he had to venture out in one or more directions. Researching his closest competitors and their strategies provided him with the following options to pursue. Kapoor now had to decide which option would best grow his revenues and strengthen his brand:

- Geographic expansion into nearby towns
- Expansion of product range to include antigravity desserts and chandelier cakes which were becoming increasingly popular
- Creation of an overarching digital strategy including starting a loyalty program
- Incorporating a thematic photography option

Source: Kalia, S. and Puri, S. (2017). My Kind of Cakes: An expansion dilemma." ID: 9B17A024. Ivey Business School Foundation. Distributed by www.thecasecentre.org

Summary

This chapter was devoted to addressing CRM initiatives in small- and medium-sized businesses (SMEs). By their very nature and size, SMEs across the globe face a set of specific realities different from large businesses, which require a different approach to CRM. The chapter identified the unique challenges and opportunities for SMEs in managing customer relationships, developed a set of five CRM initiatives for SMEs including 1) entrepreneurial marketing, 2) marketing knowledge management, 3) value creation, 4) social CRM and e-marketing, and 5) collaboration, and discussed the process–technology–people requirements for implementing strategic imperatives.

References

Alshawi, S., Farouk, M., and Irani, Z. (2011). "Organisational, technical and data quality factors in CRM adoption—SMEs perspective." *Industrial Marketing Management*, 40, 376–83.

Anderson, R.E. and Wen-yeh, H. (2006). "Empowering salespeople: Personal, managerial, and organizational perspectives." *Psychology & Marketing*, 23, 2, 139–59.

Aobakwe, L., Mornay, R-L., and Hendricks, B.K. (2019). "The perceived influence of relationship quality on brand loyalty." *African Journal of Economic and Management Studies*, 10, 1, 85–101.

Appiah-Adu, K. and Singh, S. (1998). "Customer orientation and performance: A study of SMEs." *Management Decision*, 36, 6, 385–94.

Ariño, A., Ragozzino, R., and Reuer, J. (2008). "Alliance dynamics for entrepreneurial firms." *Journal of Management Studies*, 45, 1, 147–68.

Biscaia, A.R., Rosa, M.J., Moura e Sá, P., and Sarrico, C.S. (2017). "Assessing customer satisfaction and loyalty in the retail sector." *International Journal of Quality and Reliability Management*, 34, 9, 1508–29.

Chaffey, D. (2022). "Global social media statistics research summary 2022", Jan. 27, www.smartinsights.com/social-media-marketing/social-media-strategy/new-global-social-media-research/#:~:text=Networks%20vary%20in%20popularity%20with,27%20minutes%20(October%202021)

De Moulin, N.T.M. and Zidda, P. (2009). "Drivers of customers' adoption and adoption timing of a new loyalty card in the grocery retail market." *Journal of Retailing*, 83, 3, 391–405.

Donotan, S. (2016). "Why brands need to skip the ads and start telling stories." *Adweek*, www.adweek.com/brand-marketing/why-brands-need-skip-ads-and-start-telling-stories-170905

Elliott, R. and Boshoff, C. (2007). "The influence of the owner-manager of small tourism businesses on the success of Internet marketing." *South African Journal of Business Management*, 38, 3, 15–27.

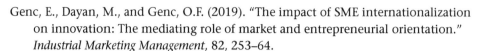

Genc, E., Dayan, M., and Genc, O.F. (2019). "The impact of SME internationalization on innovation: The mediating role of market and entrepreneurial orientation." *Industrial Marketing Management*, 82, 253–64.

Hassan, S.H., Haniba, N.M.M., and Ahmad, N.H. (2019). "Social customer relationship management (s-CRM) among small- and medium-sized enterprises (SMEs) in Malaysia." *International Journal of Ethics and Systems*, 35, 2, 284–302.

Henschen, D. (2012). "How to get from CRM to social." *Information Week*, February 15, www.informationweek.com/enterprise-applications/how-to-get-from-crm-to-social

Hinson, R. (2011). "Entrepreneurship marketing," in S. Nwankwo and T. Gbadamosi, (eds), *Entrepreneurship Marketing: Principles and Practice of SME Marketing*. Abingdon: Routledge, pp. 13–29.

Hotho, S. and Champion, K. (2011). "Small business in the new creative industries: Innovation as a people management challenge." *Management Decision*, 49, 1, 29–54.

Hutchinson, K., Donnell, L.V., Gilmore, A., and Reid, A. (2015). "Loyalty card adoption in SME retailers: The impact upon marketing management." *European Journal of Marketing*, 49, 3/4, 467–90.

Kemp, E., McDowell, P., Nwamaka, A., and Dong-Jun, M. (2021). "The impact of storytelling in creating firm and customer connections in online environments." *Journal of Research in Interactive Marketing*, 15, 1, 104–24.

Klijn, E., Reuer, J., Buckley, P., and Glaister, K. (2010). "Combinations of partners' joint venture formation motives." *European Business Review*, 22, 6, 576–90.

Konstantopoulou, A., Rizomyliotis, I., Konstantoulaki, K., and Badahdah, R. (2019). "Improving SMEs' competitiveness with the use of Instagram influencer advertising and eWOM." *International Journal of Organizational Analysis*, 27, 2, 308–21.

Law, A.K., Ennew, C.T., and Mitussis, D. (2013). "Adoption of customer relationship management in the service sector and its impact on performance." *Journal of Relationship Marketing*, 12, 4, 301–30.

Liberto, D. (2020). "Small and mid-size enterprise (SME)." *Investopedia.com*, Nov. 14, www.investopedia.com/terms/s/smallandmidsizeenterprises.asp

Lim, H. and Childs, M. (2020). "Visual storytelling on Instagram: Branded photo narrative and the role of telepresence." *Journal of Research in Interactive Marketing*, 14, 1, 33–50.

Marolt, M., Zimmerman, H-D., Znidarsic, A., and Puchihar, A. (2020). "Exploring social customer relationship management adoption in micro, small and medium-sized enterprises." *Journal of Theoretical and Applied Electronic Commerce Research*, 15, 2, 38–58.

Martin, D.M. (2009). "The entrepreneurial marketing mix." *Qualitative Market Research: An International Journal*, 12, 4, 391–403.

Morais, F. and Ferreira, J.J. (2020). "SME internationalisation process: Key issues and contributions, existing gaps and the future research agenda." *European Management Journal*, 38, 62–77.

Morteza, H.F. and Nader, S.A. (2018). "The effect of entrepreneurial marketing on halal food SMEs performance." *Journal of Islamic Marketing*, 9, 3, 598–620.

Muhammad, F.S., Muhammad, A., and Muhammad, A. (2019). "Perceived impact of e-marketing practices (EMP) by SMEs on customer relationships: Moderating role of security, privacy and weak infrastructure." *Global Management Journal for Academic & Corporate Studies*, 9, 1, 134–45.

Nguyen, T.H. (2009). "Information technology adoption in SMEs: An integrated framework." *International Journal of Entrepreneurial Behaviour & Research*, 15, 2, 162–86.

Nguyen, T.H. and Waring, T.S. (2013). "The adoption of customer relationship management (CRM) technology in SMEs." *Journal of Small Business and Enterprise Development*, 20, 4, 824–48.

O'Dwyer, M., Gilmore, A., and Carson, D. (2009). "Innovative marketing in SMEs: A theoretical framework." *European Business Review*, 21, 6, 504–15.

Orenga-Roglá, S. and Chalmeta, R. (2016). "Social customer relationship management: Taking advantage of Web 2.0 and big data technologies." *SpringerPlus*, 5, 1, 1462.

Perez, L. and Cambra-Fierro, J. (2015). "Value generation in B2B contexts: The SMEs' perspective." *European Business Review*, 27, 3, 297–317.

Phayaphrom, B., Wong, A., and Bhandar, M. (2021). "The SME survival model for the technology transformation era." *Journal of Management Information and Decision Sciences*, 24, 4, 1–8.

Sharma, N. (2016). "CRM—a tool of competitive advantage in modern management." *International Journal of Engineering Technology Science and Research*, 3, 3, 135–42.

Smith, D. (1997). "Small is beautiful but difficult: Towards cost-effective research for small businesses." *Journal of the Market Research Society*, 39, 1, 273–5.

PART III
MANAGING STAKEHOLDER RELATIONSHIPS

9
GLOBAL PARTNER RELATIONSHIP MANAGEMENT

International Partnership in the Aircraft Modification Market

Aircraft Maintenance and Engineering Corporation Beijing (Ameco) had grown steadily in the last couple of decades. It had built up a strong presence in the high-end manufacturing industry, particularly in the aircraft modification business. Its strength lay in localized management and cutting-edge technology. Apart from its main business of aircraft maintenance, Ameco also offers aircraft painting, engine repair, routine safety inspections, and business aircraft modification. However, in order to serve customers better Ameco consolidated all its multiple services into the business aircraft modification business. Around 2013 Ameco's business aircraft modification arm started to stagnate because of a decline of this industry within China and strong competition from multiple related industries. This is the story of Ameco's efforts to improve its business through international partnership.

Internationalization Efforts

Going international in the Asia Pacific region looked promising for business growth. The international aircraft service industry had significantly grown in nearby markets and many airlines were servicing their planes in these countries. Ameco had a cost advantage over other international suppliers and the more established competitors serviced much smaller aircraft.

(Continued)

Lacking the resources to enter into a wholly owned subsidiary in a foreign market and not finding other entry strategies such as licensing and franchising to be suitable, Ameco decided to export their services to international clients. Their plan was to set up contracts to service aircraft in China and send them back to their home location. Despite some initial interest Ameco was unable to land any business. When clients realized there would not be any local service, their interest significantly cooled. Ameco realized that despite their superior technology and lower prices, they needed a partner in foreign markets to be successful.

International Partnership: A First Unsuccessful Try

Seeing potential for a win–win collaboration, Ameco partnered with AAG, a US-based, renowned, Boeing-authorized aircraft modification company. Ameco would leverage the US company's expertise in interior cabin design, engineering, project management, and manufacturing while AAG seemed interested in boosting profits by utilizing Ameco's low-cost manufacturing. The two partners decided to collaborate on one-stop retro fitting services, design, technology, and project management. They also agreed to exchange information on each other's clients. When none of this materialized and Ameco learned that AAG had reached out to Ameco's clients in an effort to convert them Ameco felt deceived and retreated from the partnership. Ameco realized from this failure that it would not be attractive to other strong international competitors unless it strengthened its own competitiveness. It set about doing just that. In the ensuing years it significantly improved itself in the areas of infrastructure and employee skills. Ameco received both the Crystal Cabin and Red Dot awards and became the first Boeing-authorized conversion center in Asia.

A Mutually Beneficial Partnership

Hoping for a more successful second try, Ameco went into a partnership contract with LHT, a subsidiary of Lufthansa. LHT had significant advantages in channels, technical resources, design, and suppliers. LHT needed a partner in the Asia Pacific region to make itself more attractive. Clients could get their aircraft serviced regionally in China at Ameco's locations to save on extra costs for delivery. This would help the partnership to capture more of the international market share.

Having learned from its past mistake Ameco engaged in a year-long negotiation before signing the contract. The negotiation resulted in an agreement that included the following structures and policies:

- Specific terms of cooperation
- Modalities of reporting key progress
- Coalition committee
- Leadership and working groups from both sides
- Protection of core technologies and classified client information

To create a win–win situation the two companies established three groups targeting three areas of cooperation:

- *Group 1—Sales and marketing*: Exchange market, client, and project information, and build international brand image
- *Group 2—Project, process, and procedure*: Enlarge channels, production processes, and manufacturing technology standards that would allow Ameco to learn from LHT's experience in project management
- *Group 3—Design and R&D*: Learn from each other's design concepts—user experience expertise from LHT and knowledge of design preferences of Asian customers from Ameco

Small Hiccups but a Final Big Win

Sharing client information: Ameco was hesitant to share information because of its initial bad experience with AAG. However, once the board of directors of both sides were directly involved, collaboration went smoothly.

Design: The cultural philosophy towards design and specific design aspects differed significantly between the two parties. Ameco's design approach was subtle and was left to interpretation whereas the LHT's was more direct. Additionally, where the German company was inclined to include high-tech and smart elements in their design elements such as touch-screen-controlled lighting, their counterpart emphasized the esthetic aspects of Chinese culture such as bamboo. As the two parties worked towards understanding the differences, they were able to resolve their differences through an "East meets West" compromise design theme called Nature's Touch. This design ended up receiving multiple international design awards and recognition.

The success in collaboration in design gave Ameco reason to look forward to collaboration in market development and the technical capability to achieve competitive advantage in the global market.

Source: Chen, J., Li, C., Su, N., and Li, Z. (2020). "Ameco's international strategic alliance." ID: 9B20M204, *Richard Ivey School of Business Foundation*, Ontario, Canada. Distributed by www.thecasecentre.org

---

Introduction

In today's complex, highly competitive world of omnichannel marketing, many of the capabilities to create and deliver superior customer values and experiences lie outside the organization in the value chain. The value chain consists of organizations and channels that help to create, add to, and deliver the promised customer value and experience. Each value chain entity uniquely contributes to this effort through one or more complementary operations such as innovation, technology, research, finances, marketing, logistics, and customer service. For CRM to succeed it is important that firms, whether manufacturing or retailing, establish partnerships with value-chain entities and actively enrich these relationships. This proved beneficial for Ameco as discussed in the opening case of this chapter. Research and industry experience has amply shown that customer relationship management and organizational growth get a boost if organizations engage in nurturing partner relationships by finding ways to integrate and create entrepreneurial value (Bowen and Burnette, 2019). An interesting example is the successful Genius–Spotify partnership. Genius.com, a Web-based startup song lyric provider, partnered with Spotify, the popular music streaming service, to create the "behind the lyrics" project, a brand new idea of supplying additional details about singers, songwriters, albums, and so on to consumers. The reputation and reach of Spotify allowed the start-up company to proactively reach a large number of consumers, provide extra value to them, create a win–win situation for both partners and pre-empt competition (Rezazadeh and Nobari, 2018).

Value-Chain Partnerships and Partner Relationship Management

Value-chain partnerships (VCPs) can be defined as bilateral or multilateral collaborative arrangements between organizations in a value chain (Wolt et al., 2019). These relationships are formed with the aim of solving common problems and achieving the collective goals of enhancing customer experiences and market competitiveness (Morcillo-Bellido, 2019). To be beneficially sustained these relationships need to be actively managed by all participants.

Partner relationship management is a business model for developing strategies, processes, and systems to initiate and sustain mutually beneficial relationships among value-chain organizations.

The Importance and Role of Value-Chain Partners in Global CRM

Value-chain organizations individually and collectively add value to the consumption experience of the customer by performing interconnected value-chain activities spread across multiple areas. Table 9.1 highlights these areas.

Table 9.1 Value-Chain Activities

	New product development and innovation	Warehousing
Market research		
Research and development (R&D)	Manufacturing	Transportation
Information technology	Marketing communications	Retailing
Design	Professional selling	Customer service

Increasing access to technology and social media, and most recently the Covid-19 pandemic, have promoted omnichannel purchase and consumption behaviors, which have raised new expectations from customers in consumption areas such as delivery and product returns. In many fast growing emerging markets intense competition and higher volatility have created an increasing demand for more and differentiated resources to meet these new expectations in the hope of developing a competitive advantage. Such resources in many cases reside in strategic partnerships between value-chain organizations and are expressed in the synergistic impacts of a complementary set of knowledge and capabilities (Morcillo-Bellido, 2019). Research has shown that value-chain partnerships promote knowledge transfer and collaborative project management, helping to improve performance (Briones-Penalvar et al., 2020). For example, Phillips has created partnerships with a diverse set of companies such as Nike, LG, IKEA and Dell to enhance joint capabilities in new product development for new markets. Amazon has partnered with 7Eleven to improve its delivery options and 7Eleven's access to consumers. Amazon allows consumers to fund their Amazon accounts at 7Eleven. This provides 7Eleven with more foot traffic to its stores. Where there are no 7Eleven stores Amazon's website provides online sales opportunities to 7Eleven (Loza, 2017; Morcillo-Bellido, 2019). On average, a significant percentage of sales revenues of a brand can be indirectly attributed to contributions made by value-chain partners (Oracle.com, 2021).

Looking at value-chain partnership through the lens of the social exchange theory helps us better understand its role and the benefits it offers. Social exchange theory states that the formation of social relationships between partners contribute to long-term mutual benefits through impacts of social exchange factors such as attraction, mutual dependence, and positive collaborations (Yang et al., 2008). Social relationships also help partners to overcome market challenges and develop trust and commitment in due course (Morgan and Hunt, 1994). According to social exchange theory, the collaboration that characterizes social relationships leads to more stable partnerships (Bignoux, 2006). Mutually dependent, committed, and collaborative social relationships in a value-chain partnership also provide economic benefits by lowering transaction costs and increasing transaction value of operations by facilitating piggy backing on the capabilities of partners (Vrande et al., 2009). It is thus important to consider both economic and relational perspectives to holistically appreciate the benefit of value-chain partnerships.

As companies venture into international markets, partnerships with value-chain entities such as manufacturers, distributors, retailers, advertising and public relations agencies, and market researcher companies provide enhanced knowledge and capabilities in marketing communications and operations. Value-chain partners can thus be considered as essential pillars in achieving sustainable competitive advantages in global CRM. Table 9.2 highlights the environmental realities in global customer relationship management that make it imperative for organizations to seek out value-chain partnerships (Morcillo-Bellido, 2019).

Table 9.2 Environmental Drivers for Value-Chain Partnerships

Increasing globalization	Increasing competition in the value chain
Sophistication in consumer expectations	Resource limitations
Increasing technological development	Need for market expansion

Source: Printed with permission of IUP

Diversity in Global Marketing Channel Structures and Capabilities

Marketing channels consist of intermediaries that are part of the total organizational value chain and particularly facilitate the flow of finished goods, services, and communication between the manufacturer and consumer. Marketing channels thus play a direct and critical role in global CRM.

Economic development, culture, and laws impact multiple aspects of marketing channel structure, operations, and capabilities to create differences across countries (Zinfi.com, 2022). These differences impact the kind of role marketing channels play in global CRM initiatives.

Even though intermediaries are part and parcel of a channel structure across countries, the number of such intermediaries within the channel structure (in other words, the length of the marketing channel) and the kind of functions they perform varies. A distributor in many countries will both stock and distribute the product locally whereas in other countries they may simply stock the product. Retail structures too vary across countries. In developed countries in general retail is far more organized and centralized compared to the fragmented nature of retail structures in many developing countries. In the former, particularly in the US, Canada, and Australia, large national retailers dominate whereas in the latter small- and medium-sized mom and pop stores are the norm. Many advanced economies such as some in Europe fall somewhere in between.

Differences also exist in the type and quality of operations of intermediaries. Intermediaries by the same name (e.g. retailers) may provide different levels of support for sales and service, the quality of which may also vary. In many countries retailers do not hire salespeople and simply wait around passively for customers to inquire and purchase. Many forms of service support, such as product returns or multiple forms of payment option, are not provided by retailers in many countries.

Culture's Impact on Partner Relationship Management

Integration and collaboration between partners have been shown to be core aspects of successful partner relationship management (Cao and Zhang, 2011; Leuschner et al., 2013). However, differences in cultural norms and values make it more complicated to develop and manage value-channel partnerships across countries (Zinfi.com, 2022). Research indicates that cultural forces impact partnerships by impacting involvement, team work, communication, information sharing, risk taking, trust, and stability (Cao et al., 2015; Wolt et al., 2019). Specifically, differences in perceptions, attitudes, and partner tactics have been shown to negatively impact partnerships through exacerbating conflicts in the areas of technology, norms, and emotions (Liu et al., 2020).

Impacts of national culture on consumers and businesses are commonly seen through the lens of established cultural dimensions developed by Geert Hofstede on which countries vary. Impacts of these have remained reliable and valid over time. Table 9.3 identifies these dimensions (Hofstede et al., 2010). Chapter 2 provides more details on each of them.

Table 9.3 Geert Hofstede's Cultural Dimensions

Individualism–collectivism	Uncertainty avoidance
Power distance	Masculinity–femininity
Short- and long-term orientations	Indulgence

In most developed and individualistic countries where business culture is more policy based, transactions and relationships happen on fairly straightforward guiding principles and policies. On the other hand, in emerging countries with more collectivist cultures, just the merit of the value proposition is in many cases less important than the relationship for transactions to happen smoothly. In relationship-oriented countries with higher corruption and a specific set of ethical principles, value-chain operations are guided by power-based relationships which become complicated and expensive to manage.

As uncertainty avoidance increases in a country businesses tend to favor less risk and desire, more structure, procedure, control, and more detailed analysis of situations in order to avoid risks. Businesses tend also to keep more secrets and share less information with partners. This tendency of risk averseness in trust can be overcome in collectivist cultures such as in China and in more feminine cultures such as Turkey through reciprocal network relationships. However, in individualistic cultures such as the USA and masculine cultures such as Germany—where partnerships are viewed as more transactional than relational and businesses more aggressively pursue individual versus collective benefits—such a tendency to be risk averse towards trust is aggravated. Mutual dependency in value-chain partnerships is also difficult to achieve in high power distance countries such as Mexico where power differential is expected and partners showing a desire for mutual dependencies will be perceived as not competent. Opportunistic actions commonly happen in such countries. On the other hand, countries with long-term orientations, such as Japan and Korea, commit to long-term benefits and hence have a tendency to make more relationship-specific investments for mutual benefits. Building integration and collaboration in value-chain relationships between partners with different national and corporate cultures thus needs cross-cultural adapted management strategies for addressing issues of communication, involvement, trust, and continuity (Wolt et al., 2019). Alignment in overall values, vision and objectives for the alliance is critical for cross-cultural partnership success (Kanchel and Kahla, 2021). Conflicts will still happen but adopting a more cooperative conflict management strategy versus a more competitive one has been shown to be more effective in cross-cultural partner relationship continuity (Liu et al., 2020). Figure 9.1 illustrates the impacts of culture on value-chain relationships.

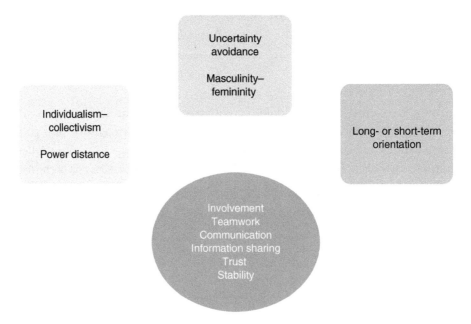

Figure 9.1   Cultural Impacts on Value-Chain Relationship Aspects

Quanxi and Business Relationships

In China, quanxi plays an important role in society both in personal lives and business partnerships (Barnes et al., 2011). It has been defined as "an interpersonal relationship that binds partners with a range of mutual obligations, expectations, and favors" (Xue et al., 2018).

Quanxi is considered a multidimensional concept and impacts through a synergistic combination of its components. Quanxi consists of three elements: mianzi (face), reciprocal favors, and affect (Kipnis, 1997). Quanxi as a business and political tie is seen as a form of social capital. If quanxi is high between value-chain partners it motivates them to take care of each other when in need.

Research has shown the multiple benefits of quanxi. Quanxi encourages partners to extensively exchange information, increases absorptive capacity for knowledge, strengthens inter-firm cooperation and trust, lowers the negative effects of opportunistic behavior that can easily crop up in cross-cultural value-chain relationships, and positively impacts partnership performance. Quanxi does not stop conflict from happening but if two parties have a high quanxi between them it convinces them that it is important to find constructive solutions to conflicts for fulfillment of mutual goals and long-term relationships. For successful partner relationship management in China, quanxi is indispensable because it promotes cooperation rather than competition (Barnes et al., 2011).

Managing Partner Relationships

Success and Failure in Partner Relationships

Given the importance of partnerships for customer relationship management and organizational growth and competitiveness, it is important to understand why some partnerships are successful and why many fail. Researchers and practitioners both say that a significant percentage of value-chain partnerships fail and a good percentage fail to achieve their goals (Morcillo-Bellido, 2019). Research has investigated the most important reasons for the failure and the success of partnerships. Academics and practitioners agree on the importance of such factors for partnership success (Alkaabi et al., 2021; De Backer and Rinaudo, 2019; Famakin et al., 2012; Morcillo-Bellido, 2019). Table 9.4 highlights these factors.

Many of the factors reflect corporate culture, which is influenced by national cultural elements. Culture and other global business environments tend to further complicate and heighten the impacts of these factors for cross-cultural partnerships (Kanchel and Kahla, 2021; Ozorhon et al., 2010; Samanta and Singla, 2019).

Table 9.4 Reasons for Success or Failure of Value-Chain Partner Relationships

Environmental contingencies
Cultural fit
Pressure to rapidly implement partnership
Employee rewards tied to implementation time frame criteria vs. other more holistic criteria
Involvement of senior management
Implementation of standardized vs. customized solutions
Analysis of potential conflicts and risks
Alignment of common objectives
Internal and partner communication
Partnership governance processes
Ability to make quick changes as needed to succeed

Partnership Management Capabilities for Competitive Advantage

The impact of a multitude of factors on partnership success makes management of partner relationship a complex initiative. The capabilities view of the firm advocates that organizations consciously develop the particular skills and abilities highlighted in Table 9.4. The core of partnership success lies in the extent of integration and collaboration, and the management of knowledge. The organization's relational capacities and abilities to manage knowledge within the alliance are thus the two most important partnership management capabilities (Chon and Shin, 2021). Structure, tools, and processes need to be in place to facilitate the development of these capabilities. Learning from repeated experiences with partner relationship management across countries helps sharpen these capabilities. Seen in the light of the resource-based view (RBV) of the firm, partner relationship management capabilities are beneficial resources that are not easily imitated and can help achieve competitive advantage in the CRM world (Ralston et al., 2020). RBV states that firms can derive advantages of higher performance from differentiated and heterogeneous resources (Barney, 1991).

Imperatives of Managing Partner Relationships

The overarching imperative is to build integrative processes that will facilitate the relationship. Integration between partners includes the three prongs of managing 1) collaboration, 2) end-to-end processes alignment, and 3) knowledge to optimize the total value in the value chain (Bowen and Brunette, 2019). Collaborative integration usually starts at the strategic level where a clear and unified understanding is developed of the value that each partner contributes to customer relationship management and then moves down to the operational level where activities are managed across multiple value-chain processes such as marketing, supply chain, manufacturing, new product development, and data management. For example, customer service may need to address both customer and partner inquiries, joint programs on promotions and training may need to be developed, and IT may need to work on integration of partner interfaces (Oracle.com, 2021). Research has shown that this active integration in managing risks and opportunities in global marketplaces increases trust and satisfaction with the relationship, helping it to thrive longer (Prihandono et al., 2021). Figure 9.2 illustrates the three prongs of collaborative value-chain integration.

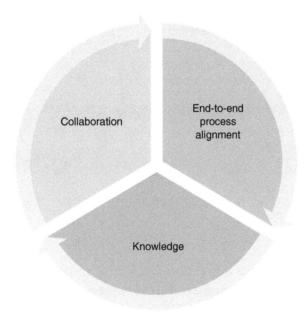

Figure 9.2 Imperatives of Collaborative Integration in Partner Relationship Management

Before starting on the process of developing, managing, and deepening partner relationship management, it is important first to find the right opportunity in the market and if and where a value-chain partnership would be beneficial, and then second to find the right partner—one that is a strategic fit and who will help take advantage of the opportunities. Good-fit partners should have the right "capabilities, culture and a willingness to engage" (Salesforce.com, 2017), so it is important for organizations to define priorities for partnership, segment the partner market, and create good-fit partner profiles (Gainsight.com, 2022; Morcillo-Bellido, 2019).

Process of Partner Relationship Management

Once prospective partners are identified it is important for organizations to do the due diligence of rigorously following the process of partner relationship management. The next few sections discuss the requirements for the steps in this process (see Figure 9.3) and a comprehensive picture of the elements and steps of the value-chain partner relationship management process.

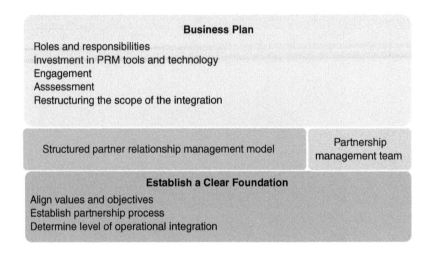

Figure 9.3   Elements of Partner Relationship Management Process

Establishing a Clear Foundation

One of the major reasons for the ultimate failure of partnerships is the rush to get into one without the prospective partners taking the time to get to know one another well and mapping the collective journey (De Backer and Rinaudo, 2019; Gainsight.com, 2022). It makes sense to set up a clear and common foundation on which the partnership can securely rest. This will help to bridge the ideological, cultural, and procedural gaps between the organizations (Schmid and Almog-Bar, 2020). Setting up a foundation includes aligning values and objectives, determining the level of integration, and agreeing on processes that will guide the partnership.

Aligning Values and Objectives

Reaching a state of shared values and coherence in the overall mission and goals of a partnership is important for streamlining agreements on processes, reducing conflicts, and facilitating management of the partnership. This effort also addresses attitudes towards the partnership and getting buy-in (Hsu and Tang, 2019).

To determine shared values and goals it is important to know the potential partner organizations well. Efforts should be made to understand each other's organizational culture and attitudes, gauge cultural similarities, compatibility, and complementarity, and assess capabilities and competence (Gao et al., 2017; Morcillo-Bellido, 2019; Rezazadeh and Nobari, 2018; Sanyal, 2018). This knowledge helps the negotiating parties assess each other's integrity, reputation, and objectives for the partnership which are key for successful governance of a collaborative partnership (Hsu and Tang, 2019). Both financial objectives, such as revenues and growth, and non-financial intermediate objectives, which directly impact achievement of the financial objectives, should be negotiated (Gainsight.com, 2022). Some examples of non-financial areas that impact CRM and on which objectives should be shared are resource sharing, customer acquisition, customer retention, innovation, portfolios, customer lifetime value, and customer success.

Establishing collective objectives for the partnership requires active involvement of both top leadership and operational personnel. This helps organizations to be on the same page strategically and operationally, signal partnership orientation, allay concerns, increase the likelihood of buy-in, and showcase robust bargaining power. To increase buy-in and bargaining power, research suggests showcasing capabilities in marketing, financial management, and technical support and services (Lee and Yan, 2019).

It is at this stage, after the objectives are agreed upon, that the following issues should be addressed (*InformationWeek*, 2001):

- Resource contribution from either partner towards fulfillment of common objectives in forms of technology, finances, employees, marketing, and sales
- Identification of potential conflicts and deviations, creation of contingency plans, and agreement upon policies for exiting the partnership

Establishing Partnership Processes

Successful partnerships agree upon a set of processes that will facilitate management of the alliance. These should include at the minimum the processes for:

- Negotiation
- Integration
- Operations
- Assessment (*InformationWeek*, 2001; Morcillo-Bellido, 2019).

Partners should compare, align, streamline, and simplify operational processes. Mapping the collective partnership journey identifying integration in tactics, technologies, and workflows is essential for a shared understanding and for enhancement of customer relationship management (Gainsight.com, 2022).

Determining the Level of Operational Integration

Strategic integration is established when shared objectives are established. To determine and negotiate optimum levels of subsequent operational integration it is important to carefully consider the collective objectives and contribution of resources from each side (Bowen and Burnette, 2019). The complexity and difficulty in integration will depend on its extent.

Mapping the value chain, identifying opportunities for creating joint value in that chain, and aligning them across organizations in the partnership help determine the extent of operational integration needed to provide the value proposition to the customer and create an economic benefit for all partners. If the primary objective for the partnership is innovation in the product sphere it will need more focused integration than exploring a new market for growth. The former will likely include integration in new product development, end of product life, demand management, commercialization, and customer relationship management whereas the latter will require integration across additional operations such as supply chain, manufacturing, sales, and order fulfillment. Depending on the extent of integration, organizational structure, policies, roles, and reporting will also need to be aligned. Additional considerations include differences in culture and capabilities, and their impacts on requirements for integration (Saleforce.com, 2017).

Once the partner relationship foundation is successfully established, it needs to be nourished and managed for sustenance. To do that partners need to set out a partnership management model and a business plan.

Structured Partner Relationship Management Model

A structured model helps to streamline the management so that the partnership works efficiently and effectively. This involves creating a management system where partner organizations are brought into the fold of the focal organization's strategies, processes, operations and structure through an alignment design (Morcillo-Bellido, 2019). This model will depend on the extent of integration that has been negotiated.

Partnership Management Team

The complex task of managing a partnership demands a team effort. It is imperative to form a team that will closely monitor and coordinate partnership operations and progress. To make sure that the team's efforts are taken seriously and their input is heard, it is important to have someone from corporate leadership teams to head the partnership team. To ensure the quality of the integration team members should be cross-organizational and cross-functional (Bowen and Burnette, 2019).

Business Plan

A detailed business plan with operational details on the following areas is necessary for providing clarity and details on joint partnership operations, for supporting smooth operations and workflows, and to avoid conflicts from arising.

Roles and Responsibilities

For smooth joint operations it is important to clearly define who performs and is responsible for which parts of the operation. This is particularly important for cross-cultural partnerships where misunderstandings can easily happen because of culture-based norms and expectations, creating undesirable gaps in processes and operations, and lowering their effectiveness (Kanchel and Kahla, 2021). Clearly defined roles help avoid conflicts and also identify and establish accountabilities, incentives, and employee development.

Investment in PRM Tools and Technology

Effective processes are made efficient through technology. For the partnership to contribute to customer relationship management in timely and smart ways, it is important to streamline and support aligned processes and operations by adopting technology. To bring partners into the fold of global CRM initiatives, organizations and their partners should adopt partner relationship management (PRM) technology that is aligned to their CRM technology tools (see the PRM software section below).

Engagement

Collaborative integration with partners should be actively nurtured. This requires change management efforts. A variety of developmental, digital, and personal interactions throughout the partnership structure should be part and parcel of this change management effort. These interactions also have the benefit of positively shaping customers' perceptions of the focal brand (Salesforce.com, 2017):

- *Investment in personnel*: Motivated and capable employees in a partnership are assets. Providing monetary and non-monetary incentives, facilitating joint operations in manufacturing, sales, distribution, and customer service by equipping employees with technology tools and enhancing skills and capabilities across partner organizations through training on technology or languages are essential investments in increasing motivation (Salesforce.com, 2017; Sanyal, 2018)

- *Knowledge sharing*: Successful partnerships know that without establishing a process for knowledge sharing and motivating everyone to share that knowledge, alliances will fail (*InformationWeek*, 2001). Sharing knowledge provides a diversity of ideas, makes employees more knowledgeable, and helps partner organizations and teams to be on the same page on CRM initiatives. All of this helps avoid costly mistakes and revisions. (Alkaabi et al., 2021; De Backer and Rinaudo, 2019)
- *Social connections*: To build trust in a partnership the organization should provide opportunities for executives and employees at all levels to socialize across the partner organizations. In successful partnerships only about 40 percent of all meetings are on business-related issues. The rest of the time is spent on connecting socially and building friendships (De Backer and Rinaudo, 2019)

Assessment

To make sure that collective partnership objectives are being met it is important to assess performance periodically at specific time periods in the relationship. Both financial and non-financial metrics that assess intermediate and final performance tied to shared objectives need to be agreed upon as well as the baseline values of these metrics. To facilitate and simplify the handling of the complexities of ongoing assessment of the partnership, partners should develop a measurement framework and rubric to generate a realistic progress report (*InformationWeek*, 2001).

Restructuring the Scope of Integration

Global market environments such as technology, competition, laws, and consumer behavior change over time, impacting market opportunities across countries. This has implications for value-chain partnerships. It is important for partners to regularly revisit their relationship structure and determine if the scope and nature needs to be reset or renegotiated or if it is time to exit the relationship (De Backer and Rinaudo, 2019). This helps to prevent the unintended breakdown of the partnership, which has negative impacts. The need to restructure the partnership will depend on its initial scope. A partnership involving the development of complementary products might need less restructuring than one that involves developing joint technologies.

Table 9.5 identifies critical success drivers for managing partner relationships discussed in this chapter.

Table 9.5 Critical Success Drivers for Partner Relationship Management

Detailed and codified partnership system based on previous partnership experience
Function dedicated to partnership support
Process for managing knowledge and learning
Risk analysis prior to partnership formation
Negotiation of entry and exit conditions
Post-partnership analysis
Partnership management separate from daily operational management
Dedicated partnership team manages the relationship process
Senior management does not impose partnerships
Senior management support for partnership execution

Success Story

Implementing Total Value Optimization

A global organization providing high-tech solutions and products had a network of 1,500 suppliers. As a result of lack of collaboration between leadership and cross-functional teams the value-chain network was neither efficient nor effective, costing the organization time and money. The following problematic symptoms surfaced:

- Established new product development policies were not being followed
- Procurement systems and processes were not rigorous
- Visibility of the end-to-end supply chain was poor

Initial analysis by an external consultant showed that the underlying problem was the way interactions with suppliers happened. The process was dominated by sales and engineering, had limited business rules and no accountability.

To correct this problem and achieve the vision of an innovative manufacturer the organization decided to apply the total value optimization approach (TVO). This involves aligning strategies and managing operations and knowledge flows, both across multiple functions within the organization and across external value-chain stakeholders to achieve shared goals based on a common understanding of the total value being created in the chain.

To implement TVO the company took the following steps:

- Leadership created a global, unified vision
- Leadership was aligned with well defined business rules
- Analytics were established to provide better end-to-end visibility of the value chain
- A new procurement management operating system was implemented to improve relationships in the value chain and bring in sustainability
- Roles and responsibilities were clearly defined across the organizations

(Continued)

- Processes for customer service, new product development, cross-functional sales, inventory, and operations planning were revamped to improve operational efficiencies
- Key performance indicators (KPI) were agreed upon

These steps benefited sourcing, manufacturing, and collaboration across all operations leading to higher financial and operational performance, visibility, and relationships in the value chain.

Source: Bowen, S. and Burnette, M. (2019). "Redefining the value from end-to-end integration." *Supply Chain Management Review*, March/April, 36–41.

PRM Software Solutions

Managing the complexity in integration and collaboration in global value-chain partnerships effectively requires a helping hand in the form of partner relationship management solutions.

Partner relationship management solutions are technology applications that consolidate and simplify how value-chain partners work with each other. These have been around for the past three decades and used by large companies for vendor relationship management but it is only recently that they have captured the interest of different industries and companies of all sizes.

PRM solutions can help the partnership to realize the full benefits (Oracle.com, 2021). A PRM solution provides a platform for cross-partner communication and knowledge sharing. It helps each partner to have a view of the other's operations that are part of the integration and to be on the same page in terms of progress (e.g. at what stage a customer is in her purchase journey, or a product is in development, manufacturing, and distribution). It also allows partners a shared view of upcoming opportunities in the channel and of which partner is taking the lead and what kind of role they are playing (McHugh, 2019). A PRM automates all of the above, allows self-service into joint operations and provides the opportunity for people in the relationship to concentrate on more strategic and relational activities. Panasonic Toughbook Europe uses Oracle's PRM to facilitate access to its distributors on market support, leads, and deals and enrollment in Toughbook University, a self-paced in-depth training program on how to use, market, and sell Toughbook devices (Banks-Louie, 2019).

A typical PRM solution includes the following functionalities:

- Partner recruitment and onboarding
- Deal registration and lead management
- Account and territory management
- Incentives and rewards management
- Marketing development and co-branding
- Training and certification
- Partner communications and reporting

Forward-looking organizations have recognized that blending PRM and CRM provides a better experience for partners and hence customers (Salesforce.com, 2017). PRM built into a broader CRM system allows partners to act on CRM issues and facilitates a more collaborative go-to-market strategy.

Given the evolution in the PRM solutions industry there are plenty of vendors to select from. The choice should be determined by the functionalities needed given the level of integration and collaboration desired in the partnership. It is important to:

- Recognize that all systems partners will need to access functions such as sales and marketing, content, IT, pricing, and inventory
- Organize data across these systems
- Work with partners to assess these systems for functionality, data accessibility, performance, scale and mobility
- Identify the desired information on deals and opportunities that will be available on a dashboard to be accessed through a centralized access portal (Oracle.com, 2021)

Table 9.6 highlights some popular PRM solutions.

Table 9.6   Partner Relationship Management Software Solutions

PRM Software*	Description
PartnerStack	Automates the most challenging parts of launching the partnership and scaling
Impact.com	Purpose-built global platform manages all kinds of value-chain relationships
ZINFI	Cloud-based unified channel management platform that seamlessly works with existing infrastructure
Impartner PRM	Fastest growing and most award-winning platform that helps companies globally to drive demands and revenues through indirect sales channels
Zift Solutions	Enterprise channel management leader that automates marketing, sales, and operations and integrates with existing systems
Allbound PRM	Mobile-friendly partner portal that arms partners, resellers, and distributors with content, training, and campaigns
Everflow	A partner marketing platform that goes beyond managing affiliates by tracking all channels, integrates tech and analyzes what delivers ROI
OneAffiniti	Global service-enabled technology platform that creates customized and scalable channel marketing programs to boost growth for brands and partners
Sales Cloud PRM&	Easy-to-use cloud-based platform for improving channel sales and identifying business opportunities
PartnerLinQ	Cloud-based supply chain visibility platform that integrates multi-tier supply chain networks, channels, and marketplaces with enhanced visibility and connectivity

Sources: *g2.com (2022). "Best partner management software." G2.com, www.g2.com/categories/partner-management
& Gartner Peer Insights (2022). "Partner relationship management application reviews and ratings." Gartner, www.gartner.com/reviews/market/partner-relationship-management-applications

TECH BOX: OPENPATH-CHANNELTIVITY PRM SUCCESS

Openpath is a fast growing player in the corporate physical security market and sells its groundbreaking technology only through integration partners. Given the importance of skills and knowledge in successfully selling this product, Openpath determined that training and certification of its partners was a core mutual objective that would help create a win–win situation for customer development.

To reach this objective Openpath chose Channeltivity's PRM solution. Not only did Channeltivity have competitive pricing and value-added resources for a comprehensive integration portal, they made interacting with them a helpful experience and provided assistance from adoption to launch.

Apart from its Training and Certification module, Channeltivity PRM also offered the following functionalities to facilitate the partnership between Openpath and resellers:

- Lead distribution
- Content use tracking
- Deal registration

Since launch, not only did Channeltivity help get all of Openpath's resellers trained, it made a first strong impression on the end users, who valued Channeltivity providing an opportunity to reconnect with Openpath.

Source: Channeltivity.com (2019). "Case studies—Openpath." Oct 17, www.channeltivity.com/customers/openpath-channeltivity-case-study

---

Case Study

International Retail Partnership

Kroger Inc., the largest supermarket chain in the US, formed a partnership with Alibaba, the Chinese e-commerce giant.

Heated competition in the grocery industry in the US was pushing companies to look internationally for growth. The biggest of these international markets is China. However, given the significant cultural differences between the US and China, few US companies were able to successfully compete in the Chinese market. To overcome this difficulty some of them were looking to form alliances with domestic Chinese companies.

Additionally, the future of grocery competition will be played in the e-commerce arena and so bricks and mortar retailers like Kroger had started to strengthen their online business through tie ups with e-commerce companies. This trend took off sharply with Amazon's purchase of Whole Foods Grocery in the US market.

A Win-Win Relationship

The partnership with Alibaba would allow Kroger to sell its private and organic brand Simple Truth on TMall Global, the Chinese e-commerce store for international products. Launched in 2014 TMall Global would be the biggest business-to-consumer (B2C) online retail market which would allow international brands which did not have footprints in China to sell to the Chinese. The mutually beneficial Kroger–Alibaba partnership would allow:

- Kroger to strengthen its digital business
- Kroger to compete more effectively with other US-based and international supermarkets
- Kroger to strengthen growth in one of the top markets. The Chinese increasingly purchase online, are attracted to healthy food choices, and have a positive perception of quality of western grocery brands, a desire borne out of some level of distrust in the safety of local Chinese brands
- Kroger to maintain its market leadership
- Alibaba to project a stronger image in the Chinese grocery market through offering international grocery products
- Alibaba to strengthen its relatively weak presence in the US market

The alliance allows Kroger to sell directly to TMall Global's buyers which includes third-party sellers and to benefit from Alibaba's strong capabilities in omnichannel marketing such as its online expertise, Alipay online payment systems, logistical and home delivery, and high-tech automated supermarkets. The alliance allows Alibaba to combine its online, offline, and logistics activities.

Industry experts said that even if the partnership did not turn out to be that successful Kroger would be benefiting anyway from trying something new and gaining experience in international investment and international consumers. This would by itself prepare Kroger better for future internationalization efforts.

Source: Javalgi, J. and Bhagyalakshmi, K. (2019). "Kroger partners with Alibaba for online retail in China." ID: 319-0035-1, Amity Research Center Headquarters, Bangalore, India, Distributed by www.thecasecentre.org

Summary

This chapter has discussed global partner relationship management. PRM is about developing and managing relationships with value-chain partners with the aim of facilitating global CRM and creating mutual growth. Partner relationship manage-ment is considered an essential supplement to CRM where value-chain partners integrate and collaborate to enhance customer experiences and relationships. The chapter addressed strategic concepts of PRM, the role value-chain partnerships play in global CRM, and the impact of culture on PRM. The chapter provided a detailed guideline on managing global partnerships through developing and implementing the partner relationship management process. The chapter ended with a discussion of technology solutions that lend vital support to PRM.

References

Alkaabi, K.M., Al-Shami, S., Rafeea, S.J., and Adil, H. (2021). "Causes of strategic alliance failure among healthcare partners: The role of knowledge sharing in alliance performance - a revew paper." *Journal of Legal, Ethical and Regulatory Issues*, 24, 1–10.

Banks-Louie, S. (2019). "Customer platform helps Panasonic crush Europe's rugged device sector." *Forbes*, Jan. 23, www.forbes.com/sites/oracle/2019/01/23/customer-platform-helps-panasonic-crush-europes-rugged-device-sector/?sh=62008e7f280d

Barnes, B.R., Yen, D. and Zhou, L. (2011)."Investigating guanxi dimensions and relationship outcomes: Insights from Sino-Anglo business relationships." *Industrial Marketing Management*, 40, 4, 510–21.

Barney, J. (1991). "Firm resources and sustained competitive advantage." *Journal of Management*, 17, 1, 99–120.

Bignoux, S. (2006). "Short-term strategic alliances: A social exchange perspective." *Management Decision*, 44, 5, 615–27.

Bowen, S. and Burnette, M. (2019). "Redefining the value from end-to-end integration." *Supply Chain Management Review*, March/April, 36–41.

Briones-Penalvar, A.J., Bernal Conesa, J.A., and Nieto, C. (2020). "Knowledge and innovation management model. Its influence on technology transfer and performance in Spanish Defence industry." *International Entrepreneurship and Management Journal*, 16, 595–615.

Cao, M. and Zhang, Q. (2011). "Supply chain collaboration: Impact on collaborative advantage and firm performance." *Journal of Operations Management*, 29, 3, 163–80.

Cao, Z., Huo, B., Li, Y., and Zhao, X. (2015). "The impact of organizational culture on supply chain integration: A contingency and configuration approach." *Supply Chain Management: An International Journal*, 20, 1, 24–41.

Chon, Y. and Shin, K. (2021). "How do alliance portfolio factors affect a precision medicine firm's innovation performance?" *Journal of Open Innovation: Technology, Market and Complexity*, 7, 3, 203.

De Backer, R.D. and Rinaudo, E.K. (2019). "Improving the management of complex business partnerships." *McKinsey*, Mar 21, www.mckinsey.com/business-functions/strategy-and-corporate-finance/our-insights/improving-the-management-of-complex-business-partnerships

Famakin, I.O., Aje, I.O., and Ogunsemi, D.R. (2012). "Assessment of success factors for joint venture construction projects in Nigeria." *Journal of Financial Management of Property and Construction*, 17, 2, 153–65.

Gainsight.com (2022). "The essential guide to Channel partner success." www.gainsight.com/guides/essential-guide-channel-partner-success/#:~:text=Successful%20Channel%20partnerships%20share%20similar,in%20place%20to%20leverage%20advocates

Gao, H., Yang, J., Yin, H., and Ma, Z. (2017). "The impact of partner similarity on alliance management capability, stability and performance: Empirical evidence of horizontal logistics alliance in China." *International Journal of Physical Distribution & Logistics Management*, 47, 9, 906–26.

Hofstede, G., Hofstede, G.J., and Minkov, M. (2010). *Cultures and Organizations: Software of the Mind*. New York: McGraw-Hill.

Hsu, T-H. and Tang, J-W. (2019). "Applying fuzzy LinPreRa cognitive map to evaluate strategic alliance partnerships for outlying island duty-free shop." *Asia Pacific Journal of Marketing and Logistics*, 31, 4, 730–58.

InformationWeek (2001). "Eight principles for managing strategic alliances." www.informationweek.com/it-life/eight-principles-for-managing-strategic-alliances

Kanchel, H. and Kahla, K.B. (2021). "Partnership success factors: Overcoming cultural misfits between Tunisian SMEs and their French partners." *Independent Journal of Management and Production*, 12, 7, 1808–35.

Kipnis, A.B. (1997). *Producing Guanxi: Sentiment, Self, and Subculture in a North China Village*. Durham, NC: Duke University Press.

Lee, Y-H. and Yan, M-R. (2019). "Factors influencing agents' bargaining power and collaborative innovation." *Asia Pacific Journal of Marketing and Logistics*, 31, 2, 559–74.

Leuschner, R., Rogers, D.S., and Charvet, F.F. (2013). "A meta-analysis of supply chain integration and firm performance." *Journal of Supply Chain Management*, 49, 2, 34–57.

Liu, J., Cui, Z., Feng, Y., Perera, S., and Han, J. (2020). "Impact of culture differences on performance of international construction joint ventures: The moderating role of conflict management." *Engineering, Construction and Architectural Management*, 27, 9, 2353–77.

Loza, C. (2017). "7 - Eleven deepens Amazon relationship." Path to Purchase Institute, Nov. *14*, https://pathtopurchaseiq.com/7-eleven-deepens-amazon-relationship

McHugh, M. (2019). "Is the channel PRM-ature?" *Computer Reseller News*, Oct., 14–15.

Morcillo-Bellido, J. (2019). "Strategic alliance trends in the Spanish food and beverage industry." *The IUP Journal of Supply Chain Management*, 16, 1, 22–36.

Morgan, M.R. and Hunt, S.D. (1994). "The commitment–trust theory of relationship marketing." *Journal of Marketing*, 58, 3, 20–38.

Oracle.com (2021). "Essential strategies for partner relationship management." Oracle, www.oracle.com/a/ocom/docs/partner-relationship-management.pdf

Ozorhon, B., Arditi, D., Dikmen, I., and Birgonul, M.T. (2010). "Performance of international joint ventures in construction." *Journal of Management in Engineering*, 26, 4, 209–22.

Prihandono, D., Wijayanto, A., and Cahyaningdyah, D. (2021). "Franchise business sustainability model: Role of conflict risk management in Indonesian franchise businesses." *Problems and Perspectives in Management*, 19, 3, 383–95.

Ralston, P.M., Keller, S.B., and Grawe, S.J. (2020). "Collaborative process competence as an enabler of supply chain collaboration in competitive environments and the impact on customer account management." *The International Journal of Logistics Management*, 31, 4, 905–29.

Rezazadeh, A. and Nobari, N. (2018). "Antecedents and consequences of cooperative entrepreneurship: A conceptual model and empirical investigation." *International Entrepreneurship and Management Journal*, 14, 479–507.

Salesforce.com (2017). "3 steps to effective partner relationship management." Salesforce, https://a.sfdcstatic.com/content/dam/www/ocms/assets/pdf/misc/3-Steps-to-Effective-PRM.pdf

Samanta, P.K. and Singla, H.K. (2019). "Factors affecting the success of joint ventures in Indian construction firms." *IUP Journal of Management Research*, 18, 3, 39–50.

Sanyal, S. (2018). "5 Best Practices in PartnerRelationship Management.", LinkedIn.com, Dec. 11, www.linkedin.com/pulse/5-best-practices-partner-relationship-management-sugata-sanyal

Schmid, H. and Almog-Bar, M. (2020). "The critical role of the initial stages of cross-sector partnerships and their implications for partnerships' outcomes." *Voluntas*, 31, 286–300.

Vrande, V., Vanhaverbeke, W., and Duysters, G. (2009). "External technology sourcing: The effect of uncertainty on governance mode choice." *Journal of Business Venturing*, 24, 1, 62–80.

Wolt, J.J., Prasad, S., and Tata, J. (2019). "Supply chain management, national culture, and refugee network performance." *Journal of Humanitarian Logistics and Supply Chain Management*, 9, 2, 109–30.

Xue, J., Lu, S., Shi, B., and Zheng, H. (2018). "Trust, guanxi, and cooperation: A study on partner opportunism in Chinese joint-venture manufacturing." *Journal of Business & Industrial Marketing*, 33, 1, 95–106.

Yang, J.L., Chiu, H.N., Tzeng, G.H., and Yeh, R.H. (2008). "Vendor selection by integrated fuzzy CDM techniques with independent and interdependent relationships." *Information Sciences*, 178, 21, 4166–83.

Zinfi.com (2022). "Why channel management varies around the world." Zinfi, www.zinfi.com/blog/channel-management-why-it-varies-around-the-world

10
GLOBAL EMPLOYEE RELATIONSHIP MANAGEMENT

Syncing Cross-Country Organizational Cultures

In 2013 Mr Ibrahim Saeed formed a new software development company SYIT in Islamadad, Pakistan to primarily cater for the needs of LMT, one of Denmark's largest publishing companies. SYIT was a relatively new entrant in the offshore software development industry in Pakistan.

The collaboration between Saeed and LMT was based on the understanding that LMT would have multiple points of contact across the SYIT team instead of just one and have more say and control over aspects of coordination such as team values, culture, and office design between people in Denmark and the project team members based in Pakistan. The quality of the working relationship between SYIT and LMT would depend on transparency between the teams in Denmark and Pakistan.

SYIT Business Model: Team Expansion

In order to fulfill LMT's needs, Saeed decided to implement the team expansion model. LMT's dedicated team would be based in Pakistan and be led by a senior manager from either Denmark or Islamabad. In theory this would help team members based in Pakistan to streamline communication and engage in quick decision making. However, this benefit depended on aligning the structures and cultures of the teams on both sides so that organizational cultural traits would supersede national cultural traits.

(Continued)

Pakistan's National and Corporate Cultures

Despite the growth in Pakistan's IT industry, offshore software organizations in Pakistan typically suffered from a poor image in the minds of foreign clients because of their autocratic management styles and corporate cultures. These reflected Pakistan's national culture. Pakistan's culture was defined by the primacy of authority where authoritative figures were not questioned. The culture expected and accepted hierarchical decision making. It started at home where children never questioned decisions of parents and grandparents. Thus to gain authority in society and be considered important in society, the values of masculinity, drive, ambition, and competitiveness were built into the minds and hearts of young people, starting at home. According to Geert Hofstede's cultural dimensions, Pakistan exhibited cultural traits of high power distance and high masculinity.

This resulted in organizations where structures are hierarchical, decision making is central-ized, and employees had little autonomy and expected to be told what to do. This autocratic management culture was welcomed by employees because it was easier for them to work on complex tasks for which clear directions were provided, and for which they were not held responsible for outcomes. SYIT employees being exposed to this typical national culture and corporate work culture expected the same.

Culture Change Challenges

In order to create a better working relationship with LMT and future European clients, Saeed wanted SYIT's corporate culture to move away from the typical "masculine" one to a "self-steering" one characterized by self-management and a desire and ability to think and make decisions independently, innovate, take risks, reap rewards for their success, and take responsibility for their failures. Saeed made an effort to implement a more employee-led culture and generate more confidence in employees to be responsive to clients by providing them with tools.

Things started to falter, however, as deadlines were missed due to technical problems. Even though the employee-led model should have helped bolster working relationships between the two firms, several culture-related phenomena on both sides created problems.

- SYIT junior team members were hesitant to correct LMT senior team members out of respect for seniority and authority even though they realized there were flaws in decision making
- SYIT junior members were unwilling to provide individual input because they were unwilling to take responsibility for any potential negative outcome from that input
- LMT senior team members were not in agreement on which workstyle works the best
- LMT senior team members in remote sites tried to control decisions
- LMT senior team members failed to create an environment of open communication where junior members would be comfortable sharing ideas without fear of ramifications

Saeed realized that simple awareness of cultural differences between Pakistan and Denmark would not be enough to bring about success. The constant contact between Denmark and

Pakistan required that both short- and long-term strategies for overcoming cultural differences be implemented. Saeed realized the importance of establishing a strong corporate culture before the company grew big. He realized the challenge in front of him.

Source: Khan, M., Alvi, K.R., and Saqib, Z. (2018). "SYIT: Changing the corporate culture." ID: 9B18C004, *Richard Ivey School of Business Foundation*, Ontario, Canada. Distributed by www. thecasecentre.org

Introduction

The ultimate and the most valuable organizational resource is its people. They are at the helm of determining and implementing processes and using technology. The resource-based view (RBV) of the firm underscores the importance of human resources. RBV states that organizational resources can be sources of competitive advantage if these resources are valuable and not easily imitated by competitors. The particular nature of individual and collective employee knowledge, skills, and capabilities, the relationships among employees at all levels, and the overarching organizational culture within which these happen are some of the most inimitable of organizational resources. Harnessed the right way they are pillars of stronger customer relationships, competitive advantage, and growth. Developing this into an effective resource is, however, a challenge for most companies, particularly when an organization is implementing strategic organizational changes such as implementing CRM and doing so globally. As highlighted by the opening, case national cultural differences create additional barriers to effective human resource development. It is thus an imperative for globally spread organizations to strategically address employee development and create an organizational culture that nourishes relationships in all change initiatives and across diverse cultures.

Role and Importance of Employees to Customer Relationship Management

Organizations that successfully implement CRM show strong enthusiasm in fulfilling their customers' needs. The path to that success lies in also deeply caring about fulfilling their employees' needs. This is because the people prong of CRM determines the ultimate effectiveness of the process and technology prongs. Creating positive customer experiences and reaping benefits of customer satisfaction and loyalty is only possible when employees are empowered, curious about customers, and empathetic towards them (Berraies et al., 2020; Miroslava et al., 2015; SHRM.org, 2021). Just as customer knowledge is considered a strategic resource crucial to CRM (Spender, 1996, so is the knowledge worker, as per the relationship management theory (Deszczyński, 2018). Research has shown that successful CRM implementation depends on both active employee support from senior management and satisfaction of the CRM project team (Al-Arafati et al., 2019; Mukherjee and Prasad, 2017). Without employee success there is no success in CRM.

Managing Employee Relationships for Customer Relationship Management

Managing relationships with employees means helping them to accept change and thrive on it. This section provides guidelines on how to bring this about through highlighting people issues of change management, discussing change management models, and underscoring particular concepts and imperatives of change management in today's new economy of employee relationships.

People Change Management for CRM Implementation

CRM initiatives force the organization to bring about organization-wide change. Organizations are always trying to create new customer values, making change in organizations a constant and its management continuous. Implementing customer relationship management is about adopting and managing changes in customer strategies and corresponding changes in organizational processes, technological systems, and human resources. Change management includes all of these types of changes. Seen holistically it is the "the process of continually renewing an organization's direction, structure, and capabilities to serve the ever-changing needs of external and internal customers" (Hornstein, 2015). Employees impact the success of all types of organizational changes but shaping change among these internal customers is the most challenging. People changes can thus be considered the most critical aspect of change management (Ng, 2013; Zeynap Ata and Toker, 2012).

Humans thrive on relationships and that's where both the challenge and opportunity of change management lie. Most of a CRM change initiative's instability and unpredictability comes from the people aspect of CRM and thus all successful CRM changes have to incorporate a relational cultural shift (Theus, 2018a). Such a cultural shift happens through change management where with the help of the best relationship-based work culture and practices that a company can build, an organization harnesses and mobilizes a positive energy characterized by high levels of motivation, enthusiasm, and commitment (Insights.com, 2022), reduces employee resistance to change, creates a positive attitude towards the change, and motivates acceptance of it (Ziemba and Obłąk, 2015). The result is strong employee–employee and employee–employer relationships that feed into creating stronger employee–customer relationships (Morrissey, 2019).

People change management is defined as all methods of preparing, supporting, and motivating employees to successfully adopt organizational changes that impact their work, relationships, and procedures.

Research has shown that relationship-based work cultures exhibit certain common traits. Table 10.1 highlights these valuable traits (Rahimi, 2017).

Table 10.1 Traits of Relationship Organizational Culture

Customer focused	Innovative
Mission and vision oriented	Risk taking
Collaborative and sharing	Learning oriented
Flexible and adaptable	Involved
Stable	

Source: Used with permission of Emerald Publishing

Managing change for CRM is both a science and an art. It is about championing change in people across the organization. In today's globally competitive business world this will need a combination of a cultural evolution, a new type of leadership development, and technological agility (Lowenstein and Alper-Leroux, 2016).

Models of Change Management

Academics and consultants have developed models of change management over the last several decades. These models have been successfully utilized in organizations to manage change and provide guiding frameworks for approaching and implementing change for global CRM. Before using any particular change model, however, organizations should be clear on the CRM issues the people change management is trying to address and that will result in desired outcomes. Examples of CRM issues lie in the areas of go-to market strategies, processes, analytical, and technological systems and can vary from organization to organization or for an organization across countries. Thus any adopted people change model needs to be adapted to the organization's specific CRM situation.

The Lewin Model

One of the earlier models of change management created by Kurt Lewin, a psychologist, includes three sequential stages of change (Smith, 2020). The change process starts with a pre-change stage called "unfreezing". In this stage employees unlearn current thinking, skills, and behavior through communicating and sharing ideas across functional boundaries and participating in training. It is meant to create a neutral vessel to allow the change to sink in. The second stage "change/movement" is where the actual change occurs,where people learn and adapt to new mindsets, skills, and behaviors through identifying and defining problems and solutions, and implementing them. This stage is usually less orderly and more chaotic as the organization goes through a transition. The third and last stage is called "freezing/refreezing" where the new ways of thinking and doing are made permanent by cementing them into the organizational culture. This stops the organization from reverting back to the older ways.

Kotter's Change Management Model

Perhaps the most well known of all models in the one developed by Kotter (1996, 2007). Kotter's model concentrates more on employee actions than on the change itself. The model consists of a virtuous cycle of eight linear sequences of actions (stages). Table 10.2 below highlights these eight stages and the significance of each.

Table 10.2 Kotter's Change Management Model Steps

Stage	Description
1 Establishing a sense of urgency	Need for organizational members to believe that performance is not acceptable and hence change is needed
2 Creating a guiding coalition	Creating a coalition team that contains power, expertise, credibility, and leadership
3 Creating the vision	Defining what change is required to help reduce uncertainty and ambiguity about the change
4 Communicating the vision	Communicating the change that is required to help reduce uncertainty and ambiguity about the change
5 Empowering others to act on the vision	Moving obstacles in the guise of structures, systems, skills, and supervision to facilitate change
6 Planning for and creating short term wins	Rewarding change agents and discouraging cynics helps keep the motivation up
7 Consolidating improvements and producing more changes	Sustaining acceleration of the change
8 Institutionalizing new approaches	Anchoring the change to stop reverting to pre-change states

To help capture the complexities in change management, scholars have suggested revisions to Kotter's model. Research has stressed that the stages can overlap each other because of the different pace of change and that organizations in some cases may need to go back and forth on the stages (Pollack and Pollack, 2015; Weiss and Li, 2020).

Figure 10.1 showcases the application and revision of Kotter's model to a case of change management for CRM at an automotive company. For each stage it highlights overall change management competencies that the organization had to develop and the important issues (in italics) that the organization had to address for CRM to be successfully implemented (Sittrop and Crosthwaite, 2021).

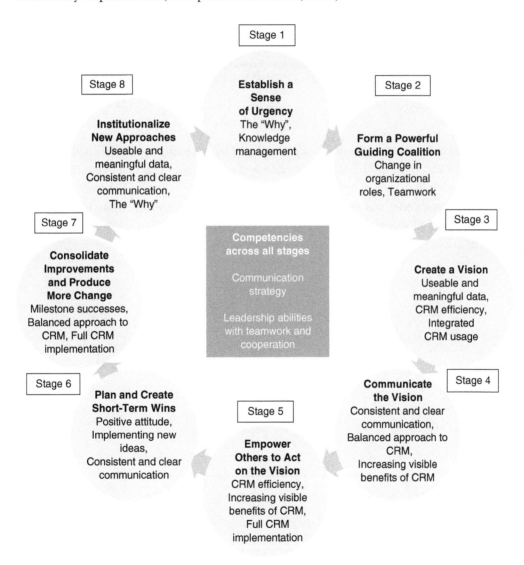

Figure 10.1 Application of Kotter's Change Management Model

The ADKAR Model

Developed by Prosci, a change management consulting company, this is one of the modern models that is easy to apply. It is a five-step framework (Smith, 2020). Table 10.3 describes these five steps.

Table 10.3 ADKAR Change Model

Step	Description
Awareness	Communicate about change details (why, what, and how) to organization
Desire	Motivate employees to buy into the change by highlighting the meaningful organizational and personal benefits
Knowledge	Provide employees with appropriate tools and training to develop required knowledge and skills for the change
Ability	Help employees demonstrate the knowledge and skills through application
Reinforcement	Reinforce new behaviors and thinking through incentives and other mechanisms

The McKinsey Model

The seven-construct McKinsey model developed by the namesake of the consulting firm concentrates more on the areas to be addressed rather than the actual steps of action like the models above (Smith, 2020). The areas of focus move from hard (concrete) topics to soft (capabilities and relational) ones and from organizational to more personal ones. Changes in all seven areas are necessary to create the positive energy needed to successfully adopt change. The seven areas of the McKinsey model are illustrated in Figure 10.2.

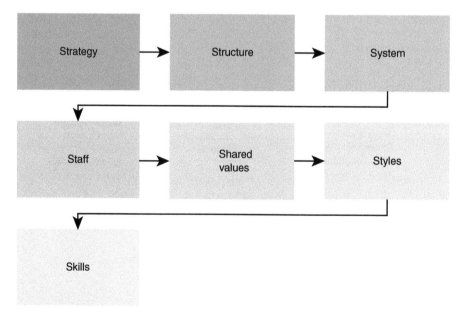

Figure 10.2 McKinsey Change Management Model

These change management models are effective but they do require the right set of organizational conditions to exist. Where organizations fail to successfully implement change it is more a case of the right conditions not being created consciously than that the models failed (Theus, 2018a).

To create the right organizational conditions for successfully managing people change for CRM, organizations have to critically understand and analyze the realities surrounding four interconnected factors. These factors are listed below (Jami Pour and Hossienzadeh, 2021):

- *Context*: This includes external and internal realities facing the organization that impact the success of a change initiative. External conditions for CRM implementation include the technology, competitive, customer, and value-chain environments and internal conditions include organizational culture, structure, procedures, and processes.
- *Content*: This includes the success factors for the change initiative. Knowing this will allow the organization to understand which employees will be affected, how, and their possible reactions to the change.
- *Individual*: This concerns employees both individually and collectively across all levels in the organization. It includes their mindsets and approach towards the change, current skills, and skills required for the change such as mentoring and teamwork.
- *Process*: This involves how the change can occur and how to best implement it given the contextual and human resource realities. It includes specific ways to present the value of change to employees, justify the change, get buy-in, and develop clear and common goals.

The Employee Relationship Economy

The concept of work has transformed over the last decade and so have employee/employer expectations and relationships. The new work concept includes trends such as boomeranging (the return of a former employee as an employee, consultant, or vendor), frequent job changes, and different work "tours" within and across organizations. Employees may see the completion of one job as a stepping stone to expanding on their professional passion and growth. Employers may see departing employees as future employees, brand ambassadors, customers, or future hire references. Now and in the future "the employee/employer relationship is no longer end to end but beginning to beginning" (Ranstad Risesmart, 2020). In this new concept of work, an evolving employee relationship economy has emerged that reframes the employee/employer relationships by considering employment as the entire journey of the employee into, within and out of the organization, and moves away from a transactional employment model to one that is built on trust and transparency (Ranstad Risesmart, 2020). In order to secure, develop, and engage talent for implementation of CRM in this employee relationship economy, organizational and human resource leaders are engaging in growth hack innovative strategies. Growth hacking is a process and a set of cross-functional skills that are employed to rapidly improve performance of multiple organizational operations. The following are examples of growth hack innovative strategies in the area of employee relationships management:

- Allowing part-time and freelance working
- Harnessing and delivering talent as a service (Taas) across all types of employees (full-time, part-time, former, freelance, vendors, and partners). Taas can be defined as "fast delivery of on-demand, high-skilled workers who are accessible to companies through a cloud-based platform" (Trajanov, 2020)
- Emphasizing technology usage to enhance work life and providing training in technology
- Redefining managers' role as employee experience coaches
- Facilitating employee transition both within and outside the firm

Developing a transparent, trust-based, flexible, and caring employment model to handle continuous organizational changes needs several inputs. It needs creation of a foundational organizational culture that works towards enhancing employee experience, and with its support development of initiatives to reduce employee resistance to change, engage employees in the change, and empower them to handle the change effectively. The following sections discuss these strategies.

The Employee-Experience Organizational Culture

An organizational culture that recognizes and nourishes employees as a core strategic resource is the cornerstone of successful change management for any organizational initiative. In his people-centric book *The Customer Comes Second*, Hal Rosenbluth states, "We're not saying choose your people over your customers. We're saying focus on your people because of your customers. That way, everybody wins" (Lowenstein and Alper-Leroux, 2016).

Culture is created from the top and so the first to change has to be leadership. Leaders and managers have a direct impact on the workforce in inculcating the desired cultural identity. The role of leaders and managers needs to change from a control focus to a coaching focus, one that provides caring and personal attention. The concept of servant leader that has been an established core of leadership from centuries ago needs to be applied where leadership impact is significant but subtle, and employees can take full ownership of success (Lowenstein and Alper-Leroux, 2016). The servant leadership model revolutionizes traditional leadership by putting employees at the top of the organizational hierarchy and leaders at the bottom. Leader serves the employees at the top. Servant leaders serve instead of command and are focused on empowering and nurturing employees (Tarallo, 2018).

An employee-experience organizational culture prioritizes communication from all employees and believes that the "voice of the employee" is the "voice of the customer." It propagates the culture of active listening by leadership and acting on that feedback to enhance employee relationships and experiences. Employee experience impacts customer experience.

Employee Engagement and Empowerment

Resistance to change: Research in neuroscience has shown that the human ancestral brain is configured to have automatic and habitual pathways in order to 1) minimize cognitive overload and 2) minimize threat and maximize safety and reward. Any change in the physical and social environment can be seen as a threat and puts more cognitive pressure on the brain by taking processing away from habitual pathways. This tends to create stress and discomfort (Hppy, 2021).

The feelings of stress and discomfort that accompany any change create a natural resistance towards the change (Theus, 2018a). To be able to engage employees in the change, make them feel empowered to handle it and secure their commitment; organizations have to reduce this resistance first. In order to do so, they must find ways to minimize the perception of the change as a threat and maximize the perception of it as safe and rewarding. Organizational leaders need to provide employees with clarity about what will change, with certainty that the change will happen and will benefit the organization, and with confidence about having autonomy and ownership of the change. The ability to do this depends on relationships as humans are born to connect. It calls for continuity in communication and consistency and fairness in cooperation from managers and leaders (Hppy, 2021). These efforts will, however, only bear fruit when employees sense and know that managers and leaders have addressed their own change resistances and are actively seeking out and addressing resistance to change in employees (Theus, 2018b). This is a tough challenge as it is and especially so when employees are from different cultures and countries where leadership and human resource processes and expectations of behavior tend to vary. To cope with this managers should be trained in two things: 1) emotional intelligence, which facilitates awareness, emotional regulation, interpersonal communication and conflict management (Theus, 2018a), and 2) cultural intelligence which facilitates effective functioning in culturally diverse environments (see Chapter 11).

Employee engagement: Engaged employees are more productive and loyal and contribute to higher revenues (Insights.com, 2014). A recent Gallup poll has shown that despite a rise in employee engagement 60 percent of employees are still unengaged (Ranstad Risesmart, 2020). This is not good news for CRM. If employees are disengaged how can they engage customers?

A straightforward path to employee engagement includes finding ways to make employees feel valued. One way to achieve this is to actively involve them in the organizational change efforts.

Engagement is a "a heightened emotional connection an employee feels for his or her organization that influences him or her to exert greater discretionary effort to his or her work" (Lowenstein, 2016). It has three core areas which can be further broken down into more specific sub areas (Insights.com, 2014; Lowenstein, 2016). Table 10.4 highlights them. Any engagement initiative should target these areas.

Table 10.4 Areas of Employee Engagement

Engagement Area	Description	Sub Areas
Intellectual	Involvement in the technical aspects of the job for improvements	• Stimulating nature of the job • Understanding the contribution of the job to organizational performance • Career growth prospects
Emotional	Having a positive feeling and attitude towards the job and the organization	• Trust in the integrity of leaders • Pride in the organization • Opportunities for development
Social	Actively sharing job-related issues with other employees and leaders	• Co-workers and team members • Relationship with managers

The following have been identified as best practice for increasing employee engagement (Hppy, 2021; Insights.com, 2014; Theus, 2018b):

- Strategic and poignant narrative of the organization by leadership about where it has been and where the change will take it. Dan Gilbert, the founder of Quicken Loans helps create engagement by sharing the story of the company at yearly employee orientations in a book he wrote about it and which he updates yearly (Hppy, 2021)
- Employee coaching by leaders and managers
- Opportunities for employees to contribute to change decisions, such as reasons for change, ways to change, how roles might change
- Opportunities for employees to own the change initiative through sharing accountability for seeing the change through

- Opportunities for employees to tell their own positive stories through feedback, reviews, or surveys. Zurich insurance company Canada created a virtual engagement forum called "Coffee Roulette" to help create informal conversations (HRReporter.com, 2021)
- Opportunities for employees to voice issues in an open forum
- Opportunities for employees to share experiences through group activities such as picnics, movies, games, sporting events. Zurich Canada gathered employees around a volunteering initiative to provide community support for senior citizens isolated by the Covid-19 pandemic (HRReporter.com, 2021)
- Opportunities for employees for outside-of-work entertainment and activities such as exercises and walking
- Utilization of games and other experiential learning activities to bring in a fun aspect

Employee empowerment: Engagement initiatives provide employees with an internal motivation for CRM change, and autonomy and participation in decision making surrounding the change. However, for motivated and engaged employees to meaningfully and effectively implement the change, the organization needs to provide organizational structures, procedures, and policies that nurture professional skills and personal wellbeing (Insights.com, 2014). This idea was popularized as empowerment. Human relations theory contends that both employee engagement and empowerment positively impact change success through employee success (Jo and Park, 2016). Research has shown that in CRM implementations, empowered employees are more committed, and they positively impact customer experience, perceived quality of service, customer satisfaction, customer loyalty and tendency to engage in word of mouth (Berraies et al., 2020). Table 10.5 highlights different areas of structural and procedural changes that are aimed at increasing employee empowerment. These need to be consistently applied till change is cemented into the culture of the organization.

Table 10.5 Organizational Empowerment Initiatives

Empowerment Initiative	Description
Management and governance	Good quality and transparent management that standardizes and integrates all aspects of change throughout the organization with a common thread (Ares Prism, 2018; Insights, 2014)
Two-way communication	Clear communication that allows both leaders and managers to share change-management-related information and expectations, and employees to provide input, share, and discuss change issues (Ares Prism, 2018; Insights, 2014)
Flexibility and adaptability	Anticipating and supporting differing needs of employees and teams for adapting to work-related and personal changes (Rahimi, 2017; SHRM, 2020)

(Continued)

Table 10.5 (Continued)

Empowerment Initiative	Description
Roles and policies	Clear and easily accessible human resource roles and policies that all levels of management have committed to (Insights, 2014)
Mentoring	Employee development-oriented mentoring to inspire employees by providing structured, fair, and customized coaching from leaders and managers who exhibit emotional intelligence and use social language (Hppy, 2021). Zurich Canada has Accelerated Development and Accelerated Leadership Engagement Programs where participants are matched with leader mentors (hrreporter.com, 2021)
Physical workplace	A comfortable and safe workplace (private space for complex tasks, ergonomic chairs, help with workplace organization, etc.) for increased job focus (Hppy, 2021)
Teams	Change teams that are cross-functional and include senior leaders. This provides credibility to the change initiative, allows employee ownership and identifies operational and processual obstacles (Al-Arafati et al., 2019)
Recognition and rewards	Frequent and ongoing recognition tied to customer value, customer experience, and other high-priority organizational goals. The city of Vernon in British Columbia, Canada has an everyday recognition program "random acts of awesome" (hrreporter.com, 2021)
Learning and training	Continuous, customized, and fun learning opportunities for change leaders and employees at all levels involved with the change. Micro learning that breaks down learning into easily digestible capsules, learning from each other in teams, personalized leadership learning, and technology and digital capability enhancement learning (Ares Prism, 2018; Hppy, 2021; McMahon, 2018; SHRM, 2020)
Performance management	Continuously updated and fresh performance management that 1) is aligned with the developmental focus of management and governance and 2) ties performance and rewards to customer engagement and experience and other organizational change goals
	Involving employees in determining criteria for evaluation and supplementing annual performance reviews with short regular employee performance surveys (hrreporter.com, 2021; Lowenstein and Alper-Leroux, 2016; Triznova et al., 2015)

Ultimately, change at its core is personal change. Change initiatives aimed at reducing resistance and increasing engagement and empowerment are successful when they help individuals change at the personal level. Individuals undergo various stages of change within themselves and progress through and process different emotions that facilitate emotional commitment to the change. Figure 10.3 illustrates a personal change acceptance model with five personal change stages accompanied by the emotions that accompany each of them, leading to ultimate acceptance and commitment to the change (Theus, 2018a). The change acceptance cycle is iterative and for each stage change takes place in two phases with different emotions accompanying each iteration. The first phase of emotions happens during preparation for the change and the second phase during implementation.

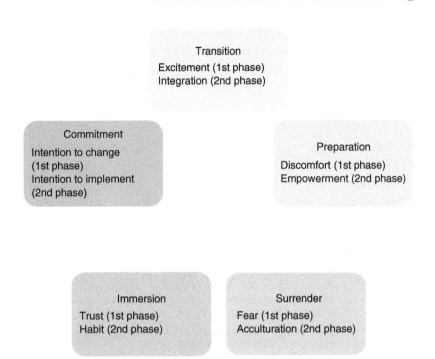

Figure 10.3 Personal Change Acceptance Model

Employee Ambassadorship

The service profit chain model stresses that happy employees make for happier customers (Heskett et al., 2008). Given this connection, initiatives for people change management for CRM implementation should have the goal of enhancing employee relationships to actively impact customer relationships. However, just making employees happy, engaged, and empowered will not automatically increase customer experience. As far as the success of CRM goes an employee relationship change initiative is not complete till employees buy into the culture of customer orientation and are motivated to be active advocates of customers (Lowenstein, 2016). Employees, whether customer facing or not, need to "live the brand and company value promise" (Lowenstein, 2016). Employee engagement and empowerment should be converted into employee ambassadorship.

> **Employee ambassadorship** is active commitment to the company, its product offering value promise, and the optimization of the customer experience.

Employee ambassadorship has the three following components:

1 *Commitment to the company*: Satisfaction, fulfillment and pride in being a fully aligned member of the company culture

2   *Commitment to the value proposition*: Active alignment with the excellence of benefits offered through the company's product offerings

3   *Commitment to customers*: Dedicated to understanding customers and acting in ways that enhance customer experiences

Employee ambassadorship helps channel engagement and empowerment in building customer value and achieving customer-related business results through directly and indirectly optimizing customer experiences.

Table 10.6 highlights employee ambassadorship initiatives at multiple organizations (Lowenstein, 2016).

Table 10.6 Employee Ambassadorship Initiative Examples

Company	Employee Ambassadorship Initiative
Hewlett Packard	"Demo Days" program where current and retired employees volunteer days at local electronic stores interacting with customers
Zappos	Training after hiring, irrespective of level or function, that includes two weeks taking phone calls from customers
NCR (high tech)	Training in customer interaction skills, company and brand information, engaging in public relations, marketing, and community events and being recognized for going above and beyond contributions

The above discussion underscores that, the subconscious positive feelings and experiences of employees that ERM generates are critical drivers of CRM success.

Success Story

Transformation of the Bank of Baroda (BoB), India

Under the capable leadership of Dr. Anil Khandelwal, the chairman and managing director, the Bank of Baroda was able to successfully implement change management to turn the fortunes of the bank around in 2005. Prior to this initiative the bank's deposits, advances, and total income growth were in steep decline. The labor union's resistance to implementing technology had a significantly adverse impact on the bank's business. Employee morale was low and many customers had left.

To find lasting solutions to the twin operational challenges of 1) technology overhaul, implementation, and acceptance and 2) to improve the performance of different product areas, Dr. Khandelwal realized he had to improve the morale of employees by engaging in people change management.

To develop an adaptive culture at the top Dr. Khandelwal initiated the following two processes:

1   A core group of executives dedicated to developing and implementing the 100-day agenda was formed. This included multiple challenging tasks such as installing ATMs, extending business hours, rebranding, restructuring the credit function and implementing IT for organizational change
2   To help develop a collaborative team-based leadership mindset Dr. Khandelwal would hold meetings every morning with the top team with the goal of engaging and motivating senior management to meet the challenges of the change

To help improve morale and reach out to the bank's 40,000 strong workforce in 2,800 national and 100 global branches Dr. Khandelwal put in motion several people change management policies:

- Face-to-face town hall type meetings and video communications with Dr. Khandelwal. In these meetings he not only communicated the need to change and the need for cooperation but also listened to employees' concerns regarding work, working environments and constraints faced in delivering services to customers
- A monthly letter to all employees from Dr. Khandelwal highlighting various developments and seeking their input
- Large groups events
- Development and sharing across employees a video that showcased the new vision of the bank
- To respond to employees' personal concerns and provide career opportunities several programs were implemented. These were: "SAMPARK" (a hotline from employees to Dr. Khandelwal) for quick problem-solving; "PARAMARSH" (professional counselling services) at large bank branches; "KHOJ" (talent search exercises)

In three years the change management was successful and the bank had significantly increased its customer base and adopted necessary technology in a vast majority of the bank's branches.

Dr. Khandelwal believes that leaders need to be both tough on performance and empathetic listeners and solvers of employee problems. He believes that connecting to human processes and developing leadership behaviors of listening to wisdom from the ground coming from employees were the primary reasons for the success of the people change management program.

Source: Panda, A. (2020). "Interview with Dr Anil K. Khandelwal: Leading transformation of a public sector bank through people processes and building intangibles." *South Asian Journal of Human Resources Management*, 7, 1, 135–43.

Impact of National Culture on People Change Management

As organizations roll out people change management for CRM in multiple operations scattered across countries it is critical to consider national cultures in operational locations. Whether it be managing change in a foreign subsidiary, an acquired company, or a value-chain partner, cultural tendencies and patterns impact the effectiveness of people change management (Cui et al., 2019; Lucia-Casademunt et al., 2018). This is because perceptions, needs, and desires for cognitive, social, and emotional workplace experiences are impacted by national culture. Cultural traits shape how employees process and react to change (Jacobs et al., 2013). The case above on successful change management at the Bank of Baroda highlighted labor union resistance as a particular challenge that leaders had to overcome for the change to successfully take place. Labor unions are common in many parts of the world. Thus any people change management framework for employee engagement, empowerment, and ambassadorship will need to incorporate policies and procedures that are adapted to the national culture. Differences across countries in areas that relate to both employees (e.g. willingness to participate in team work and their ability to do so, the desire for flexibility in work, types of recognition, and rewards), and management (e.g. performance management desired, and the type of training required) will force organizations to adapt people change management initiatives.

Geert Hofstede's cultural dimensions are commonly used to identify national cultural impacts on change management (Hofstede, 1984, 2001). All dimensions have been shown to impact perceptions, reactions to change, and acceptance but the uncertainty avoidance dimension creates the strongest impact and biggest difference across countries. Power distance and individualism relate to the impacts of change on performance and decision making and reporting structures. Where change requires working in teams, employees in individualistic countries will be more concerned about the change's impact on individual performance whereas employees from collectivist countries will be more concerned about the team's performance. Change that affects the hierarchy in decision making and reporting will impact employees differently from one country to another and to the greatest extent where there are the largest differences in power distance scores. Masculinity relates to emotional reactions to change for example anger when women are included as part of professional workforce specially as superiors, managers and decision makers in countries where on average men in particular or society in general don't want or expect women to hold professional positions of decision making. Lastly, uncertainty avoidance relates to confidence in the change as being for good, and clarity surrounding the change (Kirsch et al., 2012). Differences across countries in these dimensions result in different impacts on change perceptions and reactions. For example, whereas change that allows more employee participation in decision making, flexibility in designing jobs and determining schedules is seen as beneficial to employees from low uncertainty avoidance countries, for employees from high uncertainty avoidance countries these changes are perceived as stressful. On the other hand, where employees from high uncertainty avoidance cultures show more desire for supervisor support to boost confidence and wellbeing and help work–life balance, employees from low uncertainty avoidance look forward to learn about their leaders' expectations but need less "handholding" (Lucia-Casademunt et al., 2018).

People Analytics

To make people change management more effective organizations have recently been taking a more data-based approach to it. This has given rise to the relatively new but fast growing industry of people analytics also known by various other names such as workforce, talent, and HR analytics.

People analytics depends upon good data, statistical analytical tools, technology, and expertise (HR.com, 2021). A report published by Oracle on the adoption of people analytics by organizations shows that even though people analytics is regarded as a must-have tool for change management, a significant number of organizations are struggling and have to use the tool more effectively in order to make positive changes (HR.com, 2021).

People analytics: The process and practice of collecting, analyzing, and transforming employee data to create actionable insights for improving people change management decisions.

People analytics can be broken down into four types from lower to higher sophistication and complexity. Most organizations are struggling to utilize the last two.

1 *Descriptive analytics*: Utilizes people data to describe what has happened
2 *Insightful analytics*: Analyzes people data in a way to help organizations gain insights from it
3 *Predictive analytics*: Utilizes statistical tools on people data to make predictions for the future
4 *Prescriptive analytics*: Recommends people change management actions based on the analysis of people data

According to the survey, most organizations generally use people analytics for description and insights and only a small group moderately use the tool for driving predictions and prescriptions.

Based on conversations with people analytic teams in leading organizations, McKinsey & Company has set out six success factors for effective people analytics. They fall into three main categories: 1) data and data management, 2) analytics capabilities, and 3) strategy and process (Ledet et al., 2020). Table 10.7 highlights these factors. The first three success factors relate to the category 1, the 4th and 5th factors to category 2, and the 6th factor to category 3.

Table 10.7 Success Factors for People Analytics

Success Factor	Description
Data engineering resources	Substantial resources and a dedicated team allow for creation of a strategic and thoughtful foundation of quality data, analytical solutions, and quick testing
Breadth and depth of data sources	Data from multiple sources across the organization from human resources, finances, project management, surveys help to create multidimensional models for a richer picture of employee behavior such as engagement, teamwork, and collaboration
Data science skills	Data analysts with all-around and specific skills help create a nimble and robust team for evolving analytic needs
Integrator skills	Experts who bridge the gap between business leaders and technical experts help translate strategic challenges into analytical questions and help interpret insights from analytical output
Data analysis innovation	Opportunities for analysts to explore and innovate to help create new insights for business leaders
Alignment with organizational priorities	Mechanisms for the people analytic team to get an in-depth understanding of strategic priorities to make sure that the team is working on and learning about high-impact topics. This is facilitated through mechanisms of trust, empowerment, and ownership

Table 10.8 below highlights some popular and highly rated software applications that automate, facilitate, and streamline the process of people analytics.

Table 10.8 People Analytics Software Applications*

Software Application	Description
Rippling	Easy-to-manage platform for HR, benefits, payroll, and IT that consolidates employee data from all systems
Tableau by Salesforce	Facilitates creation of insights from consolidated data from all systems and sharing through interactive dashboards and visuals
Kudos	Facilitates engagement, culture development through reinforcing peer-to-peer recognition, values, and communication
Paylocity	Mobile friendly comprehensive platform facilitates decisions on talent, benefits, core HR, workforce management and engagement
7Shifts	Simplifies team management for all restaurants by facilitating engagement and retention, communication, scheduling, and complaint resolution. Mobile friendly and integrates with payroll and POS systems

*Sources: Capterra.com (2021). "The 2021 Capterra shortlist: HR analytics software." www.capterra.com/hr-analytics-software/#shortlist

Capterra.com (2022). "The 2022 Capterra shortlist: Employee recognition software." www.capterra.com/employee-recognition-software/#shortlist

Capterra.com (2021). "The 2021 Capterra shortlist: Employee engagement software." www.capterra.com/employee-engagement-software/#shortlist

Case Study

Cross-Cultural Communication for Customer Intimacy and Change Management

In 2016, GeoSoft Inc. launched a new technology strategy called the "customer intimacy strategy" to adapt to the global economic downturn and stay ahead of the competitive curve. This strategy would transform the way GeoSoft communicated with its customers. To roll out this strategy successfully across all five major geographic operational regions—Asia, Latin America, Australia and Asia, Europe, and North America—would require coordinated communication of change across multiple stakeholders including customers and employees representing vast cultural differences.

GeoSoft Culture

Based in Toronto, Canada, GeoSoft is a privately held, employee owned, medium-sized global organization that provides earth scientists with innovative data solutions and services. The company had stable growth over three decades and won international business awards for top performance and best places to work.

GeoSoft's organizational culture of commitment, motivation, and collaboration was spread across geographic boundaries and helped to drive their value proposition of providing innovative customer solutions with exceptional customer intimacy. Supporting this was employee ownership and consensus-building leadership behavior that put emphsais on the message that employee potential drove corporate potential. Leadership behavior created trust, engagement, and productivity. To deliver this core value proposition efficiently and effectively, Geo targeted only specific segments and focused on customizing customers' current and future needs.

GeoSoft's New Customer Intimacy Strategy

The primary focus of the new strategy was to have employees engage with more productive activities for better customer service and to concentrate more on high-value business segments. The new strategy rested on three core customer-centric pillars:

1 Customization of services and solutions to address unique needs. This made customer relationships more interactive and focused on value addition
2 Proactive and timely commitment to customer learning and customer experience enrichment through training
3 Utilization of customer data and business intelligence to proactively anticipate future customer needs

Managing the Change

To roll out the new strategy globally raised a challenge for GeoSoft, which not only had to uniformly and effectively communicate this change in strategy but also lead the change across countries with diverse cultures. This was of particular concern to senior management because of prior cross-cultural communication glitches, such as the following:

(Continued)

- Over-the-top "we are best" promotion in modest cultures
- Insensitivity to the needs of high-contact cultures such as in Latin America where it is normal to extend hospitality to visiting senior executives
- Insensitivity in scheduling meetings without due consideration of time zone differences
- Communications that presented Geo as Toronto-centric rather than a global organization

To avoid such glitches Geosoft made several changes to communication and collaboration. These changes were based on findings from surveys, and were characterized by greater diversity and inclusiveness, higher frequency, more distributed leadership, and use of multiple and relevant communication channels.

At the leadership level the following changes were implemented:

- *Distributed leadership*: Some regional managing directors were given global responsibilities for different operational areas such as exploration and energy
- CEO traveled to multiple locations to work with regional directors and to meet with customers frequently and collaboratively
- Regional managers reported to the CEO regarding communications in their regions and the CEO kept them up to date on initiatives that would impact them
- At the regional level directors communicated with stakeholders on relevant issues via channels that were best suited given the culture and the geographic location

Based on findings from surveys conducted with employees across the globe, the following people change management communications were undertaken:

- Monthly CEO forum for updates and discussions
- A weekly pulse survey to enable more frequent and timely feedback
- Face-to-face or electronic quarterly town hall meetings at all locations across the globe. These were recorded and made available to all employees
- One-on-one meetings with each employee once a year
- Regular communication via video conferencing

Senior leadership hoped that these changes that rested on diversity and inclusion would help to bring benefits such as improved engagement, innovation, reputation, and ultimately performance, to both the people and the business.

Source: Reddin, C.P. (2017). "GeoSoft Inc: Leading across cultures." ID: 9B17M064, *Richard Ivey School of Business Foundation*, Ontario, Canada. Distributed by www.thecasecentre.org

Summary

This chapter discussed ways of developing a strong and committed workforce for CRM implementation through employee relationship initiatives. Employee relationships are critical to customer relationships. CRM implementation brings about significant organizational changes that impact employees. To effectively implement these changes organizational leaders need to engage in people change management to solidify employee relationships. The chapter discussed the approach, elements, processes, and technologies of people change management for CRM.

References

Al-Arafati, A., Abdul Kadir, K., and Al-Haderi, S. (2019). "The mediating effect of output quality on the relationship between top management support and customer satisfaction on the implementation of customer relationship management system in public sector." *Academy of Strategic Management Journal*, 18, 2, 1–11.

Berraies, S., Chitioui, R., and Chaher, M. (2020). "Customer-contact employees' empowerment and customer performance." *International Journal of Productivity and Performance*, 69, 9, 1833–59.

Ciu, Z., Liu, J., Xia, B., and Cheng, Y. (2019). "Beyond national culture difference: The role of cultural intelligence in cooperation within international construction joint ventures and insights from Chinese companies." *Engineering, Construction and Architectural Management*, 26, 7, 1476–97.

Deszczyński, B. (2018). "The integrated relationship management framework." *Ekonomia i Prawo. Ecomomics and Law*, 17, 1, 17–31.

Heskett, J.L., Jones, T.O., Loveman, G.W., Sasser Jr., W.E., and Schlesinger, L.A. (2008). "Putting the service-profit chain to work." *Harvard Business Review Magazine, July–August*, https://hbr.org/2008/07/putting-the-service-profit-chain-to-work

Hofstede, G. (1984). *Culture's Consequences: International Differences in Work-Related Values*. Beverly Hills, CA: Sage.

Hofstede, G. (2001). *Culture's Consequences: Comparing Values, Behaviors, Institutions and Organizations Across Nations*, 2nd edn. Thousand Oaks, CA: Sage.

Hornstein, H.A. (2015). "The integration of project management and organizational change management is now a necessity." *International Journal of Project Management*, 33, 2, 291–8.

Hppy (2021). *Neuroscience in the Workplace, ebook*, https://gethppy.com/wp-content/uploads/2016/08/eBook-Neuroscience-in-the-workplace-How-understanding-the-brain-can-transform-your-business.pdf

HR.com (2021). *The State of HR Analytics 2021*, https://www.oracle.com/human-capital-management/analytics/?source=:ad:pas:go:dg:a_nas:71700000093268355-58700007781724640-p70699857207:RC_

WWMK160606P00037C0001:MainAd&SC=:ad:pas:go:dg:a_nas::RC_
WWMK160606P00037C0001:MainAd:&gclid=Cj0KCQjw1N2TBhCOARIsAGVHQc
6A2VYV4hbRNIzZ0szdYmuHQJqojDGSZZ_fOA3CYltfSREyzO9pBIEaAoEGEALw_
wcB&gclsrc=aw.ds

HRReporter.com (2021). "Best places to work: Top employers focus on employee
success." www.hrreporter.com/best-in-hr/best-places-to-work/360215

Insights.com (2014). Employee Engagement. *Insights white paper*, www.insights.com/
us/resources/employee-engagement-whitepaper

Insights.com (2022). *Managing Change, Insights white paper*, April 16, www.insights.
com/us/resources/managing-change

Jacobs, G., Van Witteloostuijn, A., Christe-Zeyse, J., and Polos, L. (2013). "A
theoretical framework of organizational change." *Journal of Organizational Change
Management*, 26, 5, 772–92.

Jami Pour, M. and Hossienzadeh, M. (2021). "An integrated framework of change
management for social CRM implementation." *Information Systems and e-Business
Management*, 19, 43–75.

Jo, S.J. and Park, S. (2016). "Critical review on power in organization: Empowerment in
human resource development." *European Journal of Training and Development*, 40, 6,
390–406.

Kirsch, C., Chelliah, J., and Parry, W. (2012). "The impact of cross-cultural dynamics
on change management." *Cross Cultural Management: An International Journal*, 19,
2, 166–95.

Kotter, J.P. (1996). *Leading Change*. Boston, MA: Harvard Business School Press.

Kotter, J.P. (2007). "Leading change: Why transformation efforts fail." *Harvard Business
Review*, 85, 96–103.

Ledet, E., Mcnulty, K., Morales, D., and Shandell, M. (2020). "How to be great at people
analytics." *McKinsey & Company, Oct 2*, www.mckinsey.com/business-functions/
people-and-organizational-performance/our-insights/how-to-be-great-at-people-
analytics

Lowenstein, M. (2016). *You've Gotta Have Heart: An Introduction to Employee
Ambassadorship*. Beyond Philosophy, https://beyondphilosophy.com/white-papers/
youve-gotta-have-heart-introduction-employee-ambassadorship

Lowenstein, M. and Alper-Leroux, C. (2016). *The Employee Experience Playbook*.
Ultimate Software, https://webcdn.ultimatesoftware.com/static/pdf/whitepapers/
Employee-Experience-Playbook.pdf?from=hcm-hot-topics

Lucia-Casademunt, A.M., Cuéllar-Molina, D., and García-Cabrera, A.M. (2018). "The
role of human resource practices and managers in the development of well-being."
Cross Cultural & Strategic Management, 25, 4, 716–40.

McMahon, S. (2018). "Make the most of micro-learning." *Training*, Jan./Feb., https://
trainingmag.com/make-the-most-of-micro-learning

Miroslava, T., Matova, H., Dvoracek, J., and Sadek, S. (2015). "Customer relationship
management based on employees and corporate culture." *Procedia Economics and
Finance*, 26, 953–9.

Morrissey, P. (2019). "Relationships and revenue." *Training*, May 23, Training Journal, (May 23) 22–24 https://www.proquest.com/trade-journals/relationships-revenue/docview/2304075051/se-2

Mukherjee, H.S. and Prasad, U.D. (2017). "Definitions of project success in implementation of customer relationship management (CRM) information technology (IT) solutions: Perspectives of consultants from India." *South Asian Journal of Management*, 24, 4, 142–57.

Ng, C.S.P. (2013). "Intention to purchase on social commerce websites across cultures: A cross-regional study." *Information Management*, 50, 8, 609–20.

Pollack, J. and Pollack, R. (2015). "Using Kotter's eight stage process to manage an organisational change program: Presentation and practice." *Systemic Practice & Action Research*, 28, 51–66.

Rahimi, R. (2017). "Customer relationship management (people, process and technology) and organizational culture in hotels." *International Journal of Contemporary Hospitality Management*, 29, 5, 1380–1402.

Randstad Risesmart (2020). *The Employee Relationship Economy*. https://info.risesmart.com/hubfs/Assets/wp-ere-employee-relationship-econ_020518.pdf

SHRM.org (2020). "In First Person: Satya Nadella", People + Strategy Journal, Fall, www.shrm.org/executive/resources/people-strategy-journal/fall2020/pages/in-first-person.aspx#:~:text=Satya%20Nadella%2C%20Chief%20Executive%20Officer,of%20purpose%20and%20Microsoft's%20transformation.&text=Satya%20Nadella%20is%20Chief%20Executive%20Officer%20of%20Microsoft

Sittrop, D. and Crosthwaite, C. (2021). "Minimising risk—the Application of Kotter's change management model on customer relationship management systems: A case study." *Journal of Risk Financial Management*, 14, 496–516.

Smith, C. (2020). "The Mega-Guide to Change Management: The Only Guide You'll Ever Need" (Oct 29), Accessed at https://www.changemanagementworld.com/2021/05/the-mega-guide-to-change-management-the-only-guide-youll-ever-need-2/

Spender, J. (1996). "Making knowledge the basis of a dynamic theory of the firm." *Strategic Management Journal*, 17, 45–62.

Tarallo, M. (2018). "The art of servant leadership." *Society of Human Resource Management* (May 17) https://www.shrm.org/resourcesandtools/hr-topics/organizational-and-employee-development/pages/the-art-of-servant-leadership.aspx.

Theus, D. (2018a). "A new change management model: Change from inside-out." InPower Coaching, Feb. 20, https://inpowercoaching.com/new-change-management-model-change-inside

Theus, D. (2018b). "Creating space for change." *InPower Coaching Whitepaper*, 1–30, www.InPowerCoaching.com https://community.inpowercoaching.com/making-space-for-change.

Trajanov, T. (2020). "The rise of talent as a service." *Forbes Innovation* (Jun 30), https://www.forbes.com/sites/forbestechcouncil/2020/06/30/the-rise-of-talent-as-a-service/?sh=13af5e161c74

Weiss P.G., and Li, S-T.T. (2020). "Leading change to address the needs and well-being of trainees during the Covid-19 pandemic." *Academic Pediatrics*, 20, 735–41.

Wikipedia (n.d.). "Growth Hacking," https://en.wikipedia.org/wiki/Growth_hacking

Zeynap Ata, U. and Toker, A. (2012). "The effect of customer relationship management adoption in business-to-business markets." *Journal of Business and Industrial Marketing*, 27, 6, 497–507.

Ziemba, E. and Obłąk, I. (2015). "Change management in information systems projects for public organizations in Poland." *Interdisciplinary Journal of Information Knowledge Management*, 10, 47–62.

PART IV
IMPROVING GLOBAL CRM IMPLEMENTATION

11
GLOBAL CRM AND CULTURAL INTELLIGENCE

Case Study

Overcoming Cultural Barriers for Organizational Change

This is the story of a young adventurous American who found herself in a conundrum about how best to handle cultural practices and challenges she faced working for an American construction management company in a foreign country. Anna was hired to lead and manage human resources, particularly recruiting and hiring, for the firm's business in Doha, Qatar. She was very excited about meeting this professional and cultural challenge.

The rapid economic development of Qatar, a small Middle Eastern country, largely fueled by natural gas and oil resources, has attracted businesses and employees from all across the world for career prospects and good pay. Less than 20 percent of Qatar's population are Qatari nationals.

Typical of many foreign companies operating in Qatar, the American construction company's employees are also diverse. Employees in the company hail from different countries such as Greece, India, Jordan, Lebanon, the Philippines, Oman, the UK and the US, and Yemen.

Anna was made welcome by multiple employees in the organization, particularly by Linda, her Dubai-based human resource manager supervisor, the Lebanese general manager for the Qatari office and her direct supervisor Mohammad, and Omanian business development manager Abdul. Anna was settling in her job and enjoying learning about the industry and her work environment. It did strike her as strange, however, that there was no formal process for recruitment recorded anywhere that she could have fallen back on for reference. She was having to learn everything through informal verbal communication.

A few months after Anna joined the Qatari office the company landed a major client in Qatar. Local sheikhs approached the construction company to find them suitable talent for their AquaZoo project—a combined floating zoo and aquarium. They needed an architect with significant experience of amusement parks and other technical requirements.

(Continued)

Despite the challenge in finding a suitable candidate in a short week's time, Anna was excited to report to Mohammad after a thorough review that she had found an Egyptian who fulfilled all the requirements, only to be told to continue the search because the sheiks were unwilling to work with someone from Egypt despite excellent qualifications. Mohammad also told Anna not to consider anyone from Pakistan because the government had a temporary hold on visas for Pakistani nationals. When Anna mentioned that this could be perceived as discrimination by their US-based company, Mohammad explained that things in Qatar were done differently from the US.

In an effort to get to know her international colleagues she would frequently have tea or coffee with project managers, engineers, administrators, and contract managers. As they got to know her better some of these employees started sharing with her problems with employee welfare at the Qatari office. Being the only human resource employee at that office she was naturally concerned. Some of the problems shared with her were about treatment of subordinates and hours worked.

One issue in particular that troubled her was that of sexual harassment that Rosa, a Filipino secretary, said she had faced. Anna made Mohammad aware of this, but he was unwilling to open a formal inquiry despite the fact that policies for employee empowerment, sexual harassment, and transparency were formally built into the core values of the organization. Mohammed told Anna he would speak to the alleged perpetrator and agreed to transfer Rosa to another site. Anna started to feel that Qatar's "institutional idiosyncrasies" were determining the organizational culture at the Qatari office and were violating the values of openness and transparency of the organization. She felt strongly that unwillingness to work with people of specific nationalities was not only unethical, it also made the company uncompetitive in attracting and retaining qualified talent.

Anna was uncomfortable with the whole situation but was unsure of how to proceed. She wondered during her weekly telephone call with Linda whether she should share this and get some advice or whether she should contact headquarters in New York even though she did not want to betray Mohammad's trust.

Source: Connell, M. (2015). "When does culture become a barrier for change?" ID: 415-120-1. *Cambridge Judge Business School, University of Cambridge*. Distributed by www.thecasecentre.org

---

Introduction: Cultural Competence for Global CRM

The above case highlights culture-based dilemmas and challenges that organizational leaders and employees face in international markets. Anna felt herself unprepared to deal effectively with the culture-based realities she faced in human resources and customer management practices in the organization's Qatar office. The case also underscores the need for cultural competence for global business and CRM initiatives.

As organizations venture into international markets to reach and satisfy new customers they inevitably face obvious and not so obvious culture-based realities—different languages, attitudes, beliefs, customs, and business practices. For organizations to be successful in global CRM initiatives, cross-cultural competence is needed in managerial decision making concerning customers, employees and value-chain partners, and in communicating and negotiating with them (Thomas and Inkson, 2017). The typical western rational decision making which is based on logic and analysis may not be effective in many cultural settings where decisions are made keeping in mind the human element, tradition, or consensus. In such a cultural setting who you know and their goals and motivations are more important for decision making than what you know. This may seem unethical to other cultures but ethical standards themselves vary across cultures, adding another layer of cultural complexity to cross-cultural decision making. Culture also shapes verbal and non-verbal aspects of communication and negotiation styles, creating variations across countries in both areas and impacting success.

How intelligently a leader, an employee or an organization thinks about, strategizes and manages these cross-cultural operations will determine the effectiveness of the outcomes. There are different kinds of intelligences that help humans thrive in their professional and personal lives. Howard Gardner in his theory of multiple intelligence identified eight types (Gardner, 2011). In defining intelligence Gardner states that "Intelligence is a biopsychological potential to process information that can be activated in a cultural setting to solve problems or create products that are of value in a culture" (Gardner, 1983: 34). Two of these intelligences, intrapersonal (emotional) and interpersonal (social) together help us navigate the social and cultural environment we are part of. However, as we step outside the boundary of this environment into the social and cultural environments of other countries and cultures, we need another form of intelligence for us to effectively communicate and function. This is called cultural intelligence (CQ) (Earley and Ang, 2003).

As an organization grows internationally, growing cultural intelligence becomes a prerequisite for working effectively in cross-cultural teams, leading a diverse set of employees and being led by equally diverse leaders. CQ at both individual employee and organizational levels becomes an essential component of surviving and thriving in the global social village. Chapter 10 helped us understand the crucial impact employees have on customer satisfaction and loyalty and the importance of empowering employees. Developing CQ becomes another empowerment imperative for leadership as CRM goes global. In order to do so leaders have to understand and tackle issues that vary across cultures such as ideas of leadership, expectations from employees and what motivates them, appropriate leadership styles, group norms, processes, and performance of culturally diverse teams.

This chapter helps us understand what cultural intelligence is, what role it plays in global CRM and how to develop it in organizations.

Cultural Intelligence (CQ): Foundations

Cultural Intelligence (CQ): an individual's, group's or an organization's capacity and ability to effectively function in culturally diverse environments.

It includes the set of knowledge, skills, and abilities for effectively operating and interacting in new and unfamiliar cultural settings. Based on the concept of multiple intelligences, Earley and Ang (2003) came up with a multi-factor cultural quotient construct known as cultural intelligence, which was further revised by Ang et al. (2007). This conception of cultural intelligence rests on four interconnected foundational components that combine to create CQ. These are the cognitive, the motivational, the behavioral, and the metacognitive dimensions (Ang et al., 2007). Figure 11.1 illustrates the CQ construct.

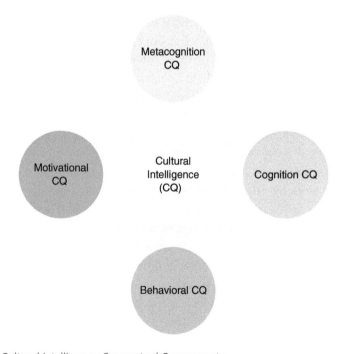

Figure 11.1 Cultural Intelligence Conceptual Components

Cognitive-CQ reflects culturally specific technical knowledge. Motivational-CQ reflects the desire to know more about the culture and use it effectively. Behavioral-CQ reflects the actual verbal and non-verbal behaviors to function and interact in diverse cultures effectively and Metacognitive-CQ reflects the thinking, processing, internalizing, and creating of mental models of cultural knowledge. Metacognitive CQ is seen as a critical link between knowledge and ensuing motivation, abilities, and behaviors (Ang et al., 2007). All four components are conceptualized to be connected and to be equally important in shaping CQ. Table 11.1 highlights the characteristics of each of these dimensions.

Table 11.1 Cultural Intelligence Dimension Characteristics

Dimension	Characteristics
Cognitive CQ	Ability to form cultural knowledge from objective and subjective information and the structure of such knowledge
MetaCognitive CQ	Ability to consciously think about, internalize, and form mental models of cultural knowledge
Motivational CQ	Drive and ability to learn about culture and to function in cross-cultural settings
Behavioral CQ	Ability to adapt verbal and non-verbal behaviors to suit cross-cultural interactions

Source: Printed with permission of Cambridge University Press

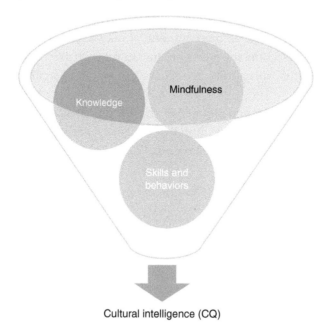

Cultural intelligence (CQ)

Figure 11.2 Cultural Intelligence Action Components

A parallel conception of cultural intelligence by Thomas (2006) and Thomas et al. (2008) takes this conceptual system of CQ and expresses it more as an action-based system of knowledge, skills, and behavioral components that interact to allow people to adapt their behaviors in culturally diverse environments. Similar to Ang et al.'s (2007) component of metacognitive CQ, Thomas (2006) proposes that an overall mindfulness component is necessary to connect CQ knowledge, skills, and behavior components. Mindfulness includes "focusing attention on the knowledge of culture and the processes of cultural influence as well as an individual's motives, goals, and external stimuli" (Thomas, 2006: 86). Figure. 11.2 illustrates the four forces of this parallel action-based CQ system.

An example to illustrate the process of developing CQ

A German customer relations manager of an office supplies firm wants to effectively engage with her Indian customers. She has the drive and ability to learn about the Indian culture and acquire new information (motivational CQ). She will first acquire knowledge of the Indian consumer and business culture (cognitive CQ). As she is gathering knowledge of the culture she will think about similarities and differences with the German culture and other cultures she has been exposed to and will form a mental model about the Indian culture so that she knows how to adapt to Indian customers and partners. She becomes mindful of idiosyncrasies of the Indian culture (metacognitive CQ). In time she meets her Indian value-chain partner and showcases her skills and abilities in adapting her behavior to the Indian cultural environment (behavioral CQ).

Both these conceptual foundations of CQ have been translated into CQ assessment tools to help organizations measure individual and collective (team-based) cultural intelligence (Ang et al., 2007; Thomas et al., 2015; Thomas and Inkson, 2017; Van Dyne et al., 2008).

Role of Cultural Intelligence in Global Business and Customer Relationship Management

Research on cultural intelligence across countries has consistently shown the positive impact of CQ on individual, team, and organizational performance (AlMazrouei and Zacca, 2021). Cultural intelligence has been shown to enhance cross-cultural job performance across a broad range of operations, such as international mergers, selling, negotiation, customer service, performance events, teaching, learning among expatriates, helping to increase the satisfaction of customers, partners and stakeholders (Akhal and Liu, 2019; AlMazrouei and Zacca, 2021; Cray et al., 2018; Cui et al., 2019; Groves et al., 2015; Imai and Gelfand, 2010; Lin et al., 2018; Pandey and Lucktong, 2020; Paparoidamis et al., 2019; Rohmetra and Arora, 2012; Yikilmaz et al., 2021). This is good news for global CRM where success critically depends upon cross-functional organizational processes, particularly those in marketing, sales, and customer service. Research finds that CQ positively impacts the outcome from these processes variety of performances by strengthening certain factors that are beneficial to cross-cultural operations and relationship building, and helping to weaken others that are harmful. Table 11.2 highlights these factors.

Table 11.2 CQ enhanced factors that improve job performance

Employee perception of organizational image	Market orientation
Customer perception of quality and image	Flexibility and adaptability
Productivity	Job satisfaction
Display of cross-cultural appropriate behavior	Cooperation
Management of emotional process	Creative confidence
Effort and control in displaying appropriate and expected emotions	Turnover intentions

Impact of Individual CQ Components

Even though overall CQ has a positive impact on performance, this varies when the four conceptual components of CQ (Ang et al., 2007) are considered separately. Some research has shown a stronger impact of the motivational and/or metacognitive components (Chua et al., 2012; Crotty and Brett, 2012). Motivation to learn more about other cultures and thinking about this more critically is likely to positively impact the collection of additional cultural information and engagement in cross-cultural behavior, leading to an overall higher positive impact of CQ. Despite the overall positive impact of CQ on market orientation (a foundational concept in global CRM) impacts of individual CQ components on its aspects (information acquisition, information sharing, and strategic response) vary. Whereas multiple CQ components positively impact information acquisition, information sharing is positively impacted only by metacognitive CQ and strategic response only by cognitive CQ (Galati, 2016). Experts argue that behavioral CQ is particularly salient in global business and CRM initiatives because many of the cultural pitfalls happen in the area of actual behaviors (Ang and Inkpen, 2008).

Impact of Organizational CQ Culture

Chapter 10 argues that global CRM will not succeed unless employees succeed. CQ's impact on CRM success happens through the individual and collective efforts of employee empowerment and ambassadorship. Employees and value-chain partners of an organization implementing CRM globally will in most cases include people from multiple cultures. This makes developing CQ as a part of employee relationship management crucial but challenging. To meet this challenge will need active CQ leadership initiatives to create a CQ organizational culture (Cabral et al., 2020). This should permeate the organization from the top to all levels of the organization and even beyond to value-chain partners. A CQ culture should motivate employees to learn about other cultures. Thus a consciously developed CQ organizational culture lays the foundation for global CRM success. Coca-Cola, one of the most global of all companies firmly emphasizes CQ across its thousands of employees. The company realizes that just as a leader needs to have a high CQ to establish an appropriate organizational culture, the truck driver who delivers its products to restaurants and grocery stores/outlets also needs to have at least a moderate level of CQ because of their interaction with clients (SHRM, 2015). Nurturing employees and partners to develop motivational CQ should impact the other dimensions of CQ. Additionally, cognitive CQ and the knowledge it contains can be enhanced by using CRM technology, which helps employees gain more information about the market. This too should positively impact other dimensions of CQ, enhancing the influence of overall CQ on CRM initiatives. CQ helps develop cross-cultural competence and ensures that customer and stakeholder touch-point interactions are culturally intelligent.

Even though CQ is mostly studied and applied at the individual level it is important to develop it at the level of the organization. This is because the optimum benefits from CQ over the long term come through individual and organizational CQs reinforcing each other. This reinforcement helps embed CQ firmly into the organizational culture whereby all cross-country decision making, behaviors, and interactions are culturally intelligent. Research supports the importance and feasibility of such reinforcement. It has been found that in a team, individual members' CQ impact the quality of teamwork (Scholz, 2012) and overall team performance (Khani et al. 2011). The individual CQs of those working in a diverse multicultural team have also been shown to improve the overall team's CQ (Iskhakova and Ott, 2020). The importance of this team-based and organizational CQ cannot be overstated for international business success. Higher quality of overall organizational intelligence makes international performance efficient and effective (Huber, 1990). In international mergers and acquisitions, strategically developed CQs of negotiating partners positively impact both pre-integration phases through increased cooperation and post-integration phases (Cui et al., 2019; Ramkeesoon, 2019).

CQ's Impact on Global CRM Competitive Advantages

To better understand and appreciate the impact of CQ on global business and CRM we look at it through the lens of the resource-based view of the firm (RBV). RBV states that tangible and intangible resources and capabilities that lead to sustainable competitive advantages are valuable, difficult to imitate, not that common, and are embedded within the organization (Barney, 1991). It has also been found that the quality of organizational intelligence determines organizational effectiveness (Huber, 1990). So can intelligence and cultural intelligence in particular, resident in an organization, be considered a scarce resource that impacts competitive advantage? It can be argued that it possibly is.

The better the firm is at gathering international market information and generating new knowledge the more culturally intelligent it will be (Huber, 1990). Competitive advantage in the arena of global CRM rests on gathering and generating new information from the market to improve competitive offerings and differentiated customer experiences. Cross-cultural interactions and behaviors (verbal and non-verbal) are salient in developing differentiated value-chain partner and customer experiences and relationships. Cognitive CQ facilitates knowledge development and behavioral CQ promotes adaptive behaviors. Both cross-cultural knowledge development and adaptive behaviors do not, however, happen by themselves. Cognitive and behavioral aspects of CQ need to be supported by their motivational and metacognition siblings. Providing organizational cultures, systems, structures, and incentives to motivate employees to learn, think about, and engage in cross-cultural communication and behaviors, help develop metacognition and motivational CQs. So CQ certainly can be argued to be valuable and has been consistently shown to be so. Its inimitability and scarcity, however, lie in how it develops within the organization as a competitive weapon. The development process happens organically and consciously within each organization that includes a combination of culturally intelligent leadership, managerial abilities to develop competitive resources such as customer loyalty, and structural capacities such as reporting hierarchies. These together help embed CQ within the organization (Ang and Inkpen, 2008). Despite the recognition of CQ's importance to global customer and partner loyalty, the complexity of being involved in developing CQ in organizations with culturally diverse employees and leaders and globally dispersed operations, makes its existence relatively uncommon (Ang and Inkpen, 2008).

Table 11.3 consolidates the individual and organizational benefits that CQ can provide for furthering global CRM initiatives and achieving competitive advantages.

Table 11.3　CQ Employee and Organizational Benefits

Employee Benefits	Organizational Benefits
Ability to adjust cross-culturally, repeatedly, and without burnout	Ability to successfully expand in culturally diverse markets without compromising corporate mission
Ability to make insightful judgments across cultures	Ability to provide superior service to culturally diverse customers and value-chain partners
Ability to make mutually acceptable decisions across cultures	Ability to efficiently operate cross-culturally
Ability to negotiate effectively across cultures	Ability to successfully complete expatriate assignments
Ability to trust and share across cultures	Ability to attract and retain global talent
Ability to creatively collaborate across cultures	Ability to make cross-cultural teams perform effectively
Ability to perform effectively across cultures in multiple functions	Ability to positively impact profitability

Success Stories

CQ in China

China today is one of the most important markets for multiple industries. The unique culture of China forces companies to engage in CQ strategies to be successful in the market. For the leaders of China social stability overrides economic considerations. In China many organizations are asked to sacrifice for the sake of the nation and put Chinese government interests first. Organizations that want to crack the Chinese market thus have to use CQ negotiation strategies to balance organizational policies, goals, and strategies with the outlook, interests, and demand of the Chinese government.

Amway is one such company that has been successful in achieving this balance and has reaped benefits in the Chinese market. When the Chinese shut down Amway's operations after the company had spent over one hundred million dollars in that market on the grounds that China was not ready for direct sales to consumers, Eva Chang, the then executive vice president for Amway Asia applied CQ to get the company back on its feet. She was able to convince Amway's US executives to get on board with the Chinese government's wishes and the Chinese government to change its policy on direct selling. CQ culture at Amway helped Chang and the organization to recognize the value of a long-term approach when developing cross-cultural relationships and work towards building trust and local ownership.

Source: (SHRM, 2015).

Assessing and Developing Cultural Intelligence (CQ)

Organizations need to actively set CQ goals, assess the current state of CQ within the organization and then create strategies and processes for developing it. This initiative should be targeted at individual employees, teams, and the overall organization. CQ development at the organizational and team level is more strategic, targeting organizational culture and competitive moves, whereas at the individual level it is more tactical, geared to meet requirements such as being able to engage in culturally adapted communication in a foreign language.

Assessing CQ Readiness

To assess if both individual employees and the organization as a whole exhibits cross-cultural competence it is important to select the correct measures and tools. Cross-cultural competence is impacted by multiple factors which can be grouped into the following three areas:

1 Individual traits and personalities that impact intercultural interactions
2 Beliefs, attitudes, and implicit biases that are often unconscious
3 Cross-cultural individual and organizational capabilities (CQ) that facilitate cross-cultural interactions

To come up with effective CQ intervention and development strategies, it is important to assess all three areas. The first two are particularly relevant for new hires, and for selecting employees to lead international operations and cross-cultural teams. It is the last area that is probably the most important because it is most amenable to change to effective development programs and is also critical to global CRM success. This area can be assessed by three instruments: 1) by measuring the four conceptual components of CQ at the individual level (meta-cognitive, cognitive, motivational and behavioral) (Ang et al., 2007), 2) by measuring the action components of CQ (knowledge, mindfulness, skills, and behaviors) (Thomas, 2006; Thomas et al., 2008), and 3) by measuring CQ at the organizational level (Ang and Inkpen, 2008). These instruments are academically sound, have been rigorously validated by the academic community and are generally accepted by practitioners.

Table 11.4 highlights some of the tools that can be used to assess these three areas of cultural competence (SHRM, 2015).

Table 11.4 Cultural Competence Assessment Tools

Assessment Areas	Assessment Tools
Individual cross-cultural personality traits and values	• Cultural values profile, https://culturalq.com/products-services/assessments/cultural-values-profile • CultureWise Platform, https://culturewise.com • GlobeSmart Platform, www.globesmart.com • Multicultural Personality Questionnaire (MPQ)
Individual world view (beliefs and attitudes)	• Harvard University Implicit Association Tests (IAT), https://implicit.harvard.edu/implicit/takeatest.html • Intercultural Developmental Inventory (IDI) https://idiinventory.com
Cross-cultural knowledge, skills and abilities	• Cultural Intelligence 4 Factor Scale (CQS)—20 items (organizational and individual levels)* • Short Form Cultural Intelligence Scale (SFCQ)—10 items** • Firm Level Cultural Intelligence Scale—28 items***

*Ang et al., 2007; Van Dyne et al., 2008

**Thomas et al., 2015; Thomas and Inkson, 2017

***Ang and Inkpen, 2008

Developing CQ

Culture experts state that there are multiple ways to improve upon individual and organizational CQ (SHRM, 2015; Thomas and Inkson, 2017). Results of CQ assessment should highlight which areas need to be improved upon. This will need customized development plans based on the unique realities of an organization, teams, and individual employees. Table 11.5 highlights broad strategies and specific tactics commonly utilized for developing individual and team CQs.

Table 11.5 CQ Development Strategies and Tactics

Strategies	Description
CQ Culture	Creating a CQ culture underscores the importance of CQ and its development to the company, and motivates employees. Leaders should: • Demonstrate their own CQ abilities • Provide support for establishing CQ culture through systems, structures, and processes for CQ culture
Recruiting and hiring	To ensure, secure, and promote organization-wide CQ initiatives, hiring policies should include assessment of CQ-related personality traits, attitudes, beliefs, and intercultural personal and professional experiences

Strategies	Description
Recognition and rewards	To promote CQ, leaders have to create policies that recognize and reward employees for CQ achievements and serve as incentives for employees to develop their CQs
Cross-cultural experiences and interactions at home or in the workplace	Exposure to and interactions with other cultures within the current location through following suggested activities: • Cultural activities organized by ethnic organizations • Community meetings with belief systems different from the participants' • Religious service or cultural ceremony (e.g. wedding) of a culture different from that of the participant
International experience	Exposure to international markets, social, and professional interactions with varying degrees of exposure: • Short-stay flying visits to multiple locations • Short- to medium-term visits to multiple cultures • Longer-term expatriate assignments to one specific location
Being part of or observing multicultural teams	Exposure to how multicultural team members behave and interact during operations such as: • Assignment of roles • Selecting a team leader • Imposition of deadlines
Training	The following types of training are recommended with experiential training being the most effective in developing all dimensions of CQ. Training can be targeted towards specific cultures or for broad cross-cultural applications. Training should be iterative allowing for attention, retention, and reproduction of CQ knowledge, skills, and abilities: • Technical: Develops objective knowledge of cultural dimensions and processes through videos, books, lectures, and briefings • Analytical: Develops cognitive and metacognitive (mindfulness) CQs through discussion, analysis of case studies, and going through programmed self-administered training manuals • Experiential: Develops metacognitive (mindfulness), motivational, and behavioral (skills and abilities) CQs through cross-cultural interactions and conflict resolution, utilizing simulations and field trips • Local training sessions for expatriates
Coaching	Coaches complement formal training by helping employees to strengthen weaker CQ areas through discussion, feedback, and creation of customized CQ development plans with specific goals and accountability for achievement of such goals
Reflection	Reflecting on cross-cultural training, coaching and actual experiences helps develop metacognitive CQ and mindfulness. Keeping a journal where reflections and meditations are noted down and revisiting these periodically is recommended

Both IKEA, the Swedish furniture manufacturer, and Samsung, the South Korean electronics manufacturer, utilize an interesting but effective way of developing CQ. Representatives of the companies frequently conduct home visits in new international markets to understand how people live, what products they use, and how they use them. These provide close-up views into cultural values and motivations.

Developing CQ in individual employees and teams does not guarantee that this will be automatically transferred to the entire organization. To make an organization culturally intelligent needs senior leadership efforts, and processes and structures to be in place.

Developing organizational CQ is a complex initiative involving managerial and organizational processes that use the most effective assets (e.g. motivational leadership and technology) and available pathways and venues (e.g. local mentoring for expatriates) (Ramkeesoon, 2019). Ang and Inkpen (2008) developed an organizational CQ model and tool to address the development of firm-level intercultural capability needed for international operations. The model states that organizational CQ can be enhanced by enhancing CQ in three mutually reinforcing organizational components. These are in the areas of managerial, competitive, and structural abilities. Developing organizational CQ depends upon hiring and training a culturally intelligent senior management team. Who senior management is, how they think, the teams they work in, and what strategies they develop, together impact organizational performance. The more culturally intelligent decision-making the senior management team engages in, the stronger the organizational CQ should be. The firm must support decision making by teams by acquiring and attaining competitive resources that impact global CRM. These resources need to become part of the processes and routines of the firm that help them become competitive. A competitive resource that would be seen as valuable for global CRM is strong customer loyalty. This can be attained through culturally intelligent decision-making in marketing, sales, customer-service and product development areas. Finally, to help embed a CQ leadership culture and competitive resources within the organization, it needs to structure itself in a way that allows processes and routines for reporting and hierarchies to develop CQ. An organizational structure beneficial for global CRM would prioritize relationships over legal contract governance with the help of particular psychological processes and business practices. Psychological processes in relational contracts help create perceptions of mutual reciprocity in contract obligations and should help strengthen the CQ actions of senior management and the impact of competitive resources. Together, these three forces should over time help develop and strengthen CQ within the whole organization. Figure 11.3 illustrates this model.

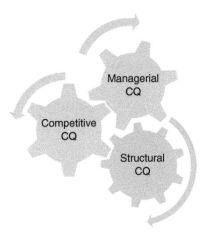

Figure 11.3 Model for Developing Organizational CQ

Based on the above discussion, implementing the following three actions items will help develop CQ at the organizational level (SHRM, 2015):

1   *Committed leadership*: Senior leaders and team leaders should show commitment to CQ through their actions and strategies. One way is to take the CQ assessment themselves to demonstrate that the organization takes CQ development seriously. Leaders should also develop processes and structures that will allow all employees to develop CQ, helping to develop a CQ culture

2   *Perform CQ audit*: This should pertain to the overall organization and should assess the extent:

    - to which cross-cultural customer and partner communications are culturally intelligent
    - of representation of diversity in the organization
    - to which teams are equipped to handle multiculturalism
    - to which leaders promote and support CQ efforts
    - to which CQ is considered for hiring, promoting, and rewarding

3   *CQ strategy and process*: Leadership should develop a strategic plan with specific developmental actions and steps, milestones, and completion dates. So that the plan is implemented effectively and leads to CQ, leadership should provide structural support through organizational processes and systems (e.g. training, coaching, and hiring) for acquiring competitive resources such as skills in new product development for new markets and cross-cultural marketing communications. For CQ to take a firm hold in the organizational culture, the CQ strategy should be embedded in overall employee relationship management and human resource strategic initiatives

Figure 11.4 illustrates the steps in the process of developing organization CQ.

Leadership
commitment

CQ Audit

CQ strategy
and process

Figure 11.4 Organizational Cultural Intelligence Development Imperatives

Whether it be developing CQ in individuals or the whole organization, it is important to realize that the process is slow and senior leaders need to stick to any initiative steadily and for the long haul. True CQ develops through iterative social experiences and learning. This involves paying attention to cross-cultural experiences, retaining the knowledge gained, reproducing and applying it again in the future and receiving reinforcement about the effectiveness of CQ behavior through feedback.

Case Study

Meeting Russian Roulette with Cultural Intelligence

CPA was facing a business problem in Russia that needed to be fixed. Its local Russian competitor was trying to create ill will towards the company by spreading negative information and making disparaging comments. CPA was opening a new establishment in Russia which was an important part of their global growth strategy. Sophia, a 15-year veteran with the company, was given charge of turning around this situation in Russia.

CPA, a US-based multinational industrial company, offered a broad range of products such as plastics, chemicals, agricultural products, and services. Being a global organization,

CPA regularly faced challenges in balancing consistency in their corporate brand with being sensitive and relevant to country-level stakeholders, across a vast range of organizational functions such as product development, sales, marketing, service, and human resources.

Sophia, originally from Canada, was considered a rising star of the organization and was responsible for public affairs and government relations. Part of Sophia's role was to resolve conflicts and challenges to corporate brand reputations. Having worked in Canada, the company's global headquarters in New Jersey, US, in Hong Kong, and in Europe, Sophia had built up a strong resume by successfully leading transformational change management across multiple functions and businesses. A tried and tested strategy of hers that had worked well had been to fall back on documents, and international experts, colleagues, contacts, and mentors with whom she had built relationships over the years. Coming from a non-Christian, mixed ethnic and cultural upbringing, Sophia had developed a knack for successfully navigating gender-based, cultural, national, and religious barriers. She had developed the ability to navigate being "different" from others in many settings. In other words she had developed CQ.

The typical western strategy to deal with the kind of conflict the company was facing in Russia would be to involve external parties such as journalists to cover stories in newspapers and on TV where the company engage in public communication to assert its global brand reputation and strength, contradict the assertions of the local Russian company, and emphasize the contributions to job creation and community development that CPA's investment would bring.

Typical of her style Sophia decided to listen to what Petar, CPA's country manager in Russia had to say. He had built up a credible reputation in a few short years in CPA's European operations and was known as an astute business person. Petar stressed that the typical western style of conflict resolution would fail but a "local" way might succeed, which would not only resolve the conflict but also leave CPA on a more firm footing in Russia. Russia was known as a country with a difficult and fluid business culture which outsiders find hard to navigate well. The "local" way would not include going public but finding a "within network" solution where highly influential people in the business and political sphere would speak to others to find something that was mutually agreeable.

At a second dinner with these influential businessmen Petar and Sophia were able to successfully diffuse the situation and find a resolution. In order to succeed Sophia engaged in the following behavior. She:

- Changed from office attire to more formal dinner attire
- Was attentive and engaging at the meeting with the help of translations from Petar, and indicated appreciation for the inputs from the Russians at the table
- Assured the Russians that CPA was learning the Russian way and that it would take some time for the company to adapt to it
- Made sure to put Petar as the primary decision maker but also took care to communicate the expectations from headquarters in the US and the necessity to keeping the superiors in the US comfortable

The whole encounter and experience in Russia left Sophia both pleasantly and unpleasantly surprised despite her years of successfully navigating culture.

(Continued)

The unpleasant surprise involved Sophia inviting her mentee Vlad Goldstein, a Russian-born financial wizard who had shown great promise, to the first dinner even though Petar suggested otherwise. Sophia realized to her dismay that Vlad's last name made him a liability at that dinner. Vlad was Jewish and the anti semitic leanings of the Russians at the table made Goldstein feel unwelcome. This was an exhibition of a cultural trait in Russia of evaluating someone not just on performance but more importantly by who one is, position, and family name.

The pleasant surprise included the topic of ice hockey sports and how stronger connections can be built on sudden revelations of commonality from unexpected quarters. One of the Russians at the dinner table revealed that he had played a role in the Red Army hockey team in the Super Summit with Canada. This led to Sophia having an animated and enjoyable discussion of the sports played historically between Canada and Russia and helping to break the ice.

Source: Blanchard, K. (2017). "Working cross-culturally: Forget 'business as usual'." ID: 9B17C013, *Richard Ivey School of Business Foundation*, Ontario, Canada. Distributed by www. thecasecentre.org

Summary

Chapter 11 has wrapped up the discussion of global CRM by introducing the topic of cultural intelligence (CQ), which has recently been growing in importance for global business in general and global CRM initiatives in particular. The chapter started by describing the foundational concepts of cultural intelligence and then explained why and how cultural intelligence is important for organizations engaged in global CRM, highlighting multiple benefits. The rest of the chapter provides practical guidance on how to assess and develop cultural intelligence in employees, teams, and organizations.

References

Akhal, K. and Liu, S. (2019). "Cultural intelligence effects on expatriates' adjustment and turnover intentions in mainland China." *Management Research Review*, 42, 7, 818–36.

AlMazrouei, H. and Zacca, R. (2021). "Cultural intelligence as a predictor of expatriate managers turnover intention and creative self-efficacy." *International Journal of Organizational Analysis*, 29, 1, 59–77.

Ang, S. and Inkpen, A.C. (2008). "Cultural intelligence and offshore outsourcing success: A framework of firm-level intercultural capability." *Decision Sciences*, 39, 3, 337–58.

Ang, S., Van Dyne, L., Koh, C., Ng, K.Y., Templer, K.J., Tay, C., and Chandrasekar, N.A. (2007). "Cultural intelligence: Its measurement and effects on cultural judgment and decision making, cultural adaptation and task performance." *Management and Organization Review*, 3, 3, 335–71.

Barney, J. (1991). "Firm resources and sustained competitive advantage." *Journal of Management*, 17, 1, 99–120.

Cabral, A.M.R., Carvalho, F.M.P.O., and Ferreira, J.A.V. (2020). "SMEs' international strategic groups and top managers' psychological characteristics." *Administrative Sciences*, 10, 92, http://dx.doi.org/10.3390/admsci10040092

Chua, R.Y.J., Morris, M.W., and Mor, S. (2012). "Collaborating across cultures: Cultural metacognition and affect based trust in creative collaboration." *Organizational Behavior and Human Decision Processes*, 118, 2, 116–31.

Cray, D., McKay, R., and Mittleman, R. (2018). "Cultural intelligence and mindfulness: Teaching MBAs in Iran." *Journal of International Education in Business*, 11, 2, 220–40.

Crotty, S.K. and Brett, J.M. (2012). "Fusing creativity: Cultural metacognition and teamwork in multicultural teams." *Negotiation and Conflict Management Research*, 5. 2, 210–34.

Cui, Z., Liu, J., Xia, B., and Cheng, Y. (2019). "Beyond national culture difference." *Engineering, Construction and Architectural Management*, 26, 7, 1476–97.

Earley, C. and Ang, S. (2003). *Cultural Intelligence: Individual Interactions across Cultures*. Palo Alto, CA: Stanford University Press.

Galati, S.R. (2016). *Entering the Global Engineering Market: A Correlational Study of Cultural Intelligence and Market Orientation*. Dissertation. www.proquest. com/dissertations-theses/entering-global-engineering-market-correlational/ docview/1765700916/se-2

Gardner, H. (2011). *Frames of Mind: The Theory of Multiple Intelligences*, 3rd edn. New York: Basic Books.

Groves, K.S., Feyerherm, A., and Gu, M. (2015). "Examining cultural intelligence and cross-cultural negotiation effectiveness." *Journal of Management Education*, 39, 2, 209.

Imai, L. and Gelfand, M.J. (2010). "The culturally intelligent negotiator: The impact of cultural intelligence (CQ) on negotiation sequences and outcomes." *Organizational Behavior and Human Decision Processes*, 11, 2, 83.

Iskhakova, M. and Ott, D.L. (2020). "Working in culturally diverse teams." *Journal of International Education in Business*, 13, 1, 37–54.

Huber, G.P. (1990). "A theory of the effects of advanced information technologie." *Academy of Management.the Academy of Management Review*, 15, 1, 47–71.

Khani, A., Etebarian, A., and Abzari, M. (2011). "The relationship between cultural intelligence and group effectiveness in Mobarakeh Steel Company." *African Journal of Business Management*, 5, 17, 7507–10.

Lin, C.C., Chen, F-P., and Chen, H. (2018). "The influence of cultural IQ and performer's involvement on organizational attraction." *International Journal of Business and Information*, 13, 4, 427–56.

Pandey, A. and Lucktong, A. (2020). "Contribution of social media and cultural intelligence on Indian-Thai B2B." *AU-GSB E-Journal*, 13, 1, 90–111.

Paparoidamis, N.G., Tran, H.T.T., and Leonidou, C.N. (2019). "Building customer loyalty in intercultural service encounters: The role of service employees' cultural intelligence." *Journal of International Marketing*, 27, 2, 56–75.

Ramkeesoon, S.A. (2019). *Cultural Intelligence: Amplifying Success for International Mergers and Acquisitions Executives*. Dissertation. University of Maryland, University College https://www.proquest.com/dissertations-theses/cultural-intelligence-amplifying-success/docview/2291631557/se-2

Rohmetra, N. and Arora, P. (2012). "The interface between cultural intelligence and customer satisfaction: The hospitality 'PERSPECTIVE'." *UFHRD Annual Conference*. www.ufhrd.co.uk/wordpress/rohmetra-n-and-arora-p-the-interface-between-cultural-intelligence-and-customer-satisfaction-the-hospitality-%E2%80%98perspective%E2%80%99

Scholz, T.M. (2012). "Talent management in the video game industry: The role of cultural diversity and cultural intelligence." *Thunderbird International Business Review*, 54, 6, 845–58.

SHRM (2015). *Cultural Intelligence: The Essential Intelligence for the 21st Century*. Alexandria, VA: SHRM Foundation. www.shrm.org/hr-today/trends-and-forecasting/special-reports-and-expert-views/Documents/Cultural-Intelligence.pdf

Thomas, D.C. (2006). "Domain and development of cultural intelligence: The importance of mindfulness." *Group & Organization Management*, 31, 1, 78–99.

Thomas, D.C. and Inkson, K. (2017). *Cultural Intelligence: Surviving and Thriving in the Global Village*, 3rd edn. Oakland, CA: Berrett-Koehler Publishers.

Thomas, D.C., Elron, E., Stahl, G., Ekelund, B.Z., Ravlin, E.C., Cerdin, J., and Lazarova, M.B. (2008). "Cultural intelligence: Domain and assessment." *International Journal of Cross Cultural Management: CCM*, 8, 2, 123.

Thomas, D.C., Liao, Y., Aycan, Z., Cerdin, J.L., Pekerti, A., Ravlin, E., Stahl, G., Lazarova, M., Fock, H., Arli, D., Moeller, M., Okimoto, T., and Van de Vijver, F. (2015). "Cultural intelligence: A theory based short form measure." *Journal of International Business Studies*, 46, 9, 1099–118.

Van Dyne, L., Ang, S., and Koh, C. (2008). "Development and validation of the CQS: The cultural intelligence scale," in S. Ang and L. Van Dyne (eds), *Handbook of Cultural Intelligence: Theory, Measurement, and Applications*. Armonk, NY: M. E. Sharpe, pp. 16–38.

Yikilmaz, I., Tasdemir, D.D., and Cekmecelioglu, H.G. (2021). "The assessment of the intermediation role of emotional labor dimensions in the relationship between cultural intelligence and individual work performance." *Business and Economics Research Journal*, 12, 1, 157–72.

INDEX